The New Found Land of Stephen Parmenius

THE NEW FOUND LAND OF
Stephen Parmenius

The life and writings of a Hungarian poet,
drowned on a voyage from Newfoundland, 1583

Edited and translated with commentaries by
DAVID B. QUINN & NEIL M. CHESHIRE

UNIVERSITY OF TORONTO PRESS

©University of Toronto Press 1972
Printed in Scotland for
University of Toronto Press
Toronto and Buffalo
ISBN 0-8020-5212-6
microfiche ISBN 0-8020-0027-4
LC 78-151386

Preface

THIS WORK IS A BELATED TRIBUTE to a young Hungarian scholar and explorer, who was the first from his country to write about North America in the international language of the European classical Renaissance. But he was more than just another academic word-spinner. Although he originally intended to return to his homeland and turn his literary skill to the subject of her misery, he changed his mind (we do not know why) and became the first of his countrymen to sail to the promising New World which he had acclaimed in his verse. It was his ill fortune eventually to drown in what are now Canadian waters.

Parmenius deserves some recognition in the record of European expansion overseas and in the early modern history of Canada and the United States. Contemporaries of his, Richard Hakluyt and Edward Hayes among them, regarded him as an exceptional, even heroic, figure; and certainly he was far from a nonentity. Yet he has not in recent times received much notice from scholars in England and North America. The account of his life, circumstances and writings makes an appealing chapter in the discovery story; but very little is known about his earlier years, and we can only hope that the publication here of what is to be found at present about his stay in England and his fatal American voyage may stimulate fruitful inquiry into his youth in Hungary and his student travels in Europe.

Sir Humphrey Gilbert's voyage to Newfoundland in 1583, which is the focus of our study, is important for Canadian history in spite of its tragic outcome in the wrecks of both the *Delight* (in which Parmenius went down) and the *Squirrel* (with which Gilbert perished). Although it failed to fulfil its promise either as a major reconnaissance of the eastern coast of North America or as the spearhead of a great colonizing movement, it is nevertheless a major episode in the slowly developing relationship between England and the North American continent.

The book began as the result of a coincidence. Some years ago D.B. Quinn wrote a short article on Parmenius for the *Dictionary of Canadian Biography*, and at the same time N.M. Cheshire happened to be translating, quite independently, one of the poems at the suggestion of Dr E.J. Devereux (now of the University of Western Ontario). After an inquiry by Cheshire, the Hakluyt Society put the writers in touch with each other. Three subsequent events gave the project additional impetus and enlarged its scope: Quinn discovered that the only known American copy of the major poem bore an inscription in Parmenius' own hand, Cheshire found that a copy of the shorter poem had been similarly treated by Parmenius when presenting it to an Oxford friend, and Quinn came upon some letters at Longleat House which had been written by Captain Maurice Browne with whom the Hungarian sailed on his fateful last voyage. Extracts from these last throw new light on the atmosphere in which Sir Humphrey Gilbert's venture of 1582–83 was planned and executed. In the light of all this Parmenius emerges as a figure of sufficient interest to justify our collating what is known about him and his setting with reprints and translations of his three surviving works – two poems and a long letter. From internal evidence, and from his inscription on presentation copies of his poems, we know the names of several people with whom Parmenius was brought into contact in England, and can speculate on his possible relations with some others. Indeed his Latin poems and his co-operation with Richard Hakluyt in the intellectual preparations for Sir Humphrey Gilbert's American expedition imply a busy period of association with Puritan-inclined elements at London and Oxford.

The original plan was that Cheshire would produce the translations and the literary-linguistic commentary to go with them, and that Quinn would write the introduction and historical notes. But this distinction, though broadly maintained, has been blurred in the practice of collaboration so that each of us owes much to the other.

Inevitably, the way in which a Latin text is printed is to some extent a matter of convention; in the case of quasi-classical Latin of the Renaissance, the problems are multiplied by the need to consider the conflicting interests of two relatively separate traditions, Graeco-Roman and Elizabethan. And when the material in question is being presented both as a literary composition in its own right and as a documentary source for historical argument, whatever conventions are decided upon will reflect an arbitrary compromise and displease somebody. As far as orthography is concerned, we have followed the general usage of modern editions of classical texts with respect to 'u', 'v', 'i', and 'j'; but not all spellings have been 'classicized' in other ways (see p. 26 below); standard contractions have been expanded silently and we have rationalized the often chaotic Elizabethan punctuation. The 'accents' which were scattered inconsistently over some texts have been abandoned. In the case of English texts, we have tended to retain rather more of the original punctuation.

The authors owe many acknowledgments. For first putting us on the track of Hungarian material, we are grateful to Mr P.M. Barbour, Professor E.S. Donno,

Dr György Pajkossy of the National Széchényi Library, Budapest, and Professor S.H. Thomson of the University of Colorado. Dr István Gál, in spite of poor health, and Mr Tivadar Ács, both of Budapest, have taken a great deal of trouble on our behalf in bringing us up to date on what is being done in Hungary; Dr Gyula Haraszty, Head of the Department of Manuscripts of the National Széchényi Library, has also given us every assistance. Our consultants on Hungarian, in which we have no competence, Miss Betty Hudson, Mr N.C. Masterman and Dr R.A. Markus, have shed invaluable light. Professor Jan van Dorsten of the University of Leiden searched the university archives for us and Dr J. van Groningen those of the University of Leiden Library. Professor Gavin Townend of the University of Durham, Mr T.C.W. Stinton of Wadham College, Oxford, and the University of Toronto Press reader have made important suggestions about the Latin translations and commentaries. We have been helped in various ways by the late Dr George W. Brown, Dr Roy Strong, Professor G.B. Parks, Professor Leicester Bradner, Dr Alastair MacFadyen and Mr K. Lloyd-Jones.

Many librarians have assisted personally in our researches: Dr J.R.L. Highfield of Merton College and Dr J.F.A. Mason of Christ Church, Oxford; Mr P. Morgan of the Bodleian Library; Mr Patrick Strong of Eton College. The librarians of the Bibliothèque Nationale, Paris, and the Deutsche Staatsbibliothek, Berlin, have searched without result for works of Parmenius said to be amongst their collections. We are grateful for permission to publish material or illustrations from the British Museum, the Bodleian Library, the Henry E. Huntington Library, the National Széchényi Library, Her Majesty's Stationery Office, the National Portrait Gallery, London, and the Provost and Fellows of Eton College. We are indebted to the Marquess of Bath for permission to print letters from Maurice Browne, and to Mr R.H. Ingleton and Mr M.F. Tiffin for enabling us to examine the manuscripts at Longleat.

Alison Quinn worked on many of the notes, typed the first draft of the manuscript and compiled the index. Our typists, who did so much of the labour, did not find it always easy and we are grateful to them.

DAVID B. QUINN
NEIL M. CHESHIRE
Liverpool and Bangor, 1968

Contents

Illustrations

page 9

1 / Hakluyt, "A particuler discourse" (1584), references to Parmenius
Reproduced by permission of the Manuscript Division,
the New York Public Library, Astor, Lenox and Tilden foundations

between pages 20 and 21

2 / Henry Unton as a young man. British school, artists unknown
Reproduced by permission of the Tate Gallery, London

3 / Sir Henry Unton: extract from his memorial portrait
British school, artist unknown
Reproduced by permission of the National Portrait Gallery, London

4 / Laurence Humfrey, president of Magdalen College, Oxford
Engraving from Henry Holland, *Herwologia Anglicana* (1620)
Reproduced by permission of the Bodleian Library, Oxford

5 / Sir Humphrey Gilbert. Engraving by Robert Boissard
from the copy of Henry Holland, *Basilwilogia* (1618) in
the Ashmolean Museum, Oxford

6 / *De navigatione . . . Humfredi Gilberti . . . carmen* (1582),
title page, with an inscription by Parmenius to Geoffroy Brumen
Reproduced by permission of the Henry E. Huntington Library,
San Marino, California

7 / *Paean . . . ad psalmum Davidis CIV* (1582), title page,
with an inscription by Parmenius to Thomas Savile
Reproduced by permission of the Provost and Fellows of Eton College

INTRODUCTION

STEPHEN PARMENIUS: HIS LIFE & WRITINGS

Preliminaries

THE ODYSSEY of a young sixteenth-century scholar from his home in Hungary, through Europe, to an unexpected country of adoption far across that continent (as space was reckoned then), was not an unusual event. The medieval student had frequently moved about Europe until he found an acceptable abode, and the new humanism of the sixteenth century was also international. A Hungarian or a Pole, nurtured on the revived glories of Greece and Rome, was as likely to find congenial company among like-minded intellectuals in Paris or Oxford as he was in his own country. The religious convulsions of the century, too, added an ideological impetus to the movement of scholars, especially of those who were Protestants. Exile, and the search for an ecclesiastical setting appropriate to his beliefs, might send a scholar far afield and root him firmly in a community which, but for his religious allegiance, would have remained alien to him.

It was unusual, however, for a scholar, unless he was a member of a Catholic missionary order, to venture beyond the Atlantic to the new lands which had been opened up to European penetration and exploration in the fifteenth and sixteenth centuries. Many of the explorers and conquerors from Italy or from the Iberian lands were educated men, and a number of them left highly literate records of their experiences. By the later sixteenth century clerical missionaries were devoting scholarly attention to the American civilizations, such as that of the Aztecs, which their soldiers had ruined. Yet there had been few explorers whose interests were primarily literary, whose purpose in going overseas was first of all to obtain inspiration for poetic creation and whose considered intention it was to record in epic verse or prose the deeds of the exploring hero. The great exception, who stands out among his contemporaries as the poet of the European expansion, was Camões. And it was for this reason, first of all, that our young Hungarian left England for America.

Parmenius' intention was to write an epic of the exploration of eastern North America by the English: but his performance was not to match his hopes. For he was lost at sea on 29 August 1583, on the sandy bars of Sable Island, when the ship in which he was sailing, the *Delight,* went aground and broke up. As a

3

result, we have only two pieces on his chosen subject. One is a poem, which was to have been merely his first essay in the celebration of the New World; it is based on second-hand knowledge filled out with classical myth and convention, but nevertheless shows substantial promise of greater achievement. The other is a short prose epistle recording his experiences on first landing on American soil, which was a hopeful augury of his capacity to observe and comment on the New World. He might, we can guess with some confidence, have done much to reveal North America both to the reason and to the senses of the learned. Instead, he must remain for us a lost pioneer like his hero Sir Humphrey Gilbert, who was himself a somewhat tragic figure, a victim of his own optimism as well as of his pioneering spirit.

There is uncertainty at the very start of this biography, for it is not clear what precisely to call the person concerned. His name was in print from 1582 in England in the Latin form *Stephanus Parmenius Budeius*; William Camden, the English historian, in the same year referred to him as *Dominus Parmenius Budensis*; Richard Hakluyt anglicized him in 1589 as "Stephen Parmenius of Buda". In his native Hungary he was unknown until 1889. In that year Lajos Kropf published the English evidence of his stay at Oxford and of his death in North American waters. He also found a Hungarian name for him, *Paizs*, or *Pajzs*, a recognized surname which literally means 'a shield' as does the Greek *parme*. Under this name he appeared in the Hungarian biographical dictionary in 1905, and has so far been called by this name,[1] or, more recently, and more conservatively, *Budai Parmenius István*, since no evidence linking him with a family called Paizs had been found and it is, in any event, a possibly unsatisfactory rendering.[2] It is true that a recent claim has been made that he can be identified with a sixteenth-century family named *Peis*,[3] but this has been in no way authenticated. Most recently of all, the

---

1 Lajos Kropf, "Budai Parmenius István", *Egyetérétes* (4 January 1889), and more extensively in *Századok*, XXIII (Budapest 1889), 150–4. Biographical article in *Magyar írók*, ed. József Szinnyei, x (Budapest 1905), cols. 409–10.

2 There are two difficulties with Kropf's argument: first, etymologically a Greek nominative of this form does not readily generate the required ending -*enios*; second, we should expect someone who was Latinizing the name "Shield" to use the perfectly good Latin equivalent *parma* and produce something like *Parmarius*. We may, however, observe that P. is unorthodox elsewhere in forming word-endings: in *NL* he compounds a Greek verb irregularly from the corresponding noun, and the Untons' house called "Wadley" seems to become in his Latin *Wadlenianum*. If the latter is sufficient evidence that P. tended to introduce the letter 'n' idiosyncratically, then Kropf's case is strengthened. See p. 29 below, Fig. 6, *NL*, note to l. 4.

3 Dezső Láng, "Budai Parmenius István", *Magyar Hirek* (Budapest), 23 November 1967. This article, in a weekly periodical, without references, makes many statements which

Latin form, *Stephanus Budaeus*, has been found in a Hungarian manuscript for a man who is almost certainly he. It is probably simplest to call him, as Hakluyt did, Stephen Parmenius.

What little we know of Stephen Parmenius is derived from his dedicatory epistle to Sir Humphrey Gilbert of his Latin poem on his approaching voyage.[4] There he explains the circumstances under which the poem came to be written, but the biographical material it contains, though invaluable, is far from being specific or circumstantial.

Stephen Parmenius was born in Buda under Turkish rule: that is in the capital of the *pashalik* of Buda founded after its capture in 1541. He evidently left Hungary in 1579 and is unlikely to have been, at that time, under twenty or over twenty-five years of age, which would bring his date of birth roughly between 1555 and 1560. His prejudices against the Muslim were strong, and probably explain why he emphasized that he was born of Christian parents, but by "Christian" he meant, it seems, Protestant.[5] He was, by many indications from his writings and contacts in England, a Calvinist by conviction, and his parents are therefore most likely to have been Calvinists, whose church inside the Turkish sector of Hungary was well organized. It seems likely that he belonged to a family of some position or wealth, for he received a classical education in occupied Hungary at the hands of scholars he respected, and it sounds as though he was taught privately rather than institutionally. But he does also refer to the flourishing of humane scholarship in the unconquered parts of Hungary, meaning Austrian Hungary, or even Transylvania, where the Calvinists had more freedom and consequently more chances of receiving a liberal education. Though we do not know who Parmenius' own teachers were, we may be sure that among the eminent Hungarian scholars of whom he speaks in general terms he had in mind at least János Sambuc (Johannes Sambucius), who taught mainly in the university of Vienna and had produced an

are quite inaccurate. Láng calls the metre of *DNC* "Sapphic"; he says that Edward Hayes brought the poem back from Newfoundland and that in the epistle P. thanks Gilbert for inviting him to join the expedition (cp. *DNC* 157–64); he makes the expedition sail from Wales (cp. *NL*, l. 7); he mentions "impressions" and "editions" of the texts as being in libraries where inquiry has shown they are not and never have been. When he states, therefore, that P. was a son of János Peis, a Calvinist of Buda, who moved to Nyitra in northern Hungary, where he and his three sons, János, Gabor, and Marton, were condemned by the Dominicans for heresy and sent to the galleys in 1574 while Stephen escaped, he must be treated, until evidence for his statements is forthcoming, with the utmost scepticism.

4 Pp. 76–9 below.
5 For hostile references to Muslims, see *DNC* 49, 72–3, and note to l. 50; and to Roman Catholics, see p.8, n. 1 below.

annotated paraphrase of Aristotle's *Poetics* in 1564, and János Sylvester, the Lutheran who first (in 1541) translated the New Testament into Magyar.[6]

After what we might call his undergraduate education had been taken as far as possible in Hungary itself, he was sent, as he says was customary with Hungarians, to continue his studies in the universities of the Christian (which we should probably again interpret as "Protestant") world. He was expected to obtain on his tour what he could from institutions of learning, to examine the Protestant churches which he would encounter, and to glean some measure of statecraft. His programme was to extend over three years. England was the last, or almost the last, stopping point on his progress. He evidently left his home to go first to one of the leading Protestant universities in Germany, that of Heidelberg. The sole record of him which can be identified with any confidence in Hungary is a seventeenth-century list of Hungarian Protestants who attended foreign universities. They are arranged university by university and in most cases the entries contain detailed biographical notes, but in this case the entry is simply "1579. Stephanus Budaeus", in the long list of Heidelberg students.[7] The date fits in very well with what he tells us in his dedicatory epistle to Sir Humphrey Gilbert. He must have been in England, we judge, by the autumn of 1581 at the latest, though he could have come earlier; in the spring of 1582 he was seriously considering returning to his native country and he indicates that he had spent well over two years (*ferme triennio*) on his continental journey before landing in England.

Heidelberg, we may take it, was the first stopping point on his journey, but many wandering scholars left little or no trace of themselves in the universities where they sojourned for a time, so that we do not know how long he stayed, nor have we picked up his trail between the banks of the Neckar and the North Sea. But from Heidelberg in the Palatinate, the main German centre for intellectual Calvinism, we can plan a possible – though only imaginary – itinerary for him. Up the Rhine he would find his way first to Strasbourg, where he would find congenial professors and students, and thence to Zürich, with its Zwinglian heritage through the Carolinum, and from there to Calvin's Academy of Geneva, the first full Calvinist university, though no trace has yet been found of him in Switzerland. It is then most probable that he went on to Italy. Without a knowledge of Italy no humanist's education was complete. Rome, though it could be dangerous for Protestants; Florence with its Renaissance glories; Venice with its grandeur and its unique form of government; Bologna for its authority in the field of law: these

6 We are particularly indebted to Dr István Gál for his correspondence with us on the Hungarian humanists.
7 This entry was discovered in the National Széchényi Library, Budapest, MS Fol. Hung, 1734, by Mr Tivadar Ács, who kindly communicated his discovery to us.

were places to which the itinerant scholar was most likely to go. Parmenius tells us that he was intending to study not only the past but the present, and to learn the character of the places and the peoples he encountered. To this end he endeavoured to obtain introductions to persons of eminence in the places he visited. If he remained for any length of time at a university in Italy it is likely to have been in Padua, where under the protection of cosmopolitan Venice a truly international university society had gathered and where the lectures of the professors, particularly in law and medicine, were widely attended by foreigners. There had been an outbreak of plague late in 1578 and the entries of Hungarian students in the university's records – in which Parmenius does not appear – are relatively scanty for the late 1570's.[8] But there were Englishmen there in 1580 or 1581 with whom Parmenius may well have made some contact.[9]

On his way from Italy to northern Europe, a humanist and Calvinist would have been reluctant to avoid Paris; he would have found it almost impossible, too, not to visit the painfully resurgent scholarship of the rebellious Netherlands. Did he, for example, go to Leiden, the location of a new and vigorous university created as recently as 1575? But even if he did, the records there also tell us nothing of his stay:[10] we still do not know where precisely he went, after Heidelberg, and when he crossed to England.

8 See Endré Veress, ed., *Matricula et acta Hungarorum in universitate Patavina studentium, 1264–1864* (Budapest 1915); on the plague in 1578, see p. 215. Veress's collections on Hungarian students in other European universities were never published but are now deposited in the National Széchényi Library. Mr Tivadar Ács who has consulted them there informs us that he has found no reference to Stephen Parmenius in them.
9 See below, pp. 17–18.
10 Professor Jan van Dorsten has most helpfully but vainly made search for him in the university archives.

Parmenius in England

T HOUGH WE DO NOT KNOW precisely when Parmenius reached Oxford, he was certainly there by the autumn of 1581, because when we meet him early in 1582 he has an assured knowledge of the university and of England. He was clearly well advanced in his educational programme. An accomplished Latinist, he commanded a range of verse and prose styles, and had evidently decided that he should aim at a scholar's life. He came directly to Oxford for that reason, re-garding himself only secondarily as a courtier who must meet men in high places in government. It is possible that when he left Hungary he had thought of himself as destined for the ministry, but there is scarcely a trace of this intention in what he wrote in England.[1] The classics, the world of scholarship, the activities of states – these were his first preoccupations. In England he set himself especially to do two things. The first was to explore the Anglican church settlement; the second, an interest which may have developed after his arrival, was to study the new geography – the realm opened up by the recent growth of theoretical and practical knowledge, particularly about the New World.

Oxford attracted many foreign scholars like Parmenius. Some came to visit briefly a famous place of learning; others settled down to take a degree. Parmenius did neither one nor the other. He entered Christ Church and associated himself with a senior member of the college, living in his rooms for an extended period,[2] although he does not appear in the college records nor did he make any recorded contact with the university. Nevertheless, by going to reside with Richard Hakluyt he embarked on a serious, if unofficial, course of instruction.

The younger Richard Hakluyt, so called to distinguish him from his elder cousin, Richard Hakluyt of the Middle Temple, had been at Christ Church since

---

1 He does make fleeting references, if we have understood him correctly, to the iniquities of the Roman Catholic priesthood and the virtues of their English (Reformed) counter-parts; he also protests at the worship of idols and intermediaries which he attributes to Roman Catholic practice: see *DNC*, lines 50–1, 80–3, 91–2, 252–61, and their re-spective notes.

2 See Fig. 1, p. 9 for text.

1   Hakluyt, "A particuler discourse" (1584), references to Parmenius

1570.[3] Graduating B.A. in 1574, he was incorporated M.A. in 1577, and gave his lectures as regent master in 1577–79 in the new field of geography. He then settled down to teach and study as a Student (i.e. a fellow) of the College, holding this office actively until 1583 and passively thereafter until 1587. Whether Hakluyt instructed Parmenius further in classical literature we cannot say, but there is little doubt that he introduced him to the literature of geographical speculation and none at all that he brought the literature of geographical exploration firmly to his notice. Sharing his rooms and his bed, Parmenius cannot have avoided sharing in his master's preoccupations, which at that time had been diverted into geographical research of a practical character.

Another Oxford friend of his of whom we know was the eminent and active Dr Laurence Humfrey.[4] As we shall see, Humfrey could well have been Parmenius' original contact in Oxford. President of Magdalen College and Dean of Winchester, Humfrey was a vigorous Protestant, frequently in trouble for desiring the further reform of the Church of England. He was Calvinist in theology, and a staunch Puritan, but not a wholly uncompromising one. He was, too, an ardent

3 On the younger Hakluyt's life up to 1583 see G. B. Parks, *Richard Hakluyt and the English voyages* (1928), pp. 56–86, 242–8; E. G. R. Taylor, ed., *The original writings and correspondence of the two Richard Hakluyts*, I (1935), 11–13; Richard Hakluyt, *Principall navigations, 1589*, ed. D. B. Quinn and R. A. Skelton, I (1965), xiv–xv.
4 Pp. 55, 168 below.

9

admirer of Queen Elizabeth and so he retained the headship of his college throughout almost the whole of her reign. Like many scholars of his time, he was interested
in the sea and, when he wrote Latin verses, his conception of the maritime role of
England and her Queen was frequently evident. When he addressed a Latin poem
to the Queen at Woodstock in 1575,[5] he associated in it, as E. C. Wilson has
pointed out,[6] sea-imagery, a virgin queen, classical mythology, and a Protestant
God:

> Now having launched our Ship we plough across
> The Ocean; now may you provide fair winds,
> Fair goddess. Be both poop and prow to us,
> Be our ship's anchor and direct the sails
> Of this our craft in all her voyaging.[7]

Equally, his poem on Sir Henry Unton's death in 1596 plays on maritime themes.

> O foolish men who daub their empty verse
> In vain upon the sombre monuments
> Of nobler souls! Do you suppose your lines
> Would please a man of Unton's widespread fame
> And many qualities? Does one whose wealth,
> Whose life, whose shining name so lavishly
> Enriched his fatherland require no more
> Than song? And yet they go together well
> These two, virtue and verse: they complement
> Each other – there's no third.
>   Let Walsingham
> Disperse his riches over every land
> And thus appropriate their destinies
> To his own country: Drake may fly at once
> Across to India, that source of gold,
> Charting his vessels' distant course among
> Uncharted seas: let Sidney make again
> For Zeeland, Unton sail to France and Grey

---

5 *Oratio ad serenissimam Angliae reginam Elizabetham* (1575: S.T.C. 13960), sig. A5[r];
  reprinted in John Nichols, *Queen Elizabeth's progresses*, I (1788), p. [739] (translation
  by N.M.C.).
6 E. C. Wilson, *England's Eliza* (1939), p. 278.
7 Translated by N.M.C. *Nunc mare sulcamus, mare nunc ingressa Carina est; / flatibus aspires,
  o bona Iova, bonis. / Sis prora et puppis, nostrae sis ancora navis, / peregrinantis dirige vela ratis./*

> Return to Ireland, reaping great rewards.
> These two they'd surely win, – Death and a Song:
> What else? For, as you see, the present age
> Produces nothing more ...[8]

Humfrey had known Richard Hakluyt since at least 1575 when, shortly after the younger man had received his B.A. degree, the elder had transmitted to him a small payment from a scholarship fund.[9] It is likely that he encouraged Hakluyt's geographical studies, and therefore probable that it was he who introduced Parmenius to him, even though Hakluyt, since taking orders, had become a stout supporter of the Church establishment as it was. Indeed, we might even suggest that Parmenius had arrived in Oxford already interested in the study of geography as well as of literature and that the choice of Christ Church rather than Magdalen was made, under Humfrey's guidance, to further this objective. As we shall see, there are lines which may have led Parmenius to Humfrey from members of the Unton family or from Charles Merbury. Humfrey also had many contacts among foreign Protestants, which he had renewed as recently as 1578 at the Diet of Smalcald, and these could have brought Stephen an introduction to him.

Humfrey had, too, a close sympathy for the trials and sufferings through which so many foreign Protestants were passing. As he wrote to Abraham Musculus at Zürich on 5 June 1578, "having been a stranger myself I have learned to befriend strangers; and I have only to report that my ability does not correspond with my inclination."[10] As recently as 9 October 1581, Humfrey had written to Godfridus Wing, minister of the Dutch church in London, urging him to help a poor German scholar who had come to Humfrey with a recommendation from a Strasbourg professor.[11] So many refugee Protestant scholars flocked to Oxford, he stressed, that he was unable to assist them all. There is no reason to believe that

8 *Funebria nobilissimi ac praestantissimi equitis, D. Henrici Untoni ... à musis Oxoniensibus apparata* (Oxford, J. Barnes, 1596: S.T.C. 24520), sig. E1ᵛ, translated by N.M.C. Text reads: *O stultos homines, vanis qui versibus ornant / frustra magnanimi maesta trophaea viri, / creditis Untono, modo tot virtutibus amplo / tot titulis magno, vestra placere metra? / Fortunas, vitam, splendorem nominis omnem / largitus patriae, carmina sola petit? / Sed bene conveniunt virtus et versus: utrumque / alterutri dos est, tertia nulla datur. / Walsingamus opes per cunctas dissipet oras, / (10) deferat ut patriae quaeque futura suae; / transvolet auriferos confestim Dracus ad Indos, / navibus immensum per mare mensus iter; / Belgas Sidnaeus repetat, dux Greius Hybernos, / Celtas Untonus. Praemia magna ferent: / haec duo nimirum, – Mortem Carmenque. Quid ultra? / Amplius ecce nihil secula nostra creant. / ...*
9 Parks, *Hakluyt*, p. 246.
10 *Zürich letters*, second series, ed. Hastings Robinson (Cambridge 1845), p. 301.
11 J. H. Hessels, *Abrahami Ortelii et virorum eruditorum ad eundem et ad Jacobum Colium Ortelianum epistulae* (Cambridge 1887), pp. 711–12.

11

Parmenius came penniless to England, but he is not likely to have had, after several years' travel, much money to spare. He would need friendships and introductions as well as monetary aid. Such a man as Humfrey was, by interest and inclination alike, precisely the one to help and encourage Stephen in England. There is every indication, indeed, that he did so, and that at least part of Stephen's enthusiasm for the new geography and for the life of an explorer came from Humfrey. It was to Humfrey that he first thought of writing when he reached Newfoundland. It was he whom he asked, before he decided to write an independent letter to Hakluyt, to inform him of the details of his transatlantic voyage. Thus Humfrey stands alongside Hakluyt as a major influence on Stephen's geographical enterprise.

But Humfrey, though an especially influential name in Oxford, was only one of a group of scholars who were in close contact with one another, and who overlapped the boundaries of the university to take into their circle men who lived in London as well. Its members are represented, typically, in the correspondence of Jean Hotman, Sieur de Villiers St. Paul,[12] a Huguenot scholar who had come to Oxford some time before Parmenius as tutor to the children of Sir Amyas Paulet, a former English ambassador in Paris. From this correspondence it is clear that William Camden, Richard Hakluyt and Thomas Savile, as well as Humfrey, were in close touch with each other during the period when, individually, they were making the acquaintance of Stephen Parmenius. We do not find that other members of the group, Jean Hotman himself, Richard Garth, a friend of Hakluyt's, and Scipio and Alberico Gentili, amongst them, were known personally to Parmenius, but this is almost certainly for want of evidence.

We can trace one step only in this process of assimilation. The historian William Camden, though Second Master of Westminster School and continually working on his *Britannia*, found time to engage in vigorous correspondence both with his friends at Oxford and with those on the continent. Early in April 1582 he sat down in London to draft an answer to a letter, sent to him on 11 March, which had not reached him until the 23rd. It was clearly from a close friend, but as we have neither the name of the man to whom it was addressed nor the final letter, we remain in the dark about some aspects of it.[13] He acknowledges a query from

---

12 Jean and François Hotman, *Epistolae* (Amsterdam 1700), pp. 260–314. The ramifications of this group over the years are shown by the Camden correspondence in *Viri clarissimi Gulielmi Camdeni et illustrium virorum ... epistolae*, ed. Thomas Smith (1691), and by the letters in B.M., Cotton MS, Julius C.V. and the drafts in Additional MS 22583.

13 Brit. Mus., Additional MS 36294, f. 2. The draft has several false starts as Camden set down the names of two other people to whom he may have thought of writing –

Thomas Savile which his friend had passed on to him; but, although we can identify this almost certainly as a rather dull one (about road-blocks in Caesar's *Gallic War*) which is printed, with the date 11 March, in a much later collection of Camden's correspondence, it gives no clue to who was acting as go-between.[14] Camden sends back to Savile, via his correspondent, the friendly greeting of "many good wishes" and a copy of some poems associated with an anonymous tract about the martyrdom of the Jesuit Edmund Campion, who had been exe-cuted in London the previous December; Camden comments that the tract had been recently printed in London.[15] He also asks his correspondent to pass on greetings to one of the Hotmans, presumably Jean, who must have been staying in Oxford.

Camden has had hot news from the eminent Flemish geographer Gerard Mercator – "the good Mercator", as he affectionately calls him (he was also a friend of Hakluyt) – on the attempted assassination of the Prince of Orange at Antwerp as recently as 18 March, which he apparently believed to have suc-ceeded. Near the end comes the isolated phrase which touches our subject directly: "*Dominum Parmenium Budensem, quod mihi commendasti beneficiam*", – that is to say "I will look after Master Parmenius of Buda since you have commended him to me". But we cannot tell, as we have just seen, from whom this commendation comes; obviously, however, it is from an intimate member of the circle who is closely in touch with Thomas Savile and Jean Hotman. It could be Humfrey, though per-haps it would not have been wise for Camden to send the Catholic material to Savile by way of that strongly anti-catholic president of Magdalen, lest it make him too angry. One or two other members of the circle are possible, but most likely is Richard Hakluyt himself.

So Parmenius is seen being taken into a community of scholars scattered between London and Oxford but remaining very close in spirit and embracing from time to time a continental newcomer: in a letter of the following month Camden brackets Thomas Savile with Hotman as "my very closest friends" (*mei imprimis intimi*), and we have the one in which Savile commends the Italian refugee lawyer Alberico Gentili to Camden's care on his first visit to London.[16] Though the members of this group were naturally interested in both academic gossip and

Drite Sterston and Janus Gruter: see Fig. 8. Appendix III contains text, translation, and commentary.
14 *V. cl. Gulielmi Camdeni*, no. xi, p. 13.
15 *A true reporte of the death and martyrdome of M. Campion Jesuite and prieste, ... Whereunto [sic] is annexid certayne verses made by sundrie persons* (London 1582; S.T.C. 4537); authorship attributed to Thomas Alfield. See Appendix III, note to l. 29.
16 Brit. Mus. Additional MS 36294, f. 3; and see pp. 211–16 below.

13

current events, the main links between them – and they included both established scholars and young aspirants to scholarship – were humanistic studies. This principal bond led them, even Englishmen to Englishmen, to correspond in Latin. In their company Parmenius' range of interests rapidly widened and some depth of scholarship began to emerge in his poetical writings. This brief record of a commendation is the only one to survive, in any form, from what must have been a sheaf of such introductions, from his Oxford friends to a still wider circle in the capital, which he took with him on the visit to London which he mentions in his preface to *De navigatione*.

Thomas Savile was a particularly interesting member of the group both for his youth and for his connections. In him Parmenius found a friend who was some years younger than he was, but who was already writing familiarly to Hakluyt, Camden, and Hotman. This young member of a family which was to become famous for its scholarship went up to Merton in October 1580. It cannot have been a matter of many months before the Hungarian himself arrived at Christ Church. Thomas Savile was to be appointed an "M.A. fellow" of his college in 1584 (the year after Parmenius's death) and a university proctor in 1592.[17] He shared with Parmenius some interest in political systems, and for one of his college dissertations was later to dispute the thesis that "the most excellent form of State is cooperative" (or, "participatory").[18] He earned a considerable reputation as a classicist and an authority on British antiquities, in the latter capacity corresponding extensively with Camden. As an undergraduate he knew Hakluyt well enough to complain, in a letter to Camden of June 1580, that the geographer owed him a letter: the fact that Hakluyt had gone to London was no excuse, says Savile, because it was "only his taste for novelty" (*sola novitatis cupido*) that had lured him there. Two years later he jokingly expresses concern to Camden that Hakluyt's latest publication, said to have been in the press for some time, must have got crushed to death (. . . *iniquius pressa excessisse e vivis*) because he had heard nothing of it recently. The work must have been the *Divers voyages*, but his concern for it was misplaced as it had appeared in London the previous month.[19] It was through this friendship with Hakluyt, no doubt, that Savile developed sufficient interest in travel literature to acquire in his

---

17 The first two dates, drawn from the Merton College Register, conflict with those given in *D.N.B.*

18 The titles of three "variations", or disputations, which Savile presented on 2 March 1587–88, are preserved in the Merton records. The second "position" which he considered was "*Mistam rempublicam esse praestantissimam*" (cp. P.'s interest in *sapienter institutae republicae*, expressed in the epistle to *DNC*, l. 10). We are indebted to Dr J. R. L. Highfield, librarian of Merton, for making these materials available to us.

19 See pp. 20–1 below.

last years his own copy of Ramusio's *Navigationi et viaggi*, the first volume of which, in the 1563 edition, he signed on the flyleaf with the date 1592.[20] He died the next year.

We can see from the handful of Thomas Savile's letters to Camden which survive that his religious sympathies would have been well in tune with those of Parmenius, and that he was already accustomed to taking a refugee scholar under his wing. The Italian protestant, Alberico Gentili, had reached England in 1579, had lectured in law at Oxford (where he was paid by Merton College), and eventually became Regius Professor.[21] On an early visit to London he took with him a letter from Savile to Camden commending him to the latter's care on the grounds of his religion and learning. In another letter Savile is provoked to a vividly outspoken anti-Catholic tirade by what he regards as the dishonest victimization of a Puritan candidate for university office.[22] The luckless man came from Yorkshire, was Savile's former tutor, and was regarded as one of the Puritan elite. His academic qualifications outshone his rival's as much as the moon does the lesser stars, but "that fanatical Catholic gang" (whoever they were) had forged all sorts of deceptions and, following their principle that "you needn't keep your word to a heretic" (*Fidem haeretico datam non esse servandam*), had, he says, rigged the voting and caused the goddess of Justice to flee the university. Honest scholarship is not far from being packed off to another island, perhaps, he suggests, remembering his friend from Buda, to one in the New World. Did Thomas Savile entertain the ironic thought that St. John's would be a good site for a Puritan university?

20 Now Bodleian Library, *Savile*, o.10.
21 Alberico and his brother Scipio shared P.'s interest in translation and in paraphrase of the Psalms (see p. 31 below).
   There are fifteen letters by Thomas Savile in *Viri clarissimi Gulielmi Camdeni ... epistolae*, ed. T. Smith (1691), those mentioned being on pp. 7, 14–15, and the originals in B.M., Cotton MS, Julius C.V.
22 The year-date of these two letters does not survive; but the first must almost certainly be mid-1580 (i.e. shortly before P. himself is likely to have reached Oxford), because by 1581 Gentili is sending Camden his greetings *via* another letter of Savile's; *op. cit.*, p. 17. If we are to understand from the first words of the second letter quoted that Savile was himself a proctor when he wrote it, then its date is probably 1592; though he may simply have been a member of some committee on which proctors also sat, and certainly his hand is steadier in this letter than when he signed his Ramusio in that year. Part of the passage referred to runs: ... *vera et genuina doctrina sordida obsolescit, fugit Astraea virgo iam nunc ab Academiis ...; virtus debito exuta honore languescit, et parvum abest quin literarum studia in insulam, non Angliam sed novi orbis aliquam, amandentur. Homo ... moribus ac doctrina ornatissimus, sola honestatis nimiae ... causa, candidatus cecidit; et quod pessimum est, nequissimorum animalium (Catholicos illos bullatos dico) fraude circumventus. ... Quas furialis illa Catholicorum turba fraudes cuderit, quo Catholico axiomate. ... XL minimum illi suffragia subtraxerint, certiorem te faciet ... N. Whitalk.*

Thomas Savile was a younger brother of the more celebrated Henry Savile, who eventually became both Warden of Merton and Provost of Eton. It is the school's library which has preserved the copy of Parmenius' work, his *Paean*, presented by Parmenius to Thomas Savile as a token of his friendship. This doubtless came with others of Thomas's books to Henry Savile after his brother's premature death, but it is possible that it was the symbol of an earlier association between Henry Savile and Parmenius. It could, indeed, though there are other alternatives, have been the Saviles who provided Parmenius' original introduction to Oxford. For, although there is no evidence of contact between them before the Hungarian scholar was established in England, yet we do know that Henry Savile was voted a sum of money by his Merton colleagues in April 1578 to go and study for three years in France and, more generally, "overseas" (*in partes transmarinas*). This is only shortly before the time when Parmenius was starting out from the other side of Europe on his own Grand Tour of the academic and political centres of Europe. Unfortunately the English scholar's itinerary is hardly less obscure than the Hungarian's, his own contemporaries having had some difficulty in tracing his movements at the time, and failing to find him in Paris when they expected him to be there. He may possibly have visited the Netherlands but, if so, it cannot have been for long. He turns up at Nuremberg, however, in September 1580 with Henry Nevile, Robert Sidney (Philip's younger brother) and possibly George Carew in his company. From Robert Sidney's subsequent correspondence on the tour, it is clear that he, himself, had reached Prague by the end of October, and that Savile was still expected to be with him. The party's route had been through Ingolstadt, Augsburg, Munich and Regensburg. Sidney himself was intending to continue to Vienna and Hungary after the winter, but even if he did get as far as Hungary, about which there appears to be no evidence, we do not know whether Savile was still with him.[23]

What does seem clear, at all events, is that Henry Savile was in Italy, at Venice, in 1582, and so could not be in direct contact with Parmenius while he was settling himself into the society of English scholars. Perhaps their paths may have crossed. If so it may have been at Heidelberg, where Parmenius was at the university in 1579, and where Savile had at some time made sufficient contacts to have a book published in that city in 1601.[24] But Henry Savile is not likely to have returned to England before Sir Humphrey Gilbert sailed and Parmenius was lost at sea.

23 The discussion of Henry Savile's tour draws on three main sources: J. R. L. Highfield, "An autograph manuscript ... of Sir Henry Savile", *Bodleian Library Record*, VII (1963), 73–83; A. L. Rowse, *Ralegh and the Throckmortons* (1962), pp. 84–94; A. Collins, *Letters and memorials of state* (1746), pp. 283–6.
24 *Commentarius de militia Romana ex Anglico Latinus factus* (Heidelberg 1601).

Though there are many questions about them which still remain unanswered, it is clear that Stephen's closest friends and most encouraging patrons were the Unton family, Sir Edward Unton and his second son, Henry. Sir Edward had been greatly attracted to Italy ever since he was a young man, and had travelled there, coming back by way of Mainz and Strasbourg, in 1564. A decade later[25] he took advantage of having sons of his own to educate and in 1574 obtained a three-year licence to travel abroad with his elder son Edward, though the details of their stay abroad in Italy and elsewhere are not recorded. Henry evidently did not accompany them, for he was entered at the Middle Temple on 11 February 1575. Edward seems to have stayed on in Italy after his father's return, and he was given a further licence on 22 April 1581 to remain abroad for another two years.[26] Before then, his younger brother Henry, accompanied it would seem by another young gentleman, Charles Merbury, had also spent some time in Italy, though no licences for their travel have so far been found. We may presume that Henry spent at least some time in his brother's company. Edward remained behind after Henry's return, to fall into the hands of the Inquisition in Milan and to obtain his release only in 1584.

A posthumous picture of Sir Henry Unton contains as a background a chronicle in paint of his career.[27] The stream of Unton's life is shown flowing from Wadley to Oxford, thence to an unnamed and mistily seen building, probably in the capital, either the Temple or one of the royal palaces being intended. From there it runs to Venice, Padua, and the Alps in his European tour. With Henry Unton in Italy are shown two other figures: one is most probably a servant, the other Charles Merbury (or just possibly Edward Unton). They must have reached Padua after the plague had abated and it is likely that they remained for some time at the university, hearing lectures by the many well-known scholars who taught there, mingling with the students from all over Europe who found their way to Padua, and perfecting their Italian. It seems highly probable that it was here that they encountered Stephen Parmenius (although we have no direct evidence on the

25 Richard Smith's journal, covering the greater part of the tour, is printed by A. H. S. Yeames, "The grand tour of an Elizabethan", British School at Rome, *Papers*, VII (London 1914), 92–113.
26 Public Record Office, State Papers, Domestic, Elizabeth, S.P. 12/154,5. We are indebted for this reference to Professor G. B. Parks.
27 Plate 2 is extracted from it. To Dr Roy C. Strong, Director of the National Portrait Gallery, London, we are much indebted for personal communications. His article "Sir Henry Unton and his portrait", *Archaeologia*, XCIX (1965), 53–76, constitutes a definitive study. The inscription on Sir Henry Unton's tomb in Farington Church includes the statement "*magnam orbis Christiani partem perlustravit*". Nichols, *Unton inventories* (1841), p. lix.

matter at all), and that it was here that his friendship with Henry Unton began. Stephen's friendship with Henry was so close and his respect for his family so great when our evidence becomes clear in 1582, that we would expect the two young men to have known each other for some time already. Introductions from Henry Unton could have paved the way for Parmenius' visit to Oxford, and Charles Merbury, in particular, could most easily have introduced him to his old tutor, Dr Laurence Humfrey of Magdalen. Merbury was back in England well before the end of 1581, Henry Unton most probably accompanying him. Whether Parmenius travelled to England in their company, or preceded them there, we cannot say.

Merbury and Henry Unton, on their return, soon installed themselves at court amongst the crowd of courtiers who jostled there for ministerial or royal notice. Charles Merbury felt himself under-employed, and so he put together and completed his short treatise on kingship, *A briefe discourse of royall monarchie*,[28] out of which it emerged, not surprisingly, that Queen Elizabeth's government was the ideal to be aimed at by other monarchs. He added to it a collection of Italian proverbs and phrases. If the two parts of his little book did not cohere, they at least represented very well the twin products to be expected of an Italian education: an interest in statecraft combined with an elegant knowledge of the Italian tongue. Merbury shared these interests with Henry Unton, whose "vertuous and learned companie" he praises in the book. He also acknowledges the "daily conference" with Unton, "both in the languages and in other good letters, wherein he is rarely indued", and the fact that he was the source of a number of the Italian phrases. Merbury pays a tribute as well to Dr Humfrey for his teaching while he was at Oxford.[29] Unton, in his turn, contributed an epistle in praise of Merbury, recalling "the fast friendship of the Author (whom I have long and much loved)" and his "private knowledge of the Gentlemans Intent and travailes", and saying of the treatise that it contained "a sweete joyce, and a rare Quintessence of the best framed Monarchie!"[30] The preliminaries to this short book are completed by Merbury's dedication of it in Italian to the Queen beginning: *Si come il viadante riguarda al Sole, il navigante all tramontane, & la calamita al Polo* ... The whole performance was an attempt by the two young men to advertise their Italianateness to the Queen and thus to make a bid for her attention and favour.

The book was first of all confided to Thomas Marsh to print but on 23 November 1581 it was transferred to Thomas Vautrollier.[31] The reason for the change may

28 Thomas Vautrollier, 1581: S.T.C. 17823. See Charles Sperone, ed., *Proverbi vulgari*, University of California Publications in Modern Philology, xxviii (Berkeley 1954).
29 Sig. 3^r–4^r. 30 Sig. 4^v.
31 E. Arber, ed., *Stationers' register*, ii, 403.

have been simply that Vautrollier was more used than Marsh to printing in non-English languages, though it may have been more specific. The Huguenot colony at Blackfriars was encouraged and patronized by many gentlemen, Sir Henry Sidney being one, who for the most part leaned towards puritanism. These gentle-men found the strict Calvinism in the theology of the refugees attractive, as also their tolerance in general towards the episcopal forms of the Anglican establish-ment. Sir Edward Unton was, we shall see, closely linked with puritan-minded Englishmen and French settlers alike. So the switch to Vautrollier may have been a matter of deliberately patronizing the French craftsman as well as a tribute to his capacity to print Italian elegantly.[32] Nor is this choice of printer necessarily without relevance to Parmenius, since he is found in 1582 using the same Thomas Vautrollier to publish a Latin poem of a semi-religious character. It is not at all unlikely that he was introduced to Vautrollier either by Charles Merbury or by the Untons.

If Stephen Parmenius arrived to share Hakluyt's rooms at Christ Church in the autumn of 1581 (though, as we have indicated above, p. 6, he may have come a little earlier), he would have found his master preoccupied and perhaps not paying his usual attention to his teaching duties. The young geographer had embarked busily on his first significant piece of geographical research.

Sir Humphrey Gilbert had been granted a patent, in June 1578, to search for and settle lands not hitherto occupied.[33] His objective was the eastern shore of North America on which he hoped to establish a series of English colonies. But the expedition which he led to sea in 1578 had failed to reach American waters and its failure led him into a trough of disappointment from which he found it hard to emerge. When a tiny vessel of his, the *Squirrel*, crossed and recrossed the Atlantic in 1580 bringing news of a fertile shore to the west which he might easily reach and occupy, he took heart again. He consulted the eminent geographer-astrologer, Dr John Dee, and worked out with him that Verrazzano's *Refugio*, which Ver-razzano had found on his 1524 voyage, was the best location for a settlement. They both linked *Refugio* in their minds with the *Rio de Gamas* or River of Norumbega,

---

32 For Vautrollier and his connections see W. R. Le Fanu, "Thomas Vautrollier, printer and bookseller", Huguenot Society of London, *Proceedings*, LX (1960), 12–25. Little is known of Vautrollier's movements in 1582. He was in Edinburgh for a time in 1581 and returned from there in 1583, which has led to statements that he remained in Scot-land in 1582; see G. Neilson, ed., *George Buchanan: Glasgow quatercentenary studies, 1906* (Glasgow 1907), p. 411. But Vautrollier's London press produced at least four books in 1582, and he is mentioned once in a London document: it is therefore unlikely that he was in Scotland continuously and thereby deprived of the chance of knowing Par-menius personally.

33 For Gilbert, see Quinn, *Gilbert*, 2 vols. (1940), the biography being in vol. 1, pp. 1–104.

which appeared in some maps in much the same place and was derived from the voyage of Estavão Gomes in the same year as Verrazzano's. *Refugio* is actually Narragansett Bay, whereas the *Rio de Gamas* is the Penobscot, which is separated from it by a long coastline. Geographical knowledge of America was still un-refined and Dee was able to combine the two locations on the vast map he pre-sented to Queen Elizabeth later in the year. He himself took over Gilbert's rights from 50° N. to the Pole.

Richard Hakluyt may well have been involved with Gilbert or with some of his associates as early as 1580. In that year he had a good deal to do with the appear-ance of English versions of narratives of Jacques Cartier's voyages into the St. Lawrence in 1534–36. He lent to John Florio, a young man of Italian parentage who had settled down to translate and to teach Italian to fashionable Oxford undergraduates, his set of Ramusio's *Navigationi*, where the Cartier narratives ap-peared. Moreover, he evidently revised Florio's translations and supplied him with propaganda statements on the advantages of English settlement in North America to use in his address to the reader, prefixed to the translations. With the aid of some money from Hakluyt and his friends, the elegant little book made its appearance in London in the late summer or autumn of 1580, with the title *A shorte and briefe narration of the two navigations to Newe Fraunce*. One objective was possibly to pro-mote expeditions to the St. Lawrence as a sideline to Gilbert's main preparations. There is not much evidence of Gilbert's activities in 1581, but it is clear that he enlisted the services of the younger Hakluyt in the larger research and propaganda venture which was to produce the *Divers voyages* in the following year. Hakluyt must have travelled frequently between London and Oxford, collaborating with his elder cousin, Richard Hakluyt, the lawyer, who indeed may well have guided his footsteps very thoroughly. He would have met Michael Lok, the battered but intellectual businessman who had suffered severely for Frobisher's fool's gold brought from Baffin Island only a short time before; Cyprian Lucar, a young merchant of London, who owned documents deriving from Robert Thorne the younger, a colonial theorist of the 1520s; Sir Francis Drake, William Borough, Dr John Dee; in fact, the whole range of those who had any interest in or docu-ments on the Americas, and more particularly North America, which was still so largely unknown to Englishmen.[34]

It used to be thought that *Divers voyages touching the discoverie of America*, the book which emerged from these researches, was published only about November 1582, but it is now known that it was already in print by 21 May, when it was "entered",

34 Most of what we know of the making of *Divers voyages* is contained in Hakluyt's dedi-cation to Sir Philip Sidney, himself an investor in Gilbert's expedition.

2 Henry Unton as a young man

3 Henry Unton, extract from his memorial portrait

LAURENTIVS HUMEREDUS

Rurſus ab exilio patriam complexus amatam
Papicolas ſacris fulminibus iugulo

AB

4 Laurence Humfrey, president of Magdalen College, Oxford

QVID NON:

VIRGINIA

Sr Humphry Gilbert knight
Here may yee see the pourtraict of his face
Who for his countries honour oft did trace
Along the deepe, and made a noble way
Vnto our growing fame Virginia
The picture of his minde if yee do craue it
Looke vpon vertues picture and yee haue it

5 Sir Humphrey Gilbert

DE NAVIGATIONE

ILLVSTRIS ET MAGNANIMI
Equitis Aurati Humfredi Gilberti, ad deducendam in novum orbem coloniam
suscepta , carmen
ἐπιβατικόν

STEPHANI PARME-
NII BVDEII.

faou d go
refue q

. LONDINI,
Apud Thomam Purfutium.
An. 1582,

Ornatissimo domino Gothofrido Brumannio
in testimoniu amicitie autor dd
in Watlemano 1 5 82 · 24 Juny

6 *De navigatione ... Humfredi Gilberti ... carmen* (1582), title page with
inscription from Stephen Parmenius to Geoffroy Brumen

7 *Paean ... ad psalmum Davidis* CIV (1582), title page with inscription from
Stephen Parmenius to Thomas Savile

PÆAN STEPHA-
NI PARMENII BVDEII

Ad psalmum Dauidis C IV. conformatus, & gratiarum loco, post prosperam ex suis Pannoniis in Angliam peregrinationem,
Deo optimo & ter maximo
seruatori consecratus.

LONDINI,
Excudebat Thomas Vautroullerius Typographus.
1582.

8 The first page of the Camden letter to Richard Hakluyt the younger

since Sir Edmund Brudenell inscribed his copy with the date 22 May.[35] This means that the work would have had to be complete very early in 1582, and the bulk of it must have been done during 1581. Although it was not a long book, it would have taken some time to bring together. The task of searching, copying, translating and summarizing available sources of information on North America was by no means negligible.

Hakluyt managed to search the patent rolls, where he found the 1496 patent to John Cabot and his sons, which helped greatly to justify later English ventures such as that which Gilbert had in mind. He ransacked Ramusio's *Navigationi* for information and details about Sebastian Cabot. The Verrazzano and the Zeno voyages were extracted from the same source and translated. Robert Thorne's papers, the first substantial English contribution to the problem of the northern seas, were obtained; these Hakluyt probably got from his elder cousin, who also allowed the printing (though without mention of his name) of the notes he gave to Pet and Jackman in 1580, and of the valuable recommendations on American colonization he had prepared for Gilbert in 1578. Jean Ribault's description of southeastern North America was reprinted from the scarce 1563 edition. Lists of geographical writers, and of "certain late travaylers", as well as of American com/modities, were drawn up and a stop/press note on a Portuguese voyage inserted.

Philip Sidney evidently thought the work worth while, since he apparently sub/sidized it and so earned Hakluyt's dedication which began: "I Marvaile not a little ... that since the first discoverie of America ... wee of England could never have the grace to set fast footing in such fertill and temperate places, as are left as yet unpossessed of them."[36] The book was not only a useful compendium but also a valuable instrument for publicizing Gilbert's projected voyage. We have good evidence that by the spring of 1582 Hakluyt had taught Parmenius much about the English voyages, not only to North America but to other parts. It seems highly probable that, in return, Stephen helped Hakluyt to put together the *Divers voyages*, saving him time by searching books in languages unfamiliar to the Oxford don, copying in his clear and elegant hand, and perhaps even adding his oc/casional contribution by way of comment and discussion. Such a supposition is not mere fancy but reasonable conjecture, supported by the geographical informa/tion shown by Parmenius in the poem he wrote on Gilbert's venture early in 1582.

One other person undoubtedly known to Parmenius was Edward Hayes.[37]

35 See D. B. Quinn, *Richard Hakluyt editor*, a study introductory to the facsimile edition of *Divers voyages* [and] *A short and briefe narration of the two navigations to Newe Fraunce*, 1967, I, 20, 32–33.   36 Sig. 1ʳ.
37 Cp. D. B. Quinn, "Edward Hayes, Liverpool colonial pioneer", Historic Society of Lancashire and Cheshire, *Transactions*, CXI, 25–45.

Born near Liverpool about 1550 and educated at King's College, Cambridge, he had been after 1571 in the service of the Hoby family in Berkshire. Although the Hobys' house, Bisham Abbey, was some considerable way across the county from Wadley, he may have had some contact with the Untons. In 1578, as "Master Haies, gentleman of Leerpolle", he had subscribed to Gilbert's first expedition. Shortly afterwards he had taken to the sea, though whether his interest in ships and shipping had preceded or followed his interest in the overseas world we cannot say. Before June 1580 he was already involved in litigation in the High Court of Admiralty, claiming damages from John Fisher, owner of the *Swallow* (possibly not the ship later engaged in the Gilbert voyage).[38] By November 1581 he had become owner of the *Golden Hind*, a Weymouth ship of 40 tons, in which Christopher Carleill had previously had an interest. Hayes was to contribute his recent acquisition, on hire we may assume, to the Gilbert expedition in 1583, and sailed in her as her captain. He was already known to Hakluyt when the latter was putting *Divers voyages* together later in 1581 or early 1582, for he was referred to as one of "certaine late travaylers" who were expected to have set out by the time the *Divers voyages* appeared. But, like Gilbert, he did not in fact do so for another year. Parmenius had thus every opportunity to make his acquaintance when he was in London and at the ports where the ships assembled before sailing in 1583. The evidence that he did so is contained in Hayes's account of Gilbert's voyage where he speaks of Parmenius' learning, piety, and his gifts in oratory and poetry in a manner which indicates a greater personal knowledge of him than would be gained in a few days' acquaintance in August 1583 at St. John's harbour in Newfoundland.

Hakluyt, on at least one visit to London, took Parmenius with him, introducing him to Sir Humphrey Gilbert. The two men were attracted to each other – which makes it likely that by then Parmenius was able to make himself understood in English – so that Hakluyt's precept combined with Gilbert's example to rouse some positive enthusiasm for the American venture in the mind of the young Hungarian. Parmenius began to think of going to America himself, but put the thought aside as he considered he was needed more in Hungary.[39] The meeting with Gilbert also put him in the mood for literary composition. The result was the Latin poem which is Parmenius' chief claim to reputation as an author, together with a humanistic exercise in honour of England, both of which he was to publish in 1582.

38 Public Record Office, London, H.C.A. 3/18, 24 June 1580; H.C.A. 24/52, no. 145. Cp. also Quinn, *Gilbert*, I, 83; II, 333, 413.
39 See p. 125 below.

The Two Poems

D E NAVIGATIONE ... HUMFREDI GILBERTI ... CARMEN (text and translation in Part I) is a careful eulogy (in dactylic hexameters) of England, her Queen, her social policy, and the achievements of her explorers; her project for colonial expansion is represented as a missionary rescue-operation to peoples who either are in pagan ignorance or have been positively corrupted by the church of Rome. There is, too, a certain amount of speculation about the character of the American lands which are so imperfectly disclosed; but this has had to be elaborated with classical myths and analogies. The chief of these is that Gilbert's expedition is another Argosy, which this time is to recover not a Golden Fleece for the Greeks but a Golden Age for the whole debased and war-weary world.

The achievements of previous English adventurers are reviewed: those of men like the Cabots, Sir Hugh Willoughby, Stephen and William Borough, Anthony Jenkinson and Martin Frobisher, about all of whom Richard Hakluyt had taught Parmenius, and all of whom are inscribed in the list of English travellers prefixed to the *Divers voyages*. Not that Parmenius was the only scholar of his time to celebrate such adventurers and their Queen in Latin hexameters: one of Thomas Watson's sequence of poems entitled *Amintae gaudia*, which appeared a few years later, briefly depicts the exploits of Cabot, Chancellor, Drake, Frobisher, Willoughby and Wyndham.[1] Incidentally, in the very same year that *De navigatione* saw the light of day, Watson encouraged vernacular literature by publishing a significant collection of lyric poems in English. And Parmenius himself, complimentary to his hosts and patrons, appears to make a gesture in the direction of commending the literary potential of English, in a passage which he added to the later version of his poem about Gilbert's voyage.[2]

1 For further discussion of Watson's poem, see p. 67-9 below; for the text of his catalogue of voyagers, see *DNC*, note to l. 277.
2 Watson's collection was published under the title *The Hecatompathia; or The passionate centurie of love* [1582], S.T.C. 25118a. See J. Buxton, *Sidney* (1964), pp. 197-9. P.'s own apparent allusion to the status of the English language occurs in *DNC*, 223-26.

Gilbert and Queen Elizabeth emerge in the poem as figures who, great in themselves, will add to their stature by American discoveries, sponsored by the one,
achieved by the other. Parmenius has also gleaned Gilbert's life story, either from
him in person or from Hakluyt, and he uses it, not without some imaginative
extravagance, in his verse. This sort of composition, the occasional Latin epic
about a contemporary heroic figure, was not entirely unfamiliar to Renaissance
England. In the middle of the previous century, a poem about the great Oxford
classicist Humfrey, Duke of Gloucester, had been written by an admiring Italian
immigrant.[3] Since that poem specifically celebrates the Duke's military activities
in Flanders, it rather closely foreshadows, whether Parmenius knew it or not, one
section (lines 105–33) of *De navigatione*.

Throughout this "stately poeme" (as Hakluyt was to call it), and indeed in his
two other works that survive, Parmenius' use of Latin words is classical, with the
exception of a very few which have been taken over to refer to aspects of the
Christian church.[4] His grammatical constructions also are classical, apart from a
decadent penchant for the subjunctive in subordinate clauses, evident in the
dedication to *De navigatione*. This prose passage is altogether more formal than the
colloquial, epistolary vein in which Parmenius was to write back to Hakluyt from
Newfoundland scarcely more than a year later. But then, to press a flattering
analogy which has, nevertheless, a certain relevance, Cicero himself did not write
to Atticus in the same tones that he used to record his speeches.[5] Parmenius too is
convincing when speaking with either voice.

As to verse-style, his hexameters adhere strictly to the metrical scheme ex-
emplified by, for example, Lucretius, Virgil and Statius; his elegiac couplets con-
form to the model of Ovid and Propertius. It was the current scholarly fashion, of
course, to introduce conspicuous and identifiable allusions to one's classical sources,
and Parmenius concurs. He had naturally read a good deal of Virgil, so that the
influence of both the *Aeneid* and the *Georgics* can be detected from time to time.

3 The poem, which came, as Professor R. Weiss remarks, "too early to inaugurate a
 tradition of humanist court poetry", is Tito Livio Frulovisi's *Humfroidos*. See Weiss's
 essay, "Italian humanism in western Europe", in E. F. Jacob, ed., *Italian Renaissance
 studies* (1960), pp. 69–93, esp. p. 81.
4 Such words are *superi* (*DNC*, 50, 80, 91), *genii* (91), *patres* (81); as the notes indicate,
 their meaning is not always clear. In the prose Preface to *DNC* the sequence of tenses
 occasionally departs from the classical practice of, say, the first century B.C.: see *DNC*
 notes to ll. 8, 9, 19 (Preface).
5 The relevance is that Cicero himself introduces in a letter to Atticus the same Greek
 word with which Parmenius entitles the dedicatory elegiacs of his *Paean* (see *Paean*,
 first note to "Ad illustrem . . . Henricum Untonum"); also that one of his colloquial
 constructions in the letter from Newfoundland has another letter, this time from Atticus
 to Cicero, as one of its few known classical precedents.

There are also echoes of Statius and Horace.[6] In particular, some of the themes which figure in his encomium of Elizabeth's England hark back to the spirit of the so-called Roman odes of Horace and suggest, as do his allusions to Virgil's fourth *Eclogue*, that Parmenius may have seen himself as performing for his host-country a similar service to that rendered by these classical poets who extolled the virtues of Augustus' benevolent reign at Rome. Indeed, the ways in which Rome's law-giving imperial mission were represented in contemporary literature sometimes resembled the sort of rationalizations with which Elizabethan adventurers veiled their motives for colonization. Thus Parmenius introduces, in common with Horace, a catalogue of subjected (or, at least, overawed) foreign peoples, an admiring comment on the clemency with which justice is tempered and on the absence of internecine civil strife, and a homily on the self-destructiveness of power wielded without judgment.[7]

Although there are many successful passages, yet the hand of the amateur craftsman can be detected in some features of Parmenius' writing. There are two places where he scans vowels short which would classically have been taken to be long.[8] Since they both involve assigning wrong vowel-lengths to words transliterated from the Greek, it may be that Parmenius did not know that language very well. If his Greek was in fact rather insecure, then his meretricious introduction of a Greek word towards the beginning of all three works could be seen as reflecting a wish to demonstrate to the world that he really was classically bilingual.[9] It must be remembered, however, that it was the custom of the times to make this sort of display. We know of another foreign protégé of Henry Unton who did it

6 Some of the lines involved are: *DNC*, 10, 22-3, 27, 57-60, 96, 140, 143, 150-3, 202, 204, 219; *Paean*, xi, 98. The classical passages concerned are mentioned in the relevant notes. The art of imitating or borrowing, without being merely parasitic or unimaginatively derivative, was cultivated by the practitioners and discussed by the theorists. For contemporary examples and a summary of Bembo's doctrine on the subject, see J. Sparrow's essay "Latin verse of the high Renaissance", in E. F. Jacob, *Italian Renaissance studies*, pp. 354-409, especially pp. 364-7.
7 We are indebted to the University of Toronto Press reader for pointing out the general parallel with Horace. Poems concerned are the first six or so of *Odes*, iii, some from book iv, and the *Carmen saeculare*; for particular points of comparison, see *DNC*, notes to ll. 113, 210, 223, 322.
8 The words are *physeter* and *Oenotriae* (*DNC*, 21, 261). Cp. also *Paean*, note to l. 8 (b).
9 The renaissance of Greek was still underdeveloped in England. Giordano Bruno, who lectured in Oxford in 1583, found the university as a whole deficient in the language: see Frances A. Yates, "Giordano Bruno's conflict with Oxford", Warburg Institute, *Journal*, II (1938/9) pp. 227-42, esp. pp. 231-32. The gradual acquisition of Greek texts by the college libraries had been gaining momentum from the mid-1530s: see N. R. Ker, "Oxford College libraries in the sixteenth century", *Bodleian Library Record*, VI (1959), 459-515.

with considerably less restraint.[10] Secondly, Parmenius elides long vowels and diphthongs before short vowels much more frequently than Virgil (rather seldom) does.[11] Statius, it is true, does so more often, but still does not as often as Parmenius. A further point, more difficult to pin down, is that his vocabulary seems to be somewhat pedestrian by comparison with the impression of variety and colour given, without necessarily being obscure or exotic, by Virgil, Statius or Ovid; and, indeed, even by comparison with his Scottish contemporary George Buchanan.[12] Again, there are passages of both prose and verse in which Parmenius produces some degree of congestion by trying to fit too many ideas into too few words without making the syntactical structure at all clear.[13]

He was well aware, no doubt, that his verses fell short of those of his models: he himself speaks disparagingly of his "raucous" poetic voice – *raucae carmina ... tubae*.[14] Perhaps it is little more than conventional self-depreciation; all the same, he was certainly not (and he would have known that he was not) as outstanding a poet as his countryman Tivadar Ács has represented him in modern times.[15] But we are lucky to be able to glimpse, in comparing the first version of *De navigatione* with the second, how the Hungarian scholar polished his lines to make them approximate more nearly to his ideal.[16]

For all his classicism, Parmenius uses (or his printers use) some variations from what have come to be regarded as classical spellings. Certain instances of these are recognized 'alternative' versions, current in the ancient world, but others are corruptions.[17] They have all been retained in the present edition of the texts, that of the

10 In dedicating his Latin translation of Guillaume de Saluste du Bartas, *L'Uranie* (J. Wolfe, 1589: S.T.C. 21673), to Unton, Thomas Ashley contrived to introduce in the space of two or three pages some half-dozen Greek words and three lines of Greek verse. Erasmus himself had adopted this practice in moderation. It had been a feature, of course, of Cicero's letters.
11 In the course of the 470 hexameters which survive, P. uses this device 38 times, which is an average of a fraction over 8·5 times per 100 lines; Virgil's rate seems to be about 5.
12 Cp. pp. 31-3 below and *DNC*, notes to ll. 25, 27.
13 Cp., e.g., *DNC*, notes to ll. 7 (Preface), 20, 21, 34, 195, 249; *Paean*, note to l. 12.
14 *DNC*, "Ad Thamesin", 4.
15 Tivadar Ács in *Akik elvándoroltak* (1942); "Egy tengerbe veszett magyar humanista költö a xvi. században", *Filologiai Közlöny* (1962), 115-22; and "Ki volt Budai Parmenius István", *Magyar Nemzet*, 24 January 1968, has done much (especially in the Hungarian abstract of *De navigatione* in his 1962 article) to make Parmenius known in Hungary. But he makes a number of assumptions about him, such as that he left large collections, still unexplored, at Oxford, that Parmenius was a university librarian, and that Edward Hayes brought P.'s letter back from Newfoundland to Hakluyt, and other points of this sort, which he would now admit, in the light of further knowledge, were unjustified.
16 See pp. 37, 42-4 below.
17 According to the authority of Lewis and Short (*A Latin dictionary*), the following are

De navigatione being based on the 1582 version, but incorporating from the later edition such variant readings as constitute additions or improvements.

At all events, what Parmenius produces is a highly accomplished humanistic exercise which conveys a most complimentary picture of the promoter of the newest American enterprise. The poet was able to present it to him in manuscript during the spring of 1582, probably early in March. At that time Gilbert was getting shipping ready in the Thames for his American voyage. He welcomed the poem and its compliments, and saw it as useful propaganda among the educated classes for his venture. As he was, at the time, making overtures to many landed gentlemen who had sufficient training in the classics to relish the Parmenius poem, this was sensible enough. He undertook to sponsor the poem (and to pay at least part of the cost of publication). The manuscript was sent to Thomas Purfoote, a general printer, whose association with the overseas voyages had begun as far back as 1569 when he had printed John Hawkins' account of his third West Indian voyage.[18] The poem appeared in June, some days before the 21st, and thus followed little more than three weeks after the *Divers voyages*.

We can say nothing about the reception or influence of the poem on its first appearance. But since only two copies are known to survive (one in the Huntington Library and one in the British Museum), it may have been disposed of quickly. When he was writing it, Parmenius expected that Gilbert would shortly leave the Thames for America, hence the dedicatory elegiacs "to the Thames"; but instead he had gone to Southampton in April to purchase shipping, and from then onwards directed his main efforts to completing his preparations in that port.

At the time the poem on Gilbert appeared, Parmenius was living with the Untons at Wadley, their country house near Faringdon in Berkshire, which the Queen had visited in 1574.[19] Sir Edward Unton had been in poor health. He had made a will on 14 September 1581, probably during an earlier illness. In May 1582 he had taken to his bed with a bad leg and, perhaps thinking he was dying,

examples of classically recognized alternatives, which are, however, not necessarily regarded as equally "correct": *paullum* for *paulum*, *intelligo* for *intellego*, *moeror* for *maeror*, *pene* for *paene*. On the other hand, these are non-classical: *caeptum* for *coeptum*, *foelix* for *felix*, *charus* for *carus*, *spacium* for *spatium* and *ocia* for *otia*. With regard to the last two cases, we may note that a certain interchangeability of 'c' and 't' was current in Elizabethan times: thus *deliciae* was sometimes spelled *delitiae*; and cp. also the apparent softening of the 'c' in *sceptra* (*DNC*, 229, 315). This had been a mediaeval, or even earlier, trend, which was merely consolidated by Renaissance contact with Italian. See, for example, K. Strecker, *Introduction to mediaeval Latin* (trans. and revised by R. B. Palmer; Berlin 1957), pp. 59–62. For general editorial practice see Preface, above.
18 See Hakluyt, *Principall navigations*, edd. Quinn and Skelton, I (1965), xxix–xxx.
19 *Victoria county history of Berkshire*, IV, 491.

delivered his will before witnesses on 29 May 1582.[20] Probably before this he had already called down a French apothecary from London to attend him. Geoffroy le Brumen considered himself a good apothecary, and he was evidently on close personal terms with Sir Edward from earlier acquaintance, as he also was with Sir Francis Walsingham, the Queen's secretary of state, for whom he performed various services. Sir Edward's limb got worse: it began to show signs of gangrene, so that flesh had to be removed from it. By the middle of June he had taken a turn, Brumen thought a decisive turn, for the better. But Sir Edward would not allow the apothecary to leave, even though Brumen was by then chafing to get back to other business. In a detailed and interesting letter to Walsingham on 14 June,[21] Brumen discusses various items of family business which Unton has asked him to take up with Sir Francis. He is particularly concerned to leave his younger son, Henry, for whom Brumen expresses a high regard, well off: he had arranged for him to have a good deal of money (some of it would seem an advance on what was being left to him by will). Through Brumen he asks that Walsingham should help to find an office which can be purchased for Henry. Brumen commends the young man not only for his personal qualities but also because his wife, formerly Dorothy Wroughton, is a relative of Lady Walsingham's: yet, most significantly for our purposes, he stresses his puritanism. He and his wife "strive to extend the kingdom of Christ wherein you rejoice", the evangelical impulse being strongest amongst those who were on poor terms with the establishment. Brumen also shows that Sir Edward was of the same persuasion since he proposed to commend both his sons, in the event of his death, to the care of Walsingham "and that of those of the Religion". "The Religion" here is that of men who are Calvinist in theology, evangelical in temperament, and critical of a rigid episcopalian establishment, even if not outright Presbyterians.

It was during his stay at Wadley that Geoffroy le Brumen became closely as-sociated with Parmenius. As an apothecary – and possibly as an alchemist also – Brumen was capable of making a chemical analysis, in the crude terms in which this was possible in the late sixteenth century. This ability had brought him into contact with the overseas movement some five years before. He had been called in by his patron, Walsingham, to examine some specimens of the alleged gold-bearing ore brought by Martin Frobisher from Baffin Island or, as he called it, Meta Incognita, in 1577. Brumen's report, in French, to Walsingham on 24 January 1578 is an able one.[22] Unlike other experts who examined the ore brought back, he was neither credulous nor self-deceiving and did not find a high yield of gold and

20 Nichols, *Unton inventories* (1841), p. xliv.
21 *Calendar of state papers, foreign, 1582*, pp. 87–8.
22 *Calendar of state papers, colonial, East Indies, China and Japan, 1513–1616*, p. 31.

silver, but only "quelque peu de bon metal", and the main mineral content "marchasites", marcasites or iron pyrites. Had his analysis been accepted, Frobisher need not have set sail with eleven ships in 1578 to discover on his return that all the ore previously brought home had been condemned, rather late in the day, by other mineral experts. Thus we can see that Brumen shared with Parmenius some, at least, of the concern which the Hungarian had developed for the New World, though perhaps his experience had made him sceptical of its riches in precious metals. It is, perhaps, significant that he did not invest in Sir Humphrey Gilbert's enterprise. The two men are likely to have found food for discussion at Wadley, both between themselves and with their host, Henry Unton. Parmenius too would have found books at Wadley and may have done there some of the reading which preceded the completion of *De navigatione*. In 1596 the study at Wadley, then Sir Henry Unton's, but in 1582 his father's creation, had "seven hangings of gilded leather, one table ..., shelves, with many books of diverse sorts to the number of two hundred and twenty, and one chest of vair".[23] Some of the books may well have been collections of voyages. Parmenius' poem came out in June, and by 21 June at any rate copies had come down to Wadley, no doubt leading to the presentation of copies to Sir Edward and to Henry, though neither has survived. There is, however, at least one such presentation copy still in existence, having been first in the collection of E. D. Church and now in the Huntington Library. This is the one which Parmenius inscribed as follows: *Ornatissimo domino Gothofrido Brumannio in testimoniu[m] amicitiae autor d[ono] d[edit] in Wadleniano 1582: 21 Iunii.*[24] The testimony of the Hungarian scholar's friendship with the French apothecary Geoffroy le Brumen is here kept alive.

By November Brumen had been called in to attend on the Earl of Sussex, although he was unable in the event to take much part in the treatment, being pushed out by the physicians and surgeons. This might again suggest a further widening of the circles of Parmenius' personal contact, since Charles Merbury had by now obtained for himself a post in Sussex's household. But Walsingham had work for Brumen in France, and it was there that he spent from March to June 1583. He was back in London by 9 June,[25] but by this time Parmenius had left the city and was about to sail from Plymouth with Sir Humphrey Gilbert. The friends had met for the last time.

It is not possible to know precisely how Parmenius divided his time between Wadley, London and Oxford during the months between June 1582 and May

23 Nichols, *Unton inventories* (1841), p. 3.
24 Title-page of Huntington 17387: S.T.C. 19308. Fig. 6 below.
25 *Calendar of state papers, foreign, 1582*, pp. 474–6; *Calendar of state papers, foreign, 1583, with addenda*, pp. 198–9, 217–19, 229–30, 251–2, 389–90.

1583. In his dedication to Gilbert of the *De navigatione* he had acknowledged that one of his reasons for coming to London from Oxford was to obtain introductions to outstanding men there. We do not know to whom, besides Gilbert, Richard Hakluyt was able to introduce him, but we may assume that he met the elder Richard Hakluyt whose still greater command of geographical lore would have proved impressive. He already knew William Camden. It is not at all unlikely also that he had met Philip Sidney, to whom Hakluyt had already acknowledged his debt and who was now associated in Gilbert's venture, though he later with-drew from it. Sir George Peckham, Gilbert's chief associate, is someone else whom Parmenius may have encountered. In August and September Sir Francis Wal-singham and Sir George Peckham and "dyvers others of good judgment and Creditt" were listening to various reports on America, good and bad, from Englishmen who had been there.[26] Both Gilbert and Hakluyt would naturally have been present at these sessions. It is, therefore, possible that Parmenius also may have managed to hear David Ingram relate his scarcely credible story of his alleged journey by foot from Mexico to Cape Breton, or Simão Fernandes recount how he sailed the *Squirrel* to and from America.

Whether or not Parmenius was present, it seems probable that he did acquire an introduction to Walsingham. The latter was always ready to make fresh contacts with foreign Protestant visitors who might in future be induced to send him in-telligence reports, and he could easily have heard of Parmenius from Geoffroy le Brumen as well as from Hakluyt or Gilbert. Parmenius is most likely to have waited on the Earl of Leicester, Chancellor of Oxford University, and patron of Laurence Humfrey,[27] as well as of many other Puritans in the Church of England. Humfrey could well have given him a letter of introduction. It is likely too that Parmenius was brought to court to see and admire, at least from a distance, the Queen of whom he had already written so enthusiastically. But he did not spend all his time in London.

Because he dedicated it so warmly to Henry Unton, it seems likely that Par-menius began his next piece of writing at Wadley, though he may not have com-pleted it there. It was a paraphrase, again in hexameters, of the 104th Psalm.[28] Since it was intended to celebrate his safe journeying from Hungary to England, he called it a 'paean'. It contains more classical myth and humanist expertise than

26 Quinn, *Gilbert*, II, 281–310 (especially p. 283).
27 See Eleanor Rosenberg, *Leicester, patron of letters* (1955), pp. 128–32, 260–2.
28 *Paean* (S.T.C. 4016); for full title see below, p. 140. The British Museum copy and the one at Eton which belonged to Thomas Savile (pp. 36–7 below), are the only ones so far located. The publication date on a pamphlet was usually that of the calendar year, so we should expect it to have been published before 31 December 1582. But a

either Christian doctrine or autobiographical information. To print and publish it Parmenius went to Thomas Vautrollier. Again, one reason may have been the French printer's skill in setting Latin verse, but the links between Charles Merbury, Vautrollier, and Henry Unton suggest, as we have seen, that the printer was personally known to the Untons. Then, too, in view of the dedication, it is highly probable that Henry Unton subsidized the publication, so helping in turn to keep a vigorous printer of Puritan material in business.

Latin versions of the Psalms had been in use, of course, throughout the early and medieval Church, ever since St. Jerome's pre-Vulgate translations contained in the Roman "Breviary";[29] they were therefore readily available, at the time Parmenius was writing, to anyone who did not reject their ecclesiastical and theological associations. But, as Augustin Bea remarks, "It is easy to understand that in a humanistic age there would have been a lively desire to have a translation of the psalms which was at once more comprehensible and in more cultured Latin."[30] Thus there was already in Parmenius' day quite a tradition of more 'classical' versions made in the sixteenth century – some of them done, like the famous set by George Buchanan, in a variety of Graeco-Latin verse-forms (*in carmen Latinum*).[31]

Vautrollier had specific experience in printing compositions of this particular genre. Two years previously he had put out an edition of Buchanan's celebrated version; and the following year he had published an incomplete set by Scipio Gentili, as well as a complete *psalterium* by Heobanus Hessus.[32] Seeing that the

book with "1582" on the title-page (and on occasion, no doubt, a pamphlet) could have been published as late as 24 March 1583.

29 Jerome's *Psalterium Romanum*, completed in A.D. 383, and the revised *Psalterium Gallicum* of 392, had been through various partial recensions from the sixth century onwards and were to be officially revised in 1590 under the auspices of Pope Sixtus V. It was the "Gallic" version that Coverdale had used.

30 "On comprend ... aisément qu'au temps de l'humanisme le désir ait été vif de posséder une traduction des Psaumes à la fois plus intélligible et d'un Latin plus cultivé" (Augustin Bea, *Le nouveau psautier latin* (Paris 1947), p. 21).

31 We may note those of Pagnino (1528), Gaëtan de Vio (1530), and Arias Monanto (1574); there had apparently even been a fifteenth-century version, by Giorgio Manetti (d. 1459), but it was not published. See Bea, *loc. cit.*

32 (*a*) Buchanan, *Paraphrasis psalmorum Davidis poetica* (1580: S.T.C. 3984); first published in 1566. (*b*) S. Gentili, *Paraphrasis aliquot psalmorum Davidi* (1581: S.T.C. 11730); in 1584 there followed *In xxv. Davidis psalmos epicae paraphrases*, published by J. Wolfe and dedicated to Philip Sidney (S.T.C. 11731). The Protestant brothers Alberico and Scipio Gentili had fled Italy at just about the time when P. was leaving Hungary on his European tour; for Thomas Savile befriending Alberico, the legal theorist, see p. 15 above. (*c*) Hessus, *Psalterium Davidis carmine redditum per H.H.* (1581: S.T.C. 2361).

first of these had already been through several editions on the continent, Parmenius can hardly have failed to come across it. It is interesting that numbers 1 and 104 of Buchanan's collection came to be regarded as his masterpiece,[33] so it is possible that Parmenius chose 104 after being impressed by the success of Buchanan's version. He may, however, have been more influenced by the technical consideration that its pastoral and cosmological content was closer in spirit to the *Eclogues* and *Georgics* of Virgil with which he was familiar. Parmenius' piece is in any case an altogether widerranging rhapsody than Buchanan's comparatively literal rendering, comprising 140 lines as against the latter's 83.

A further point is that Vautrollier may have been able, because of his French contacts, to supply Parmenius with the raw material for his undertaking. For it is "commonly thought" (according to Ruddiman) that Buchanan had been "chiefly directed by" the translations and commentaries which had been made from the original language by F. Vatabulus, professor of Hebrew at Paris.[34] Since Vautrollier was currently in touch with Buchanan over the production of the latter's "History of Scotland",[35] he might have been able to make a copy of Buchanan's materials available to Parmenius. On the other hand, there is Professor van Tieghem's view that Buchanan himself appears to have used the Vulgate.[36] But if the Hungarian's doctrinal sympathies had led him to scorn the text of Rome, there had been some dozen or so avowedly 'Protestant' Latin versions of the moreorless complete bible published in various parts of Europe earlier in the century. Bea says of these that they "usually take little notice of the Vulgate and try to express the meaning of the original text in a humanistic Latin that is more or less classical but not invariably felicitous".[37] One such which must just have been coming into circulation while Parmenius was at Oxford, is that of Tremellius and Junius; and Vautrollier himself printed the New Testament section of this work in 1580.[38]

---

33 This is the verdict of Thomas Ruddiman, Buchanan's eighteenthcentury editor, who was moved to write a "Vindication" defending the poet against the charge that his psalmtranslations were inferior to those of Arthur Johnson, a graduate of Padua who died at Oxford in 1641. In a long and acrimonious comparison of their versions of no. 104, Ruddiman cites several other paraphrases but is apparently not familiar with P.'s. See *A vindication of Mr George Buchanan's paraphrase of the book of Psalms* (Edinburgh 1745), pp. 284–350.

34 *Ibid.*, p. 246.   35 See *DNC*, note to l. 25.

36 P. van Tieghem, *La littérature latine de la Renaissance* (Paris 1944), p. 56.

37 "[Ces traductions] tiennent généralement peu compte de la Vulgate et cherchent à exprimer le sens du texte original en un Latin d'une humanisme plus ou moins classique, mais pas toujours heureux" (Bea, *Le nouveau psautier latin*, p. 23).

38 Tremellius and Junius, *Testamenti veteris biblia sacra, quibus etiam adiunximus novi testamenti libros* (S.T.C. 2056). Vautrollier had previously published five editions of Beza's translation.

But we happen to know that it was another translation from this group with which Parmenius would have been especially familiar.

The so-called "Zürich Latin Bible" or *Versio Tigurina* was published by Frosch-auer in 1543. It was the work of several hands. Leo Juda provided most of the Old Testament, but that part was completed (including the psalms from 103 onwards) by Theodore Bibliander; the New Testament translation was basically that of Erasmus, and the whole was edited by Pellican. Professor Gordon Rupp has commented that the influence of this version in England has not been fully studied.[39] Now, the psalter "of Leo Juda translation" had been a prescribed pos-session for Christ Church undergraduates from the middle of the sixteenth century; and it was eventually incorporated into the cathedral-college's own prayerbook. "It differs considerably from the Vulgate", writes H. L. Thomson, "and the choice was possibly due to the puritan sympathies of Dean Sampson or to the Chapter of Edward VI's days."[40] When Parmenius was at the college, the head of house was the eminent Tobie Matthew, senior, who did not conceal his liberal views; neither his vigorous but circumspect defence of the Reformation against Campion in 1581 nor his fervently Puritan wife prevented him from becoming Archbishop of York three years after the Queen's death.[41]

As for internal literary evidence, it may be illuminating to compare the vocabu-lary of Parmenius' *Paean* with the Zürich version of Psalm 104, and with the word-ing found in the Vulgate, the Breviary and Buchanan.[42] All this suggests, then, that Parmenius is likely to have worked at least partly from the version made by Bibliander for the Tigurini bible of 1543; for there seems to be no evidence of an earlier *psalterium* completed by Leo Juda himself.

In its original form, the *Paean* consists of an effective title-page, a dedication to Henry Unton on the *verso*, and a five-page poem. When putting a title to this dedication Parmenius again showed off his Greek, and the verses themselves com-prise six particularly successful elegiac couplets. The main poem is of no great im-portance in itself, except as a competent exercise in a currently fashionable idiom

39 See *British Museum catalogue of bibles*, col. 40. The Museum preserves the copy of this work which Queen Elizabeth inherited from Henry VIII. Professor Rupp's comment is in *New Cambridge modern history*, II (1958), 101–2.
40 See H. L. Thompson, *Christ Church* (1900), pp. 37–8. There seems to have been no printed form of the Christ Church prayerbook as such until 1615; in some editions, the last of which was 1726, the title varied from what Thompson gives.
41 Tobie Matthew (1546–1628) was dean from 1576 to 1584. His reply (... *concio apologetica*) to Campion's *Decem rationes* was not published until 1638. Christ Church records include a complete list of the personnel of the senior members of the college for the time that P. was there.
42 See Table of Comparative Vocabulary, p. 164 below.

by a skilled Latinist who had on this occasion no strikingly original message. It is interesting, nevertheless, as being the second of Parmenius' only two published works, and as demonstrating again his combination of Graeco-Roman humanism and Protestant theology.

We have said that Parmenius clearly knew his Virgil. If he had been familiar also with that other great first-century exponent of the hexameter, Lucretius, we might have expected to find in this work some echoes of the fifth book of his *De rerum natura*: for there are some similarities between the pictures they respectively draw of the creation of the world. More striking, however, is the allusion, in Parmenius' opening lines, to the sort of distinction between spirit and intellect which bulks large elsewhere in Lucretius' poem.[43] As we shall see below, however, there were other literary and philosophical sources also concerned with such contrasts; and it seems fairly clear, in fact, that copies of Lucretius were in short supply in the sixteenth century, although the general nature of his writing was known (if only by repute) even in England at the time.[44]

Another feature of Parmenius' intellectual environment which may have had a bearing on his selection and treatment of this particular psalm is the prevalence of Renaissance neoplatonism; or rather, of renewed Italian concern for classical philosophy in general. The humanist scholar of that era was almost bound to become acquainted with the work of those thinkers (such as Ficino, Pico and Pomponazzi) who had devoted themselves, in the latter part of the fifteenth and early part of the sixteenth centuries, to elaborating some sort of *rapprochement* between Plato and/or Aristotle on the one hand and Christian theology on the other. Linked with this project had been the endeavour to disseminate what Plato and Aristotle really said, as opposed to what Plotinus and Averroes respectively had said they said.[45]

On general grounds it is highly unlikely that Parmenius had not come across these thinkers' work in the course of his European tour (especially if he had spent any time at Florence, Padua, Bologna or Paris); and, specifically, there are a number of passages in both *De navigatione* and *Paean* where Parmenius' words remain obscure or pointless until seen against such a background.[46] At this point

43 For a comparison of particular lines about the creation, see *Paean*, notes to ll. 25, 34; and for the disjunction between *spiritus* and *mens*, see p. 35 below and *Paean*, note to l. 1.
44 See Sir Paul Harvey, ed., *Oxford companion to classical literature* (Oxford 1937), p. 249 for the report that Queen Elizabeth's physician, William Gilbert, knew and quoted Lucretius' work. For the nature of his writings being known to Philip Sidney, if only at second hand, see *Apology for poetry*, ed. G. Shepherd (1965), p. 102, line 16.
45 A valuable introduction to the objectives and achievements of such thinkers is to be found in E. Cassirer, P. O. Kristeller, and J. H. Randall, edd., *The Renaissance philosophy of man* (Chicago 1948).
46 All but one of them are directly concerned with religious or spiritual matters. The

we need only remark how in Psalm 104 the catalogue of the wonder and diversity of God's creation, and the reference to a company of celestial ministers who are "fire and flame" (verse 4), give Parmenius the chance to embroider the favourite neoplatonic theme of the human soul occupying a middle place in the hierarchy of levels of being; in this case, between God and the heavenly host above and the lower strata comprising animal life and vegetation. Plotinus had defended some such scheme against the Gnostics, and Ficino had elaborated a version rather different from his.[47] Secondly, the psalmist's initial invocation to his soul allows Parmenius to introduce into his paraphrase, by way of an aside, a sophisticated allusion to neoclassical philosophizing about the dual nature or function of the human soul;[48] and, again, in the wording of the title-page's dedication, there seems to be a concession to the current vogue for finding parallels between Christian theology and Hermeticism.[49]

In so far as the *Paean* may give the impression of marginally greater facility and flexibility of composition than does the *De navigatione*,[50] we are perhaps seeing an improvement of technique that owes something to the practical experience of writing the earlier work and something to further study at Christ Church and Wadley of his classical models. Or it may be that on a pastoral-cosmological theme he was closer in spirit to Virgilian and Ovidian antecedents; and indeed that his own heart was more in praising God and Nature than it had been in over-praising Humphrey Gilbert. (*Fortunatus et ille deos qui novit agrestes.*) It seems likely

exception is the symbolic use made of the mythical figure of Proteus (*DNC*, 22–6). For the two others which occur in the *Paean*, see below, nn. 48, 49. The remaining two come in *DNC*: one refers to the perpetuation of true (Protestant) religion in Britain (ll. 90–92), and the second to the individual believer's quest for knowledge of and communion with the Divinity (258–60).

47 Plotinus' attack on the Gnostics is in *Enneads* ii, 9, 9. Such hierarchical schemes (which may illuminate, incidentally, P.'s problematical use of the word *superi*: see *DNC* notes to ll. 51, 81, 91) provide scope for the idea of the soul trying to better itself by rising to a higher level; and they also allow the chance of discerning a link with Pythagoreanism. See *DNC*, notes to ll. 24, 50, 259; *Paean*, notes to ll. 1, 19.

48 The exposition and justification of such dualities had, of course, engaged the efforts of many speculators since Plato and Aristotle. As indicated above, there was an important Epicurean tradition rather separate from the Platonic-Aristotelian threads which the Christian classicists of the Renaissance were concerned to take up. Two major neoclassical contributions had been Ficino's commentaries on the later Plato, and Pomponazzi's reconsideration of Aristotle's *De anima*. See *Paean*, note to l. 1.

49 The suggestive phrase is *ter maximo*: see *Paean*, p. 140 and n. to l. 6 of title page, p. 156.

50 The translator, at any rate, has this impression. It is due in part, and perhaps entirely, to the more carefully balanced lines and the less repetitive use of the suffix -*que* in the fifth foot dactyl. The frequency of the latter is reduced on average from once in less than 10 lines in *DNC* to exactly once in 12 in the *Paean*.

that, whatever else may hold, Parmenius' literary skill had in fact increased, for he was able to return to the *De navigatione* after composing the *Paean* and make significant stylistic improvements.[51]

On this point it is worth remarking that, during his short association with Christ Church, Parmenius would have been in the company of some of the most accomplished Latin versifiers which Britain ever produced. There had been a productive group of Latinists, headed by the celebrated William Gager, based on the college from the mid-seventies. Their work has been discussed by Professor Leicester Bradner, and they provide eight of the contributors to the university's memorial volume in honour of Henry Unton, mentioned above (p. 11). Gager's offering is far longer than any other, running to over 300 lines and exploiting various metres. All the same, the contributors from Magdalen and Trinity colleges separately outnumber those from Christ Church, and it is to this collective profusion of academic bards that Parmenius refers when he affirms that, even if he himself has to return to Hungary, there will be plenty of other poets to write about the New World so long as Oxford stands (*De navigatione*, 162–68).[52]

From the composition of the *Paean*, however, and from the company of poets, as from the society of other great or learned men, Parmenius had now to detach himself for a time, in order to engage in the long and painful preparations for an American voyage.

He returned to them briefly at least during an interval in a long and frustrating winter, when hopes of departure were temporarily at an end, when the opening of the new year left the prospects of adventure and fame still in doubt. If we are right that the *Paean* was published in the calendar year 1582 – and in view of its Unton dedication it cannot be otherwise unless our whole chronology of Parmenius' appearance in England is at fault – it was in February 1583 that Parmenius was for a time back at Oxford and in Merton College with his friend Thomas Savile. It was then that he presented to Thomas the copy of the *Paean*, which, with its inscription by Parmenius, is now in Eton College Library.[53] The elegance and clarity of

---

51 For commentary on the main alterations see *DNC*, notes to ll. 128, 183, 220, 228, 294.
52 Professor Bradner's discussion of Elizabethan Oxford poets is in his *Musae Anglicanae* (New York 1940), pp. 60–67.
53 The copy at Eton is now bound as it was by provost Henry Savile between a work by Firminus, *Repertorium de mutatione aeris* (Paris 1539), and one by Alchindus, *De imbribus* – rather a meteorological association. But the *Paean* also shares the volume with Copernicus, *De revolutionibus orbium celestium* (Nuremberg 1543), the first edition, and with another former possession of Thomas Savile, a Latin translation by Scipio Gentili of Tasso's *Solymeidos liber primus* (1584). We are grateful to the Librarian, Provost, and Fellows of Eton for permission to inspect this volume (catalogue number Fa 4.9) and to photograph the title-page of the *Paean*.

hand with which Parmenius writes, as may be seen from Figure 7, is marred to some extent by two deletions. He starts "To his very dear friend, the young Thomas" (*Amicissimo iuveni Thomasi*), but he crosses part of this through and re- duces it "To his friend and brother ..." (*amico & fratri suo*). Even then, he struck out *& fratri*, and left the equivalent of "Presented by the author to his friend Thomas Savile at Oxford on 9 February ..."(*Thom[asi] Savillo amico suo au[tor] dono dabat oxonij 5 idus Febr.* [   ]." The ends of the lines have been trimmed to lose us the year-date, especially likely to have been present as Parmenius included it in his parallel legend on Brumen's copy of *De navigatione*.54 How long the friends re- mained together, and whether it was then that Parmenius did a little final revision of his voyage poem, we cannot say.55

54 See p. 29 above.   55 See pp. 42-4 below.

Preparations for an American Expedition

W E CAN FOLLOW Sir Humphrey Gilbert's protracted preparations through the letters of a young man-about-court, Maurice Browne, with whom Parmenius was soon to be closely associated. He was the fourth son of a well-to-do London mercer, John Browne, who died in 1571.[1] Born about the same time as the younger Hakluyt and Sir Walter Ralegh, he had matriculated from Pembroke College, Cambridge, in 1569 but had not taken a degree.[2] In May 1580, when his surviving correspondence begins,[3] he was in the service of the Secretary of State, Sir Francis Walsingham. He was also closely associated with John Thynne the younger, whose father, the builder of Longleat, that immense Elizabethan monument, was in his last illness. Over the next year or so Browne was living at Thynne's house in Cannon Row and is found doing various pieces of business for the younger Thynne who was gradually taking over the responsibilities of a large fortune. After March 1581 there is a gap in the letters of more than a year. Browne had been drawn into a significant and secret anti-Spanish enterprise, the first since Drake's return, in September 1580, from his world-encompassing voyage. Dom Antonio, the would-be king of Portugal, had been forestalled by Philip II in 1580, but had retained a foothold in the Azores. He appealed to France and England for aid. Elizabeth procrastinated, but in the summer of 1581 a small force under Captains Edward Pryn, Sachfyeld, Roberts and Henry Richards supplied a nominal English contingent to the anti-Spanish forces at Terceira. Maurice Browne accompanied the ships, apparently to maintain a measure of liaison

---

1 For John Browne, see his will in Somerset House, London, P.C.C. 30 Lyon; S. J. Madge, ed., *Abstract of inquisitions post mortem, London, 1561-77* (London: British Record Society, 1901), pp. 146–8; J. J. Howard and G. J. Armytage, *Visitation of London 1568* (London: Harleian Society, 1869), p. 24. Alison Quinn identified the family.
2 J. and J. A. Venn, *Alumni Cantabrigienses*, I (Cambridge, 1922), 235.
3 There are seventeen letters, beginning in April 1580, the relevant parts of eight of which are given in Appendix II (pp. 189-208 below). They are all contained in the Thynne Papers, volume v, Longleat House, Wiltshire. For access to them and for permission to quote from them, thanks are due to the Marquess of Bath, to Mr R. H. Ingleton, and to Mr M. F. Tiffin.

between Walsingham and Dom Antonio, and as "Master Brum" appears in the correspondence between the Portuguese and the Queen, Walsingham, and Drake. After his summer in Terceira, Browne returned to England, apparently with Captain Roberts who sailed from Terceira on 1 October, leaving behind a token force of 100 men under Richards.[4]

When he came back to London, Browne was a changed man: he was now absorbed with the prospects for Englishmen in the overseas world. John Thynne had lent him, probably during a visit to Longleat after his return from the voyage, a Portuguese chart. He resumed the correspondence with Thynne in July 1582 with a discussion of the appearance of America on the map and promised Thynne a newer and more up-to-date one.[5] He was also proposing to take lessons in cosmography and navigation from an English expert,[6] and was already involved in preparations for a new enterprise, possibly that being prepared by the elder William Hawkins for a Brazil voyage, in which he expected to sail in September. In August Browne was drawn instead into Sir Humphrey Gilbert's service. By this time, Gilbert had disposed, on paper, of great tracts of North American land to friends and associates such as Sir Philip Sidney, and to a group of Catholic gentlemen headed by Sir George Peckham and Sir Thomas Gerrard, but he had not got his ships to sea in July, as he had expected. Instead, he was at his house in Red Cross Street, in August, when Thomas Smith, son of the customer of London, came to call on him bringing Maurice Browne.[7]

Delighted to welcome the son of a rich and influential merchant and official, Gilbert spent the rest of the day talking about his plans, and sent next day to invite both his guests to a second session. There he showed them his map which has sur-

4 See Simão de Verro to Queen Elizabeth 13 October 1581; to Sir Francis Drake 14 October 1581; to Sir Francis Walsingham 20 December 1581 (Public Record Office, London, State Papers, Foreign, Portugal, S.P. 89/1, nos. 199, 201, 205), and Edward Pryn to Leicester, 16 November 1581 (B.M., Cotton MS, Vespasian C.VII, f.386).
5 The Thynne map was presumably acquired by John Thynne the elder (d. 1580). Browne's lively discussion of it has not yet led to its identification, nor can the new map he mentioned be identified (p. 189 below).
6 Who this "excellent fellowe" (p. 191 below) was who was to teach him navigation is not certainly known. Thomas Harriot, who had entered Ralegh's service shortly after he came down from Oxford in 1580, is a distinct possibility. So are, in a lesser degree, Walter Warner and Nathaniel Torporley (see E. G. R. Taylor, *Original writings and correspondence of the two Richard Hakluyts*, I, 25). Thomas Hood is, perhaps, the most likely of any. Arthur Throckmorton employed him in 1595 at 20s a week to teach him geometry (A. L. Rowse, *Ralegh and the Throckmortons* (1962), p. 197).
7 P. 192 below. Visiting customer Smith's house in December 1580, Browne had mentioned the younger Smith; in July 1582, he proposed to bring "my cosen Smith", presumably the same man, on a visit to Longleat (Longleat, Thynne Papers, v, ff. 163ᵛ, 203ᵛ).

vived and is now in Philadelphia.[8] He told of the rich promise of the country as seen by his man, the Portuguese navigator Simão Fernandes, who had crossed the Atlantic for him in 1580 in the tiny bark, the *Squirrel*,[9] to what is now New England. Gilbert also produced the evidence supplied by one of John Hawkins' sailors, David Ingram, who claimed to have walked from the Gulf of Mexico to Cape Breton in 1568–69 and who might therefore be regarded as a valuable authority on North America.[10] Gilbert said that he had two ships and three pinnaces, with some 220 men, almost ready to sail. He would attempt with them to make a settlement in America and send home as soon as possible two of the pinnaces, one with specimens of the products of the country, the other with reports on the voyage for the Queen, the Privy Council and his backers.

Sir Francis Walsingham, Maurice Browne's master, was already a strong sup-porter of Gilbert's enterprise. Browne's sudden enthusiasm for Gilbert's plans, which the two meetings had aroused, led Gilbert to wean him away from his earlier plans. The former's experience in the Azores was to his advantage; so, even more, was his close relationship with Walsingham. Consequently, Gilbert asked Walsingham for his services on the voyage, promising, if Walsingham consented, that Browne should be "the messenger (as he trusted in God) of the good newes that [he] shold send to her Majestie" and to Walsingham. Walsingham was will-ing, and Browne declared: "I was very glad to undertake the voyage in respect his honour did favor the same." He also said in writing to Thynne, that Walsingham asked that Gilbert should "have an especiall care of me, so yow se how I am dis-posed of".[11] From then onwards Browne devoted himself to the task of furthering Gilbert's preparations and preparing himself to be the reporter of the expedition's activities. Though both he and Gilbert expected to be at sea very shortly, it was to be a long and weary ten months before the ships finally set sail for North America.

Browne was soon at Southampton from which port Gilbert intended to set out, lending a hand and getting a subscription from Thynne towards the voyage. He had time to visit Longleat and see the Thynnes, John himself, and his wife Jane (daughter of Sir Rowland Heyward, whom Browne knew well), and their small son Tom. There were minor setbacks. A ship coming round from London was delayed at the Downs and so prevented the rest from taking advantage of a brief spell of favouring winds, and a Southampton merchant, on whom Browne

8 In the Free Library of Philadelphia (reproduced in Quinn, *Gilbert*, II, 374).
9 *Ibid.*, I, 50–1; II, 39–40, 282, 309. See p. 193 below.
10 *Ibid.*, II, 281–307. Ingram's account was published in 1583 but no copy is known to have survived (Quinn, *Roanoke voyages*, I, 3).
11 P. 195 below.

depended for much help with the preparations, died suddenly. Though there were still further delays, the ship at last arrived from the Downs, and the Southampton merchants, in return for trading privileges, subscribed encouragingly to the voyage. The expedition was expected to leave well before mid-winter and, after a call at Dartmouth, to clear the shores of England before the end of November 1582.[12]

A winter voyage meant a change of plans. Sir Humphrey could not hope to cross directly to North America in this season. Instead, he planned to go south-wards to the Canaries and then westward with the trades to the Caribbean and thence on the long sweep with the Gulf Stream up the North American shore. But in December they were still in port: Browne was writing defensively to Thynne, who had criticized the delays, saying that storms had made it quite impossible to put to sea.[13] Gilbert wrote a hasty note on the back of Browne's letter, fretfully rebuking rumour-mongers: "tell them from me", he said, "that I nether caer for ther lykings nor myslykynge."[14] Gilbert went back on shipboard determined to sit out the storm even if he could not ride it, and was encouraged to learn that Peck-ham's preparations for a second expedition were still going forward.[15]

All this determination and optimism were to no effect. The expedition fell to pieces at the end of 1582. Simão Fernandes, the pilot on whom Gilbert had so greatly relied earlier, had already sailed with Edward Fenton in May. It is probable that most of the men dispersed and that several of the ships were released to their owners. The winds remained steadily adverse throughout the winter. Gilbert re-turned to London and so too did Maurice Browne. There, Gilbert had to face the remonstrances of Walsingham and the Queen's proposal that he should give up the voyage, at least in person, since he was "a man noted of not good happ by sea".[16] But he refused to give in: his circle of friends rallied round him as winter turned to spring and the expedition was revived. For this dark winter season we have no letters of Maurice Browne's. He was, we may assume, too depressed to write and, perhaps, also somewhat ashamed that he had allowed John Thynne to spend his money for no return.

Sir Humphrey Gilbert now made new agreements with Peckham and his friends, whom he found, not surprisingly, more demanding than they had been. Meanwhile Walsingham set in motion a new project, aimed at backing up Gil-bert's own expedition, in the form of a further venture under his stepson Christopher Carleill. Bristol merchants had earlier wished to help Gilbert and now, in March,

---

12 Pp. 197, 199 below.
13 Pp. 200-1 below.
14 P. 202 below. This letter has not hitherto been noticed.
15 Pp. 202-3 below.
16 Quinn, *Gilbert*, II, 339.

Walsingham enlisted the help of Richard Hakluyt in bringing them to the point of equipping two ships, which he succeeded in doing. Carleill concentrated on capitalizing his own connections with the Muscovy Company which was interested in making contact with Asia by way of America.[17] Walter Ralegh, too, was now in high favour at court and, with Walsingham, urged the Queen to revive her support for Gilbert. In this they were successful, and to seal her renewed confidence she entrusted Ralegh to convey to his half-brother an elaborate gift, a valuable jewel,[18] which Browne was shortly to describe in loving detail.[19]

It was in this reviving spring of Gilbert's hopes that Stephen Parmenius was brought into the action. Most probably with Hakluyt's encouragement he took out the *De navigatione* once more and prepared a revised version of it. Its appearance in 1582 had been, after all, premature. However useful it may have proved as publicity amongst an educated circle, as an "Embarkation" poem to an explorer who failed to embark on his travels, it had turned out something of a damp squib. Now, with better prospects of an effective enterprise, it might renew its propaganda appeal and also cheer and celebrate its frustrated hero. The alterations were not extensive, affecting only about a dozen lines.[20] One of them concerns his story of Gilbert's wife's family at the point where her brother is said, like her father Sir Anthony Aucher, to have fallen at Calais in 1558 – information which was likely to have been obtained from Gilbert himself. It is curious that he should have concentrated on eulogizing Lady Gilbert's family and ignored that of Sir Humphrey, which was, in its way, not undistinguished in the Southwest. We might even guess that this was done at Gilbert's suggestion in order to flatter his wife and her relations whose money he was using so freely on his American schemes. Again, some lines relating to Stephen and William Borough were removed and those on Frobisher altered in their placing. The precise reason for interfering with the remarks on the Boroughs is unknown. E. G. R. Taylor regards William Borough as a probable author or co-author of a remarkable set of instructions for surveying the lands and coast of North America, compiled for one of the expeditions planned in 1582 which did not sail.[21] This remains inference only, since no positive evidence connecting Borough with Gilbert's enterprises has been found. It could be that Gilbert

17 Browne, p. 204 below, puts a rather different complexion on Carleill's enterprise from that in Quinn, *Gilbert*, I, 76–81.
18 Forwarded by Walter Ralegh on 16 March (*ibid.*, II, 348).
19 Pp. 204-5 below.
20 The points of discrepancy are lines 107, 128–9 (the Auchers), 183–4, 220–1, 223–6, 228, 237–41, 280–5 (the Boroughs), and 290–4 (Frobisher).
21 E. G. R. Taylor, "Instructions to a colonial surveyor in 1582", *The Mariner's Mirror*, XXXVII (1951), 48–62; D. W. Waters, *The art of navigation in England* (London 1958), pp. 164, 538–40.

had, in the interim, fallen out with the Boroughs and wished to remove their names from association with the American enterprise. A possible cause for such a breach may lie in William Borough's cruise, with Lord Shrewsbury's ship the *Bark Talbot* and another vessel, in June 1582, rounding up pirates in English waters and having a number of them hanged at London in August.[22] Gilbert had depended on sea-robbers for his crews in 1578 and had, indeed, some ex-pirates with him in 1583. It is not unlikely that Gilbert quarrelled with Borough over some of the men taken prisoner by the latter, whom he had been willing to take with him on his American venture. We can be sure, however, that it was not at Richard Hakluyt's instance that the lines were excised, since he remained a great admirer of the work of the Boroughs in the opening up of the route to Muscovy and in the early definition of the supposed Northeast Passage.

Most of the other changes in the poem were stylistic modifications in which the constructions and imagery are different but the same general sense is conveyed. The precise nature of the improvements is discussed in the notes to the text. They may be of small consequence historically but they serve to show that Parmenius had a high standard of literary discrimination. It is possible too that he added a few side-notes calling attention to individuals mentioned in the verse and giving their full titles, but they may not have been put in until Hakluyt prepared the revision for publication.[23] The passages about Gilbert's fleet going down the Thames and saying farewell to the Queen at Greenwich were left, even though they were no longer appropriate to the 1583 situation. To have altered them would have involved considerable remodelling of the poem as a whole; to leave them as they were, allowed the compliments to the Queen (no longer fully appropriate either), to stay also. Nor did Parmenius change the dedicatory epistle to Gilbert, but simply added the date "*pridie Kalen. Aprilis 1583*" (31 March 1583), which is some nine months after he had presented his friend Brumen with an autographed copy of the first version.

It is this revised edition of the poem that Hakluyt printed in 1600, after ignoring the *De navigatione* in the first edition of his *Principall navigations* in 1589. We cannot tell whether he took his text from a manuscript or a printed book. If he used the former we can envisage Parmenius preparing a copy for Gilbert's benefit during March 1583 and presenting Hakluyt with another when he returned from Bristol, probably early in April. But it is possible that Hakluyt had a printed copy of the revised text. If Gilbert thought it necessary, or if Parmenius' friends were willing to pay for it, the publication of a second edition may have taken place before the post-

---

22 John Stow, *The chronicles of England ... continued by Edmond Howes* (1631[-2]), p. 697.
23 Hakluyt or his printer, rather than Parmenius, may have altered the spelling of some proper names.

poned expedition was ready to sail. That no copies of such a second edition have survived is no clear indication that one was not published. As only two copies of the first edition (and two copies of the *Paean*) are known to be extant it would not be at all surprising if Hakluyt's reprint was the only vestige of a second edition to remain.

It might be argued that, if publicity and the attraction of subscribers were what was intended, a revision completed only at the end of March was rather late if Gilbert hoped to get away before the summer: but it would not take long to reprint, and Gilbert is known to have been collecting subscriptions almost until the end of May. As late as April, Carleill brought out an important tract to convince the public that American colonization made sense.[24] All we know, however, as distinct from what we may surmise, is that Stephen Parmenius revised his poem during the month of March and that Hakluyt printed (or reprinted) it, seventeen years after Parmenius' death, in the third volume of the second edition of his great collection, giving it the heading: "A learned and stately Poeme, written in Latin Hexamiters by Stephanus Parmenius Budaeus, concerning the voyage of Sir Humphrey Gilbert to New foundland."[25]

Hard on the revision of his poem, Parmenius himself contracted to go on the voyage. In Browne, Gilbert had the practical, hard-headed businesslike reporter whom he needed to put the result of his voyage rapidly and effectively before his backers. Parmenius represented rather something of a long-term investment. His poem may well have helped Gilbert, who always had a taste for the dramatic, to see himself as the Hero-to-be, who carried his poet and chronicler with him. Having savoured the *De navigatione,* Gilbert may have relished the prospect of featuring in an extended saga in which "*tunc eques auratus*" should replace "*tum pius Aeneas*". To Parmenius, the experience of the voyage created an opportunity to write something grander than encomia to gallant gentlemen or hospitable hosts. An expedition such as Gilbert hoped to make, one which could transform the oceanic position of England by giving her a permanent stake across the Atlantic, opened up for him the chance of writing an epic of English discovery from first-hand experience. He could go with Gilbert as a chronicler indeed, but as a poet as well, one who could distil harsh experience into imperishable words. That he had Hakluyt's encouragement we need not doubt, but he was now on sufficiently close personal terms with Gilbert not to need Hakluyt's recommendation.

At the same time, negatively, Hakluyt may have given him his chance to go. Gilbert owed much to Hakluyt for the work he had done on the *Divers voyages* in

24 Quinn, *Gilbert*, III, 351–64; three copies of the printed version are now known to have survived (see Hakluyt, *Principall navigations*, ed. Quinn and Skelton, I (1965), xxxii).
25 *Principall navigations*, III (1600), 138–43; VIII (1904), 23–33.

providing both background information and effective publicity for the voyage. It is highly probable that he gave Hakluyt himself the opportunity to go as his chronicler, and that Hakluyt might have accepted had he not received encourage-ment to fit himself for other tasks. In March, Walsingham had written to him commending his work which had "given much light for the discovery of the Westerne partes yet unknown", and urging him to "continue your travell in these and like matters, which are like to turne not only to your owne good in private, but to the publike benefite of this Realme".[26] This hint of employment in the public service may well have been reinforced in words after Hakluyt's return from his suc-cessful mission to Bristol, and it was to lead to a diplomatic appointment for him in France within a few months. If this reading is correct, Hakluyt was not available to go with Gilbert: the way was open for Parmenius instead to join Maurice Browne as joint recorder, literary rather than practical, of the voyage. Nor did John Thynne lose contact with Gilbert's men during the spring. While attending the assizes at Salisbury he was entertained by Sir Humphrey Gilbert's musicians who were evidently making a tour of towns and country places to support themselves and also, it is likely, to bring news to potential subscribers of fresh preparations for a voyage. In Thynne's personal accounts we find the entry: "Gyven in Reward to Sir Homfrye Gylbards musicions primo martii 1582[-3] – xviijd."[27]

The speed of the preparations quickened in April. Gilbert went down to Southampton once again and Maurice Browne followed him at the beginning of May. Parmenius may there have met Browne for the first time, since there had been no mention of him in Browne's correspondence so far, but they could well have encountered each other earlier in London. The two had much in common. Both were enthusiastic for the so-far-unseen America of which they had heard so much, both had an active interest in cosmography, and both embraced (to judge from what we know of their writings), a clearly Calvinistic faith. They had roles in which they could co-operate closely, but their tasks, though allied, had very different objectives. It was, indeed, essential, unless temperament stood in the way, that they should work together, combining in collecting and reporting materials on the course and outcome of the voyage, and distinguishing between what was of short-term and long-term interest.

At the end of April, just before he left London, and in the opening days of May after he had come to Southampton, Browne was able to give John Thynne a vivid picture of the preparations.[28] Walter Ralegh had bought for his step-brother a fine

26 Quinn, *Gilbert*, II, 347.
27 Longleat, Thynne Papers, LV, f.103.
28 Pp. 203-8 below. This letter is in many ways the most graphic and significant item in the Browne correspondence.

new ship (the *Bark Ralegh*) from the Southampton shipowner Henry Oughtred, which with her equipment had cost him 2,000 marks (others said £2,000). Sir Humphrey Gilbert proposed to employ her as his flagship. Another fine ship was the one that Captain William Winter, who had put up half her cost, was to command: this was the *Delight*, a vessel of tragic consequence for both Browne and Parmenius. There were three other vessels besides, "pynesses of good bourden", as Browne called them, the *Golden Hind*, under Captain Edward Hayes, the *Swallow*, of which Maurice Browne was shortly to be given the command, and the tiny *Squirrel*. Walsingham and Ralegh were doing all they could for Gilbert, and the Queen had come round: "Sir Humphrey never had her majesties favore more hyghly nor ever had so great means to contynewe the same, for the bringinge of his Actions to good effect, which God grant if it be his will." Browne tells us that, before he left London, Gilbert had given him authority "to follow all his causes here at the court as also to receyve such money as he hath here and to buy dyvers provision for him, and to send them to Hampton". Ralegh too had given Browne every possible help, especially after they had discovered a distant kinship between them. Thynne had sent him a farewell present of "butter and cheeses and marmy-lade" for the voyage. Doubtless the friends Parmenius had made at Oxford and at London were sending similar messages and gifts.

The Voyage and a Letter

THE YOUNG HUNGARIAN was at last to leave the life of the student and scholar for the life of action. Born on the wide Danube, yet never until he began his student travels near a sea, he had decided to trust himself to a fragile craft in order to record the course of an expedition and to render into Latin verse "the gests and things worthy of remembrance" on the voyage. His expectations were romantic: he imagined that the new and the strange would move him to a deeper eloquence than he had yet been able to express. He had at the same time a keen eye for the actual and a shrewd judgment. His misfortune and ours is that he did not have the opportunity to exercise his gifts more fully.

There were other delays in May but no serious ones this time. In the last days of that month and the opening days of June the ships left Southampton and made their way to Dartmouth on a first brief leg of their journey. Maurice Browne had taken up his first command as captain of the *Swallow* and with him he had as his passenger and congenial friend Stephen Parmenius. Stephen came rapidly to admire and respect his captain, whom he was soon to describe as a young man of high character (*vere generosus iuvenis*). Captain Edward Hayes shared his opinion, writing of Browne as "very honest and religious" and "a vertuous, honest and discreete Gentleman", a description which Browne's own letters bear out.[1]

The ships moved on to Plymouth, their last port of call before their final departure. A minor hitch there, the desertion of nineteen men from the *Bark Ralegh*, did not delay their assembly in Cawsand Bay and their sailing on 11 June, though it may have been this that led Gilbert to transfer his flag from the *Bark Ralegh* to the *Delight* and make her flagship of his little squadron. But this difficulty was the precursor to a major setback two days later when the *Bark Ralegh*, under Ralegh's old lieutenant Michael Butler, deserted and turned back to Plymouth. Officially, the reason was sickness on board; in fact, it was the lack of confidence of the men that their stores would last out the long voyage. Gilbert was furious but could not now turn back. His depleted force, lacking no doubt much of the specialized

---

1 Pp. 189-208 below; Quinn, *Gilbert*, II, 399, 414.

47

equipment which would have been placed in the intended flagship, sailed out to sea.[2]

If the crew of the *Bark Ralegh* had proved wholly unreliable, that of the *Swallow* was little better. The *Swallow* had originally been a Scottish merchantman which had been seized at sea by Captain John Callis and taken from him in turn by Gilbert. Her crew were mostly men who had served in the cruel trade of sea-robbery, pirates by temperament, ready to use violence at the first opportunity. Browne had taken on a tough assignment in keeping such a shipload of ruffians to the narrow track of exploration, Neither he nor Parmenius would have been too happy had they known that shortly after they sailed, official inquiries were being made for the whereabouts of the ship which had been rescued from Callis and so calmly appropriated by Gilbert. Several members of her crew, against whom piracy charges were pending, were also being sought.[3]

Sir Humphrey Gilbert's prime objective for over a year had been the eastern coast of North America between about 40 and 42 degrees North latitude; Carleill was proposing to go a little farther north, between, say, southern Maine and the mouth of the Gulf of St. Lawrence. Verrazzano's discoveries of 1524, his Bay of the Five Islands (*Refugio*) and the River of Norumbega, were the literary landmarks to Gilbert's destination. They could be reached either by the long route by way of the West Indies or by the shorter western voyage across the ocean. Edward Hayes tells us that the choice of routes was long debated but that poor victualling and the shorter passage made the choice of the northern route inevitable in the end.[4] It was, indeed, decided to sail a little farther north than was strictly necessary, partly per-haps because this track was already so well known to sailors but also to take advantage of the Newfoundland fishery.

Gilbert already knew something about the Newfoundland fishery, and Hakluyt had previously collected for him a certain amount of information on the island's resources, but it is doubtful whether, when he left England, he had any very clear intention of exploiting either in a direct manner.[5] Certainly the fishery could pro-vide a considerable short-term asset, in the form of supplies of fish to supplement the limited stores he had on board, before he beat down the long expanse of main-land shore between Cape Breton and Narragansett Bay, Verrazzano's *Refugio*. It was during the voyage, almost certainly, and probably from conversations with the master of the *Delight*, Richard Clarke, who had paid Newfoundland a by no means friendly visit in the previous year,[6] that the idea of doing something more

2 For the circumstances of the departure, see Quinn, *Gilbert*, I, 83–4.
3 *Ibid.*, II, 396–7, 399, 400, 428–31.
4 *Ibid.*, II, 392.
5 See *ibid.*, I, 34, 36–37, 52, 171–2.
6 *Ibid.*, I, 85; *DCB*, I (1965), 228–30.

with the fishery arose. Newfoundland took on a more attractive appearance in Gilbert's eyes when it seemed likely that he could take or cajole or buy from the international fishing fleets on the Banks many supplies other than fish, and when he learned too that the appropriation of the shores of the island would leave the way open to the renting of ground for drying fish, and for other associated uses, to fishermen who made an annual voyage there and who desired some prescriptive right to their usual working spaces ashore. His patent covered the whole island, and it seemed that there, with little expense, he might raise some interim revenue from his American realm. But it must be emphasized that these notions, and the pre-parations made on seaboard to put them into effect, were not ends in themselves, but only means to the larger plan of exploration and settlement centred on the main-land a thousand miles southwestward from St. John's.

However piratically inclined was the majority of her crew, the *Swallow* sailed well and was competently navigated. Rain, fog and unfavourable winds from west-northwest held the ships back and led them to sail as far south as 41° N. latitude (that is to say, almost to the Azores) before they could pick up winds that would carry them to Newfoundland. The result was that a voyage which might well have been achieved in twenty to thirty days took fifty. Yet, thanks both to good naviga-tion and to a system of signals worked out before they left England, the four remain-ing vessels kept together until, in late July, they entered the foggy zone which encloses the fishing banks and often the island of Newfoundland itself. Parmenius says that the *Swallow* kept company with the rest until 23 July, but Edward Hayes reports that the *Golden Hind* and the *Delight* lost touch with the *Swallow* and *Squirrel* on 20 July. Whichever date is correct it seems that the ships were then at about 51° N., near the northern tip of Newfoundland, having sailed well to the north of their objective owing to bad visibility and probably also to defects in their dead reckoning which should have brought them to land farther south.

On 1 August the weather must have cleared so as to allow latitude observations to be taken. It was then reckoned that they were at 50° N. and in the vicinity of Penguin Island (now Funk Island), which lies just fifteen minutes south of this latitude; but no island was seen, as the wind carried the ship southwards. Par-menius' letter, on which we have been relying, then passes over the next two days, remarking only that two of the men were lost by mischance.

We must fill in his omission by a lengthy quotation from Edward Hayes:

Here me [*sic*] met with the *Swallow* againe, whome we had lost in the fogge, and all her men altered into other apparell: whereof it seemed their store was so amended, that for joy & congratulation of our meeting, they spared not to cast up into the aire and overboord, their caps and hats in good plentie. The

49

THE NEW FOUND LAND OF STEPHEN PARMENIUS

Captaine albeit himselfe was very honest and religious, yet was he not appointed of men to his humor and desert: who for the most part were such as had bene by us surprised upon the narrow seas of England, being pirats, and had taken at that instant certaine Frenchmen laden, one barke with wines, and another with salt. Both which we rescued, & tooke the man of warre with all her men, which was the same ship now called the *Swallow*, following still their kinde so oft, as (being separated from the General) they found opportunitie to robbe and spoile. And because Gods justice did follow the same companie, even to destruction, and to the overthrow also of the Captaine (though not consenting to their misdemeanor:) I will not conceale anything that maketh to the mani⁄ festation and approbation of his judgements, for examples of others, perswaded that God more sharpely tooke revenge upon them, and hath tollerated longer as great outrage in others: by howe much these went under protection of his cause and religion, which was then pretended.

Therfore upon further enquirie it was knowen, how this company met with a barke returning home after the fishing with his fraight: and because the men in the *Swallow* were very neere scanted of victual, and chiefly of apparel, doubtful withal where or when to finde and meete with their Admiral, they besought the captaine they might go aboard this *Newlander*, only to borrow what might be spared, the rather because the same was bound homeward. Leave giuen, not without charge to deale favorably, they came aboord the fisherman, whom they rifled of tackle, sailes, cables, vitailes, and the men of their apparel: not sparing by torture (winding cords about their heads) to drawe out else what they thought good. This done with expedition (like men skilfull in such mischiefe) as they tooke their cocke boat to goe aboord their owne ship, it was over⁄ whelmed in the sea, and certaine of these men there drowned: the rest were pre⁄ served even by those seely soules whom they had before spoiled, who saved and delivered them aboord the *Swallow*. What became afterward of the poore *New⁄ lander*, perhaps destitute of sailes & furniture sufficient to cary them home (whither they had not lesse to runne then 750. leagues) God alone knoweth, who tooke vengeance not long after of the rest that escaped at this instant, to reveile the fact, and justifie to the world Gods judgements inflicted upon them, as shalbe declared in place convenient.[7]

Edward Hayes is clearly taking a righteous line about the *Swallow* and her crew. Certainly her men behaved in a cruel manner, and, besides, it was unfortunate that Gilbert, who was coming to enforce order and taxation on the fishermen, should be

7 Hakluyt, *Principall navigations* (1589), p. 686 (Quinn, *Gilbert*, II, 399–400).

burdened by a ship which displayed such lawlessness. But Hayes himself may have strayed, both before and after 1583, over the narrow line that lay between privateer⁄ing and piracy.

Early on 1 August the *Swallow*, *Golden Hind* and *Delight* made contact once again, at about 48° N., in Conception Bay which had apparently been appointed as a rendezvous. Hayes is likely to have come aboard the *Swallow* to greet Browne and Parmenius and to hear the latter say that he had enjoyed the voyage and had never felt more strong and healthy.[8] Hayes also learnt of the encounter with the foreign fishing vessel and thus of the less favourable side of the voyage, the shortage of food, and the absence of adequate clothing, which point back to faulty and in⁄sufficient provisioning before the vessels left England. Either Gilbert was deceived by his suppliers or he never obtained enough funds to equip his vessels really adequately. It may well be that both of these causes were aggravated by the long delays, and consequent consumption of stores, before the ships left England.

A short time after the three ships had greeted each other they picked up the little frigate, *Squirrel*. The reunited squadron, after recuperating, moved south to St. John's where Gilbert intended to land. This was the principal meeting place of vessels engaged in the fishery. Though dominated by the English fishermen – one of whom was annually made port admiral – Portuguese, French and Spanish Basque vessels frequently put in there. We are not told precisely how many English ships were in the harbour, but there were no less than twenty non⁄English vessels. As soon as Gilbert's squadron was sighted, the fishermen made haste to defend the narrow entrance to the harbour. A message was sent to Gilbert that he would not be admitted. The reason for this action was that Richard Clarke had brought out two men⁄of⁄war in 1582 and had piratically seized Portuguese ships and goods in Renews, a harbour some miles to the south. The hostile reaction of the fishermen was not unjustified, since Gilbert's men were quite capable of stealing by force, and Richard Clarke himself (though this could not yet be known) was acting as master of Gilbert's *Delight*. Gilbert made ready to force an entrance, but sent ahead of him a message stating that he had the Queen's commission to deal with New⁄foundland and promising to use no violence towards the fishermen.

Apparently impressed by this show of authority,[9] the port admiral gave way and prepared to admit the ships. Richard Clarke managed to ground the *Delight* on a rock in the narrow harbour entrance from which she had to be pulled by a flotilla of ships' boats.[10] This mishap robbed the entry of all its formal dignity, and

8 See *NL*, ll. 21–2.
9 On the respect shown for Gilbert's patent, see *NL*, ll. 29–30.
10 See Quinn, *Gilbert*, ii, 400. An eighteenth⁄century cartographer, John Mackeclean comments: "The Harbour of St Johns being so narrow in the Entrance and the land so very hight on each side, makes it difficult of access: you cannot expect to sail in unless

also reflected on Clarke's seamanship (or possibly that of his captain, William Winter) but it also broke the tension which had developed and established friendly and intimate relations between the fishermen and the English expedition. Once the vessels were at anchor, Gilbert, wishing to make known his plans to assume control of the island in the Queen's name, called on board the *Delight* the captains and masters of his own squadron and also the masters and owners of the English fishing vessels in the harbour. Among the latter group was Richard Whitbourne, afterwards prominent in Newfoundland's history.[11]

Gilbert told them that the privilege of assisting in the annexation of Newfound-land to the English crown had its price. He desired to have provisions sent to his ships both from the English ships at St. John's and also from those at other harbours as soon as contact could be made with them. Foreign fishing vessels were also to be taxed to the same end. From the twenty non-English vessels in the harbour provisions came in easily, the Portuguese generously adding wines, mar-malades, sweet oils and other delicacies to the basic ships' stores asked for. It was probably not wholly goodwill which prompted this hospitality, but at least partly the memory of Clarke's raid the previous summer, when indiscriminate plunder of Portuguese vessels had taken place. To avoid a repetition of this the captains and fishermen were willing, no doubt, to pay a dividend on what Gilbert requested. During the following days, too, gifts which could more easily be spared – lobsters, salmon, trout and other fish – flowed in.

Parmenius probably did not set foot on Newfoundland until Sunday, 4 August. On that day, after the morning's shipboard service, the leaders of the expedition went on shore with some English merchants from the fishing vessels. It would seem that Parmenius accompanied them to walk in the place they called "the Garden", which was confusedly, but attractively, overgrown with wild roses and brambles, possibly raspberries. Though Edward Hayes was encouraged by the prospects of the country, Parmenius was not greatly impressed. It was too wild and yet not

---

the Wind be nearly right in. When this is not the case, Ships endeavour to shoot through the Narrows as far as they can, come to an anchor and afterwards warp in, for which reason you ought to prepare yourself for that Purpose, before you attempt the Harbour. There is water enough for any ship to lay her broadside against the rocks, on the starboard side in going in but not on the Larboard." (Photostat of his map of St John's Harbour, Library of Congress, Map Division 13. 15. F. 67.) The Hydrographic chart of St John's Harbour, 1816, shows the channel in detail, with its rocky sill at the entrance, before any attempt was made to deepen it (copies in P.R.O., C.O. 700/Newfoundland 11c;W.O. 78/307).

11 *A discourse and discovery of New-found-land* (1620), pref. sig. C5 (see Quinn, *Gilbert*, II, 426–7).

romantic enough for his scholar's temperament. He wandered around looking for plants and saw, with some disappointment, that the grass there was very much like grass in Europe, though it had some rye-like ears which he thought might produce grain under cultivation. He found little else to interest him in the small space open to the walkers. What most impressed, and disheartened, him was the uniform, heavy coniferous forest which covered, so far as he could see, all the interior. Nor did the first tentative attempts to penetrate it achieve any success. Old timber had fallen and undergrowth accumulated so that any access was impossible.[12]

Early on Monday morning the visitors were again ashore. The *Delight*'s men were busy erecting a pavilion for Sir Humphrey Gilbert on an open space.[13] When they were ready, all the available fishermen, who must by now have been somewhat resentful of the interruption, were called before him. Gilbert then made a speech expounding his commission from the Queen, and probably had summaries of what he said translated into Portuguese and French. He told his audience that he was formally taking possession in her name of the harbour of St John's and all the lands 200 leagues (600 sea miles) in every direction. He was then ceremonially presented by one of his own men with a rod and a turf as symbols of possession.

He next announced that, since Newfoundland was the Queen's and he was authorized to govern it, all Europeans coming there to trade or fish or settle were to be governed by laws promulgated by him, which would be closely modelled on the laws of England. As a foretaste, he launched out at once into legislation. No religion should be publicly exercised except that of the Church of England. No one would act prejudicially to the Queen (that is, oppose himself) without becoming liable to the English penalties for high treason, which were hanging, drawing and quartering. Nobody would utter words to the Queen's dishonour (perhaps even to Gilbert's) without being liable to ear-clipping and losing ship and goods. These Anglo-Protestant innovations can scarcely have been gratifying to the Catholic subjects of other European states who were present. But all dutifully acquiesced for the moment, perhaps even showing some enthusiasm in doing so, since Gilbert went on to announce that he would soon be leaving to explore the more southerly parts of the mainland, and so would not be long available to enforce his new laws.

12 For these observations see *NL*, ll. 39-40 (berries), ll. 37-8 (grasses), and ll. 34-6.
13 See *NL*, ll. 23-6 Traditionally, to Newfoundlanders, the site was that now occupied by the Newfoundland Hotel. Early maps rarely help to indicate level spaces, so no proof can be found of this assumption. The detailed map by W. P. Ryan (*Map of St. John's*, 1932) suggests that the most level space may have lain within the 105-110-foot contour lines, which would include the hotel site.

Since Cabot, Corte Real, Verrazzano, Cartier, and probably others had already annexed parts of northeastern North America to their respective sovereigns by formal ceremonies, Gilbert's action was neither unique nor decisive. What was new was that he performed his acts of annexation before an audience consisting largely of Englishmen who were not members of his own expedition and of foreigners from Portugal, France and possibly Spain. Furthermore, this promulga/tion of laws after annexation, not to the natives of the country, but to part/time occupants of its harbour, was also without direct parallel. Penalties for the wrong kind of religious observance and for "disloyalty" to the newly established sovereign were also unprecedented in the absence of permanent settlement. They resembled the Spanish *requerimiento*, by which foreign peoples were told in Spanish that they must become Christians and good Spaniards at once on the demand of their con/querors, and were subsequently treated as if they had both understood and acquiesced.

The long/term value of these novel proceedings depended wholly on whether Gilbert could maintain some machinery in Newfoundland for enforcing the rights and authority he claimed. But there was also something to be gained in the short term. Gilbert handed out assignments of land along the slopes of the harbour to the master or owner of each ship in return for the promise of payment. These allotments were the sites of the "flakes" and stages erected for curing cod.[14] Already fishermen who came every year had been claiming rights to particular patches above high/water mark, but found that they were sometimes displaced by earlier comers. Gilbert now said he would assure them permanent possession – a promise he was unlikely to be able to fulfil. He also issued to each non/English vessel a summary of his authority and a passport entitling her to fish off Newfoundland and use its harbours. A Spanish translation of one of his passports, issued to Tomas Andre, of Aveiro, Portugal, has been found in the Archivo de Indias at Seville.[15] Whether these documents were given in return for the supplies rendered or for an additional payment is not known.

Parmenius is likely to have approved of these ceremonies as bringing something of European order into the American wilds, but during the next few days he became more and more disillusioned with his new environment. He admired the pro/fusion of fish, though he could not become enthusiastic about fishing: the smell of drying cod which was to envelop St. John's for centuries was never attractive. He inspected the pelts of bears which the fishermen showed him. White in colour and

14 The 1750 map of St. John's Harbour distinguishes between "stages" for landing, splitting, and heading fish, and "flakes" for drying them (P.R.O., MPHH 274). See also *NL*, l. 40 and note, p. 182.
15 Printed in translation, p. 210. below.

smaller than those of European bears, they were all that remained of young polar bears carried southwards on icebergs.[16]

Gilbert was very anxious to penetrate into the interior. He and Daniel, his German mineral expert, were poking around the rocks on the shore and taking specimens which gave promise of some mineral wealth, but they wished to examine the hilltops which they could see above the forests. They could at first make no entrance through the tangled timber. Parmenius and some other members of the expedition urged Gilbert to set fire to the woods so that access might be gained. He was at first willing to do this, but when he sought the advice of the fishermen they strongly urged him not to attempt it. An accidental fire at another harbour, they told him, had poured so much resin and turpentine into the water that fish had deserted it for seven years. Whatever the truth of this report, he gave up the project, which might not in any case have served his immediate purpose.[17]

At some time on Tuesday, 6 August, Parmenius, who had probably moved his quarters to the *Delight*, retired on shipboard to write letters to his friends. He wrote first of all to Laurence Humfrey,[18] as he had undertaken to do before he left England: but although his letter most probably reached its destination, it is not now, apparently, extant. Then he turned to write to Richard Hakluyt. Hakluyt had himself promised to keep in touch with Parmenius as soon as it should be possible to do so. Remembering this, the latter changed his mind, for he had first of all intended only to ask Humfrey to pass on news to Hakluyt. But his second letter would be, he said, substantially the same as that to Humfrey: he had no leisure to write something different. In it, too, he passed on commendations and good wishes to Henry Unton, to whom also he did not yet intend to write. It is not unlikely, to judge from his haste and preoccupation, that a vessel was leaving St. John's for an English port and that he was taking the unexpected opportunity of sending letters by it, though it may be that the letter had to travel much more slowly with the *Swallow*. The letter to Hakluyt is a vigorous and fluent piece of epistolary Latin, giving briefly but compendiously an account of the voyage and of his experience in the past few days since reaching the Newfoundland coast. It also clearly communicated the warmth of his feeling towards his Oxford friends.[19]

Yet, mostly, the letter reflects Parmenius' disillusionment with Newfoundland itself. "Now I ought to tell you about the customs, territories and inhabitants: and yet what am I to say, my dear Hakluyt, when I see nothing but desola-

---

16 See *NL*, l. 32 (fish), ll. 40–1 (polar bears).
17 See *NL*, ll. 43–4 (minerals), ll. 45–7 (forest fire), and pp. 183–4 below.
18 See *NL*, ll. 2–3.
19 For the text of the whole letter, see below, pp. 168–73. See also pp. 12–13.

tion?"[20] The wild, impenetrable woods, the high, bare headlands, the dubious minerals, the plentiful fish, the absence of native inhabitants – all these added up to very little.[21] He had looked forward to seeing the aboriginal Americans, apparently having had plans for their conversion. Instead, no one would admit to having seen any of the Beothuk Indians: and so Edward Hayes and he came to believe that they must have forsaken the southern part of the island. He interested himself too in the climate of Newfoundland[22] and reported it hot enough in August to make drying cod rather a difficult procedure, the fish having to be turned frequently to keep them from being ruined by the sun. He had already heard of the long winter with its severe weather, and he had picked up some information about the icebergs which were still so common in early summer. Apart from these things, his mind was set on leaving Newfoundland behind, and on finding new and more varied sights on the North American mainland. For an interim report, on the third day only of his residence at St. John's, he had done well, shrewdly and concisely characterizing his surroundings and giving an effective impression of them to his friends in England. We may regret, too, that the lighter, gossipy letters which Maurice Browne almost certainly sent home have not survived.

The expedition remained at St. John's for another fortnight. During that time something was gained and something lost. Gilbert explored a substantial part of the area round about, probably being taken by boat to other harbours from which he could explore inland. He found plenty of game, such as deer, "pheasant", partridge and swans, according to what he wrote to Sir George Peckham on 8 August[23] (two days after Parmenius had written to Hakluyt), and he may well have spent a good deal of his time pursuing what he could. His mineral man, Daniel, hacked out specimens which indicated mineral wealth. There were many stones which suggested the presence of iron, something it was scarcely possible to miss in Newfoundland, fragments of bog iron ore, and misleading indications of copper. Finally they discovered, apparently on some inland hilltop to which access had been found, an ore promising rich returns in silver, which excited Gilbert greatly. This is likely to have been a small pocket of galena, a natural lead ore (lead sulphide). Other members of the ships' company were surveying the

20 P. 171 below.
21 Parmenius had so far seen only the barren shoreland and the thick interior forest. The former was not a fair sample, the modern land-use study showing that an exceptionally high proportion of the coastal area from Torbay, north of St. John's Harbour, to Bull Head, well to the south, is classed as "unproductive"; see L. G. Reeds, *Land-use survey: Avalon Peninsula* (Canada, Geographical Branch, Department of Mines and Technical Surveys, 1953).
22 See *NL*, ll. 50-9.
23 Quinn, *Gilbert*, II, 383.

coast and drawing maps. This was done partly, it would seem, so that the letting out of stages and flakes could be organized systematically at other harbours than St. John's. Edward Hayes, though incapacitated for some time by an accident, was working hard to collect geographical and other information. Of Parmenius, who had been taken on to the *Delight*, we know nothing directly, but there is a strong probability that he was acting as Gilbert's secretary, keeping a journal of events and collecting systematic lists of data which might come in useful in future voyages. Perhaps he was also mapping out, with his limited materials, the structure of the first part of his epic.

He may, too, have become more interested in Newfoundland in the course of his work, but it is more likely that his negative attitude continued or was intensified. Gilbert himself, however, did become more and more enthusiastic. Hayes tells us that "the Generall had never before good conceite of these North parts of the world", but that "now his mind was wholly fixed upon New-foundland."[24] One reason, Hayes thought, was the hope of riches from the supposed silver ore which Daniel had found. But Gilbert also seems to have come to appreciate New-foundland for its own sake and was willing, Hayes found on the return voyage, to concentrate all his future efforts on the island.

For all that, Parmenius' hostile reaction was shared actively, even violently, by many of Gilbert's company. They did not like the country and therefore they reacted against the voyage itself; they were unimpressed by the supplies obtained at St. John's, and many of them, rather than take the risk of starvation and disaster which an extended voyage seemed to offer, determined to go no further. Gilbert and the ships' captains took to spending their nights ashore. Some of the men thereupon plotted to seize the ships at night and make off to England with them, but their plans were discovered and they were prevented from carrying them into effect. Many more slipped away into the woods, hoping to evade pursuit and to get aboard fishing vessels which were sailing home to England by ones and twos, having completed their catch. Another group moved away to another harbour, ambushed the crew of a fishing vessel there, and took their ship, marooning its crew in the woods. Hayes, who tells us this, does not say to what port the ship belonged or whether the pirates managed to take her to England. Others, apparently the *Delight*'s crew in the main, had dysentery and other diseases, some of them dying while the ship lay in the harbour. It appears that the expedition was rapidly disintegrating during the delay while Gilbert gathered still more data on the island, and that he was so absorbed as to neglect the enforcement of discipline until it was almost too late.

24 *Ibid.*, II, 418.

Shipwreck

Eventually, with an effort, some degree of order was restored. The able and willing were sorted out from the sick and unready. The latter now included Captain William Winter of the *Delight*, so he was left with the *Swallow*, which Gilbert could not now fully man, to convey the sick and unwilling back to England as best he could. Maurice Browne was made captain of the *Delight* and Parmenius was installed with him on the flagship. Many of the ex-pirates from the *Swallow* accompanied them. Gilbert himself had come to prefer the tiny *Squirrel*, which he could use effectively for reconnaissance. Finally, on Tuesday, 20 August, the depleted squadron, reduced now to the *Delight*, *Golden Hind* and *Squirrel*, sailed out of St. John's on a southward course. They kept together all Tuesday and Wednesday, and when darkness fell on the 21st they were becalmed off Cape Race at the southeasterly point of Newfoundland. While the men were catching cod in quantity by hook and line, Gilbert instructed his boy to gather various things, including notes, observations, and ore samples, from the great cabin in the *Delight*, and bring them on board the *Squirrel*. However, the boy forgot, and that was the last he was to see of them.

When the ships resumed their voyage on 22 August, they inspected Trepassey Bay and learnt that if they worked their way farther west they could come to Placentia Bay. Some men were sent ashore – Parmenius could have been one of them – to see how fertile the land was: they reported favourably, saying there was good soil and plenty of beach-peas growing on the shore. Gilbert decided to make for Sable Island rather than set course for Cape Breton at once, for he had heard that, some thirty years before, the Portuguese had put pigs and goats ashore on Sable, and that these had since multiplied. He wished to see if this story was true, since such a stock could be used to equip a colony on the mainland. It would also provide valuable stores for his current voyage. How good or bad the charts available to him were, we cannot say. The winds, at least, were not wholly unfavourable, though they did not give much help against a strong current.

By Tuesday, 27 August, the ships were on the Banquereau Bank in 35 fathoms. The wind shifted south on Wednesday evening and, in spite of an argument between Gilbert and the masters of the *Delight* and *Golden Hind*, the course was changed to west-northwest. Richard Clarke contended, so he subsequently reported,[1] that they were only 45 miles from Sable Island and that a west-southwest course would safely bring them past the island and its attendant shoals, while the course that Gilbert advocated would bring them on to Sable Island. Whether any of them knew what they were talking about is not certain, but in any event Gilbert's insistence on the course he favoured turned out to be fatal.

When day broke on Thursday, 29 August, the weather was wet and became more and more misty, while the wind "blew vehemently at South and by East", as Hayes tells us. The vessels soon found themselves caught in a series of shallow shoals and flats. As they began to sound, they found deep and shoal water alternating every few hundred yards. Cox, master of the *Golden Hind*, reported that there were white cliffs in sight, but the haze and rain were such that no one could be certain. Immediate signals were put out to warn the *Delight* to change course and run to seaward. She was ahead, and according to Hayes, was "keeping so ill watch that they knew not the danger before they felt the same too late to recover it".[2] Presently, the men in the other two vessels were horrified to see the *Delight* go aground, and such were the waves that her stern and afterparts rapidly broke up under their pounding. The *Golden Hind* and *Squirrel* were concerned first of all to save themselves. They made about – "even for our lives into the windes eye", says Hayes – and got clear. They kept a lookout to see if any boat got away from the *Delight* or whether the crew had found spars to cling to, but in the poor light saw nothing. Soon they had given up hope of any survivors.

Richard Clarke, however, master of the *Delight,* did survive to tell his tale. Slung into the water as the ship broke up at seven o'clock in the morning, he was hauled aboard the ship's boat by some members of the crew who had tumbled into her as she swung in the water at a painter's end below the ship's stern. They had got clear and were now picking up any survivors they could. Clarke was the only officer to be saved. Captain Browne went down with his ship, and with him Daniel, the Saxon miner, and Stephen Parmenius of Buda, the ores, the records, the drafts of the Parmenian epic, and all. Edward Hayes again is our recorder, and his eloquent comment is Parmenius' best epitaph:

This was a heavy and grievous event, to lose at one blowe our chiefe shippe fraighted with great provision, gathered together with much travell, care, long time, and difficultie. But more was the losse of our men, which perished to the number almost of a hundreth soules. Amongest whom was drowned a learned

1 Hakluyt, *Principall navigations* (1589), p. 694 (Quinn, *Gilbert*, II, 423–4).
2 *Ibid.,* p. 692 (Quinn, *Gilbert*, II, 413).

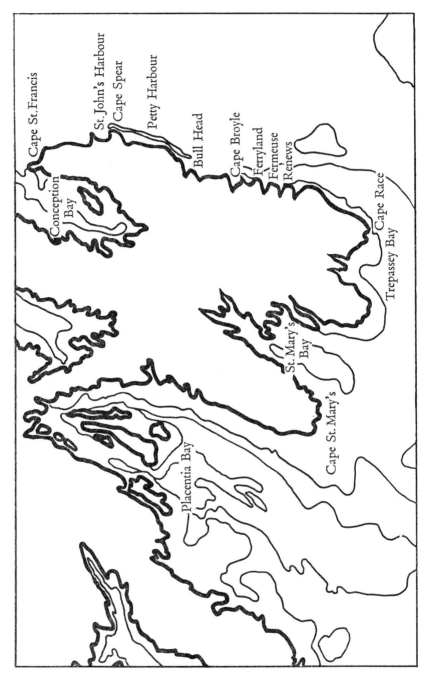

9 Southeastern Newfoundland. Scale: 1/1,162,000

man, an Hungarian, borne in the Citie of Buda, called thereof Budaeus, who of pietie and zeale to good attempts, adventured in this action, minding to record in the Latine tongue, the gests and things worthy of remembrance, happening in this discoverie, to the honour of our nation, the same being adorned with the eloquent stile of this Orator, and rare Poet of our time.[3]

That Parmenius was mentioned first in these admiring terms, before Captain Browne, shows how well Hayes knew him. In Captain Maurice Browne, too, the explora tion movement had lost a promising recruit. His gossiping letters to John Thynne show him to have been a lively and businesslike young man, adept at bridging the gaps between the merchant households of London, the Court, and the country house. His enthusiasm for overseas voyaging was not that of a brainless, jobless loiterer but of an intelligent, curious, and perceptive man. Intrigued by the new and strange, anxious to equip himself for intelligent service at sea, he was con cerned with the practical outcome of imperialism in commerce and wealth. He might well, indeed, have proved a man to make something of a success of coloniza tion, which his countrymen were slow to do. In the end he went down in disgrace, responsible for poor watch keeping (though this disgrace was shared by the ship's master), and perhaps also, if we are to believe the master, Richard Clarke, for blindly following Sir Humphrey Gilbert's mistaken orders into the eye of danger and so bringing his ship to disaster. But the warm feeling which he bred in Parmenius, in Hayes, and in the Thynne family leave him in our minds as a sympathetic and unjustly unfortunate character; in this he was not unlike Parmenius himself.

Where was the *Delight* when she was wrecked and where was Parmenius' last resting place? W. G. Gosling concluded that it was at the eastern end of Sable Island; George Patterson and H. O. Thayer thought the *Delight* was in Gabarus Bay on Cape Breton Island.[4] Richard Clarke was sure it was Sable Island: he maintained that he knew the course he followed under Gilbert's orders was a dangerous one which would bring the ship on to the island. That he knew some thing about this part of the Atlantic, and could thus tell where he was, is strongly suggested by his navigation of the ship's boat safely to Newfoundland, after

3 *Ibid.*
4 W. G. Gosling, *The Life of Sir Humphrey Gilbert* (1911), p. 258; George Patterson, "The termination of Sir Humphrey Gilbert's expedition", Royal Society of Canada, *Proceedings and Transactions*, 2nd series, III (1897), section II, pp. 113–27; Henry O. Thayer, "A pioneer voyager of the sixteenth century: Sir Humphrey Gilbert", Maine Historical Society, *Collections*, 3rd series, II (1906), 51–73 (especially pp. 61–2, 71–3). It seems unlikely that with the courses supplied by Hakluyt (*Principall navigations* (1589), pp. 691, 700 (Quinn, *Gilbert*, II, 41–112, 423–4)), an accurate location for the wreck can be obtained.

estimating, it would seem correctly, the distance and direction from Sable Island. Edward Hayes gives the courses traversed by the ships, but is undecided whether the location was Sable Island or Cape Breton. If the course being sailed at the time of the disaster was west-northwest and is thought of in connection with Sable Island, it seems more likely that the shoals and flats were encountered at early daylight as the ships were sailing along and towards the south coast of the island.[5] William Cox's "cliffs" could then have been West Point, and the *Delight*'s last resting place West Bar, the sandbank to the west of the island, on to which she herself would be heavily driven by a southerly wind, but from which the other two vessels could escape by turning southwards. It could also have been that the approach was along the northerly shore of the island, but this implies a course due west. A three-hour sail, from dawn to seven o'clock, along the south of Sable Island and ending at West Bar,[6] seems then to be the most plausible account of the prelude to the tragedy. And so Hungary was robbed of her would-be Camões, and England of a voyage narrative which would have been at the very least an important and interesting record, and might even have constituted a unique literary achievement.

Gilbert, after many heart-searchings, could do nothing but return. The *Golden Hind* was now the only effective ship left and Edward Hayes brought her safely to England on 22 September, though without Sir Humphrey Gilbert. Insisting on sailing in the *Squirrel*, he had been swamped in heavy seas on 9 September, and neither he nor any of his crew were seen again.

Gilbert appears to have talked freely when he was in Newfoundland and his own account of his plans got back to Portugal and, finally, to the Spanish government. He was intending, it was said, to make for Cape Breton and winter there, and then to make his way down the coast to Florida.[7] A decision to winter on the American coast was almost forced on Gilbert by the lateness of the season, but it explains his sorting out of his personnel at St. John's, the almost hectic drive to provision the ships adequately, and the stress which Hayes put on the value of the equipment which the *Delight* had. Clearly, in spite of the *Bark Ralegh*'s defection, much material to equip winter quarters was still being carried. A winter settlement on Cape Breton or, indeed, well to the south of it, might have proved as deadly for Gilbert's men as Tadoussac (1600-1) and St. Croix (1604-5) did for the French, but success was also possible. Even if Parmenius had survived ship-

5 Approximately in lat. 43° 52′ N., long. 59° 45′ W.
6 See Fig. 10. Sable Island has been substantially eroded since the sixteenth century. Where today only West Bar survives there was probably land then, but this does not alter the picture drawn above. We do not regard the argument as establishing firmly that the wreck took place in the way suggested.
7 What the Spaniards gathered (pp. 209-10 below) appears to be confirmed from what Maurice Browne learnt during the preparations for the voyage (pp. 192-4 below).

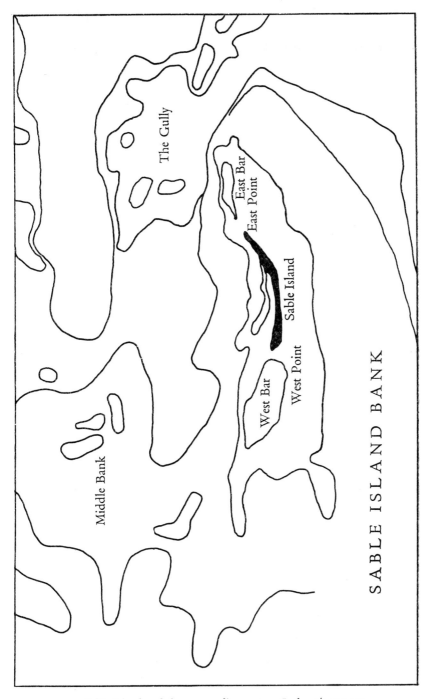

The Gully

East Bar
East Point
East Point

Sable Island

West Bar

West Point

Middle Bank

SABLE ISLAND BANK

10 Sable Island and the surrounding waters. Scale: 1/1,270,000

wreck, he might have fallen victim to the cold American winter. For the mention of Florida does not necessarily imply a destination particularly far to the south. All of North America, to 40° N. at least, went under that same name with the Spaniards. The Hudson, for example, would have been covered by this Spanish-Portuguese usage.

Gilbert has had epitaphs of varied colours. Impetuous in war, his Irish campaigns were marked by savagery; his Dutch, by impatience and lack of sophistication. His blind, ungoverned temper was liable to wreck any enterprise on which he was engaged. His intelligence was considerable; on education, on sea strategy, above all on colonization, what he had to say was worth listening to even if it was not necessarily wholly practicable. He understood – uniquely for his time – the desir-ability of uniting English merchant and gentry capital in a really extensive coloniz-ing scheme for North America, and of developing its most impressive resource, land. In this respect he was an important prophet of the successful exploitation of American soil, products, and people in the century following his own. He had a dogged persistence, even a foolhardy obstinacy, in adhering to his American plans. He was, however, a poor organizer, unable to mobilize the men, money, and materials he had called out for effective employment in America. He frittered away considerable resources in 1578, in 1579, and in 1582; he finally went to sea in 1583 with equipment inadequate to achieve even an effective reconnaissance, let alone an enduring settlement. He was liable, within his chosen American field, to switch his enthusiasms suddenly, from Northwest Passage to New England settle-ment, to Newfoundland fishery and mineral exploitation, and this touch of op-portunism made it easy for his associates to distrust him. He was an authoritarian commander even when he knew little of what he was ordering. A less good sea-man than he imagined himself, it may well be that his faulty instructions, ignorantly adhered to, led to the destruction of the *Delight*. His headstrong insistence on remaining in the tiny *Squirrel*, instead of sailing in the more shipshape *Golden Hind*, brought his own final eclipse. A stormy and dramatic figure, Gilbert has left a strong imprint on the beginnings of the modern history of North America.

The *Swallow* had been left behind at St. John's to bring home to England the sick and useless seamen from Gilbert's complement. She was presumably to be commanded by William Winter, and we might expect her to have sailed by or before 20 August when Gilbert set out with the remaining vessels. But there appears to have been some delay in getting her to sea. She may also have made a slow passage since she needed to be re-masted once she reached Cornwall.[8] Con-sequently, if she was carrying Parmenius' letters to Hakluyt and Lawrence Hum-frey, and perhaps Sir Humphrey Gilbert's to Sir George Peckham, as is quite

8 Quinn, *Gilbert*, I, 89 (though the explanation given there may not be correct); II, 428-31.

Ornatiſsimo viro, Magiſtro Richardo Hakluyto Oxonij in *Collegio ædis Chriſti,artium,& Philoſophiæ Magiſtro,amico,* & fratri ſuo.

.Non ſtatueram ad te ſcribere,cùm in mentem veniret promiſſum literarum tuarum.Putabas te ſuperiore iam Iunio nos ſubſecuturum.Itaque de meo ſtatu ex doctore Humfredo certiorem te fieri iuſſeram. Verùm ſic tibi non eſſet ſatisfactum. Itaque ſcribam ad te ijſdem ferè verbis , quia noua meditari & ἀνανεάζειν mihi hoc tempore non vacat,Vndecimo Iunij ex Anglia reuera tandem & ſeriò ſoluimus,portu & terra apud Plemuthum ſimul relictis . Claſſis

" Dominus Kalegh.

quinque nauibus conſtabat,maxima,quam " frater Amiralij accommodauerat, ignotum quo côſilio,ſtatim tertio die à nobis ſe ſubduxit.Reliqui perpetuò coniunctim nauigauimus ad 23. Iulij,quo tempore magnis nebulis intercepto aſpectu alii aliam viam tenuimus: nobis ſeorſim prima terra apparuit ad Calendas Auguſti, ad gradum circiter 50. cùm vltrà 41. paucis antè diebus deſcendiſſemus ſpe Auſtralium ventorum , qui tamen nobis ſuo tempore nunquam ſpirauêre.Inſula eſt ea,quam veſtri Penguin vocant, ab auium eiuſdem nominis multitudine. Nos tamen nec aues vidimus,nec inſulam acceſſimus ventis aliò vorantibus.Cæterùm conuenimus omnes in eundem locum paulò ante portum in quem communi conſilio omnibus veniendum erat,idque intra duas horas,magna Dei benignitate & noſtro gaudio.Locus ſitus eſt in Newfoundlandia,inter 47. & 48. gradum,diuum Ioannem vocant. Ipſe Admiralius propter multitudinem hominum,& anguſtiam nauis paulò afflictiorem comitatum habuit, & iam duos dyſentericis doloribus amiſit : de cæteris bona ſpes eſt . Ex noſtris (nam ego me Mauricio Browno verè generoſo iuueni me coniunxeram) duo etiam caſu quodam ſubmerſi ſunt. Cæteri ſalui & longè firmiores.Ego nunquam ſanior.In hunc locum tertio Auguſti appulimus : quinto autem ipſe Admiralius has regiones in ſuam & regni Angliæ poſſeſſionem poteſtatemq; vendicauit,latis quibuſdam legibus de religione & obſequio Reginæ Angliæ . Reficimur hoc tempore paulò hilarius & lautius.Certè enim & qualibus ventis vſi ſimus,& quàm feſſi eſſe potuerimus tam longi temporis ratio docuerit,proinde nihil nobis deerit . Nam extra Anglos, 20.circiter naues Luſitanicas & Hiſpanicas nacti in hoc loco ſumus : ex nobis impares non patientur nos eſurire.Angli etſi ſatis firmi,& à nobis tuti,authoritate regij diplomatis omni obſequio & humanitate proſequuntur.Nunc narrandi erant mores,regiones,& populi.Cæterùm quid narrem mi Hakluyte,quando præter ſolitudinem nihil video ? Piſcium inexhauſta copia : inde huc commeantibus magnus quæſtus.Vix hamus fundum attigit,illicò inſigni aliquo onuſtus eſt.Terra vniuerſa " montana & ſylueſtris: arbores vt plurimùm pinus : ex partim

" In the ſouth ſide of Newe founde land, there is ſtore of plaine and champion countrey.as Richard Clark found.

conſenuêre,partim nunc adoleſcunt : magna pars vetuſtate collapſa, & aſpectum terræ,& iter euntium ita impedit,vt nuſquam progredi liceat. Herbæ omnes proceræ; ſed rarò à noſtris diuerſę.Natura videtur velle niti etiam ad generandum frumentum.Inueni enim gramina,& ſpicas in ſimilitudinem ſecales : & facilè cultura & ſatione in vſum humanum aſſuefieri poſſe videntur.Rubi in ſyluis vel potiùs fraga arboreſcentia magna ſuauitate. Vrſi circa tuguria nonnunquam apparent,& conficiuntur : ſed albi ſunt,vt mihi ex pellibus coniicere licuit,& minores quàm noſtri.Populus an vllus ſit in hac regione incertum eſt:Nec vllum vidi qui teſtari poſſet.(Et quis quæſo poſſet,cùm ad longum progredi non liceat?) nec minùs ignotum eſt an aliquid metalli ſubſit montibus.Cauſa eadem eſt,etſi aſpectus eorû mineras latentes præ ſe ferat.Nos Admiralio authores ſuimus ſyluas incendere, quo ad inſpiciendam regionê ſpaciû pateret:nec diſplicebat illi conſilium,ſi non magnû incommodum allaturum videretur. Confirmatum eſt enim ab idoneis hominibus, cum caſu quopiam in alia neſcio qua ſtatione id accidiſſet,ſeptênium totû piſces non comparuiſſe,ex acerbata maris vnda ex terebynthina,quę côflagrantibus arboribus per riuulos defluebat.Coelum hoc anni tempore ita feruidum eſt,vt niſi piſces, qui areſunt ad ſolem,aſſidui inuertantur, ab aduſtione defendi non poſſint . Hyeme

The great heate of the ſunne in ſummer.

quàm frigidum ſit,magnæ moles glaciei in medio mari nos docuere. Relatum eſt a comitibus menſe Maio ſexdecim totos dies interdum ſe inter tantam glaciem hęſiſſe, vt 60.orgyas altæ eſſent inſulę: quarum latera ſoli oppoſita cum liqueſcerent , libratione quadam vniuerſam molem ita inuerſam, vt quod antè pronum erat,ſupinum euaderet, magno præſentium diſcrimine,vt conſentaneum eſt,Aer in terra mediocriter clarus eſt:ad orientem ſupra mare perpetuę nebulę: Et in ipſo mari circa Bancum (ſic vocant locum vbi quadraginta leucis à terra fundus attingitur,& piſces capi incipiunt) nullus ferme dies abſque pluuia. Expeditis noſtris neceſſitatibus in hoc loco, in Auſtrum (Deo iuuante) progrediemur,tantò indies maiori ſpe, quò plura de iis quas petimus regionibus commemorantur. Hęc de noſtris. Cupio de vobis ſcire: ſed metuo ne incaſſum.Imprimis autem quomodo Vntonus meus abſentiam meam ferat, præter modum intelligere velim: Habebit noſtrum obſequium & officium paratum,quamdiu vixerimus. Reuera autem ſpero,hanc noſtram peregrinationem ipſius inſtituto vſui futuram, Nunc reſtat, vt me tuum putes,& quidem ita tuum, vt neminem magis. Iuuet dei filius labores noſtros eatenus, vt tu quoque participare poſsis. Vale amiciſsime, ſuauiſsime, ornatiſsime Hakluyte, & nos ama. In Newfundlandia apud portum Sancti Iohannis 6. Auguſti 1583.

Stephanus Parmenius
Budeius,tuus,

11 Hakluyt, *Principall navigations* (1589), pp. 697-8; letter from Stephen Parmenius to Richard Hakluyt, 6 August 1583

65

possible, these may not have been delivered until the very end of September or early October. Edward Hayes, with the *Golden Hind*, had put into Falmouth on 22 September, conveying news of the loss of the *Delight* with Parmenius on board, and the further sad report that Sir Humphrey had probably also gone down in the *Squirrel* when she parted company with the *Golden Hind*. This information together with the Parmenius letter is not very likely to have caught up with Hakluyt before he left London.

It would have been between 20 and 25 September that he left the city in the train of Sir Edward Stafford, ambassador to the French court, to whom he had been appointed secretary and chaplain, reaching Boulogne with him on 28 September.[9] As a result, it was probably in October, in Paris, that he learnt of the disaster to the Gilbert expedition and to his Hungarian friend. Just about the time when Hakluyt was preparing to depart, another death took place. Sir Edward Unton, who had rallied under Brumen's medications in 1582, had come to London in 1583, but there he was taken fatally ill and died on 16 September,[10] being succeeded in his estates by his son Edward, but leaving, as he had promised, substantial sums to his younger son Henry. Henry was not inspired by the loss of of Parmenius and of Gilbert to step into their footsteps as an American pioneer, but turned instead to war and to diplomacy, dying on his second term as ambassador to France in 1596.

9 Parks, *Hakluyt*, p. 248; *Calendar of state papers, foreign, 1583–84*, p. 117.
10 See his will, 14 September 1583, in J. G. Nichols, ed., *The Unton Inventories* (1841), pp. xxxix–xliii.

Epilogue

P ARMENIUS WAS LOST in American waters, but not forgotten by his contemporaries. Edward Hayes had something about him in his journals, and might
also have mentioned him in the materials from them which he supplied to Sir
George Peckham, about October 1583, when briefing the latter on the course and
casualties of Gilbert's disastrous voyage. But Hayes did not write up "A report of
the voyage and success thereof, attempted ... by Sir Humphrey Gilbert knight",
with its eulogy of Parmenius, until some time later; it was done for Hakluyt to
print in 1589.[1] Hakluyt himself used the Newfoundland letter, citing it extensively
in Latin, in his "A particuler discourse", which was written in the later summer
and autumn of 1584 and included his valuable reference to "my bedfelowe at
Oxforde".[2] But this was not, of course, published at the time. For the 1589
Principall navigations Hakluyt used the letter in full and gave his own translation of
it as well.[3] For the second edition, besides reusing the material printed in 1589,[4]
he decided to add the revised *De navigatione* also, perhaps realizing he had done
Parmenius less than justice by excluding it to begin with. He did not, however,
take the space to translate either the poem or its epistle.[5] Thus in 1600 all of the
Parmenius material about America that was known to survive was assembled in
the third volume of *The principal navigations*.

But the tradition of celebrating in Latin verse the exploits of British voyagers did
not die with Parmenius. Whatever else may have been written and lost, we know
that exactly a decade after Vautrollier had put out the first version of *De navigatione*
(and some eight years before Hakluyt was to reprint it), William Ponsonby published a sequence of ten poems (*Epistolae*) composed by Thomas Watson under

1 *Principall navigations* (1589), pp. 679–97 (Quinn, *Gilbert*, II, 385–423).
2 The MS was formerly Phillipps MS 14097, purchased at Sothebys on 19 May 1913
  by Henry Stevens for £215 for the New York Public Library (A. N. L. Munby,
  Phillipps studies, IV (1956), V (1960), 64).
3 *Principall navigations* (1589), pp. 679–97; below, p. 16876.
4 *Principal navigations*, III (1600), 161–3.
5 *Ibid.*, pp. 137–43.

the title "The Joys of Amyntas" (*Amintae gaudia*).⁶ The fifth of these, adapting to a pastoral context the literary device of Homer's passage about the "shield of Achilles",⁷ envisages the shepherd presenting his Phyllis with a milking-pail on which are depicted various scenes from contemporary life and history. They include the Queen at Greenwich Palace, the Thames (lines 28–34), and London bridge adorned with the heads of Spanish sailors after the defeat of the Armada in 1588 (35–47). In the former passage (which may be compared with *De navigatione*, lines i–x and 169–75) Amyntas is made to say:

> You see the palace built with turrets joined,
> Alongside which there flows the shapely Thames,
> Turning this way and that, and winding out
> Towards the open sea? Beneath that roof
> Resides our own Diana, radiant
> Of aspect and august: so rich in wealth
> And subjects, powerful in war and feared
> By enemies, but still a godly friend
> Of peace ...⁸

But of special interest is Watson's "catalogue of explorers" (71–99), which parallels that in *De navigatione* (277–98). Like Parmenius, Watson refers to Willoughby, Frobisher, Drake, and one of the Cabots, complaining that to the last of these "the stylish Ramusio or an implacable Fate" has begrudged due recognition for his achievements.⁹

> *Illa, sub occiduo quae vitam climate ponit*
> *Immito subversa freto, miseranda Caboti*

6 Thomas Watson, *Amintae gaudia* ([Londini] imp. Gulihelmi Ponsonbei), 1592 (S.T.C. 25117).
7 *Iliad*, xviii, 483–608; for the same device in Latin see Virgil, *Aeneid*, i, 453–93.
8 "*Aspicis erectas connexis turribus aedes, | formosae Thamesis quas praeterlabitur unda, | alterno flexu veniens, remeansque sub altos | Oceani fluctus? Tectis augusta sub illis | en ubi nostra sedet vultu radiosa Diana, | dives opum, dives populi, pia pacis amica, | quamvis Marte potens, et formidabilis hosti.|*" (Trans. by N.M.C.)
9 *Amintae gaudia*, v. 71–74. The point about the reference to Ramusio is that he attributed the western voyages to Sebastian Cabot only (cp. J. A. Williamson, *The Cabot voyages* (1962), pp. 270–73), but some evidence that John Cabot, Sebastian's father, had been prominent in the discovery of America had also become available in England (Hakluyt, *Divers voyages* (1582), sig. A1–2; Williamson, pp. 207, 322–3; Hakluyt, *Principal navigations*, III (1600), 6). Watson may have been a supporter of John Cabot's claim to fame and felt that Ramusio had suppressed his achievements, but there was nothing in published sources on the death of either of the Cabots.

Cymba fuit, cuius meritis invidit honorem
Lubrica Rhamnusis, vel ineluctabile fatum.

Watson also mentions Wyndham, Chancellor, and Cavendish, envisaging (in lines reminiscent of *De navigatione*, 242–5, 315–18, Wyndham looking down from shipboard on the Aethiopians and praying that they may be brought under English rule and into the Christian faith.[10]

... Ecce novos, nostri quos ignorare parentes,
Longius explorat visu, totosque nigellos
Wyndamus Aethiopes ex prorae despicit arce:
Quos tamen, erectas tendens ad sidera palmas,
Optat in Anglorum suaderi foedera posse,
Aeternique Dei solas agnoscere leges.

These parallels do not, of course, constitute evidence that Watson had actually read Parmenius, but it is not impossible that the former was moved by the latter's work to see in the voyages of discovery a subject worthy of the revived classicism of Greece and Rome, and thus to perpetuate a *genre* which Parmenius had at least extended if not actually originated.

Another transatlantic enterprise which was celebrated by a contemporary poet is the attempt to colonize Guiana – an ill-starred project which Ralegh himself took to heart, especially at the time of his waning political fortunes. But in this case, despite its Latin title of *De Guiana carmen epicum*, the language is English; the style is blank verse and the author, George Chapman.[11] This little work, of just over 180 lines, was published in 1596, the same year as Ralegh's own account of the previous year's voyage to that region.[12] Its purpose, however, is much more exhortatory than descriptive; and it shares with *De navigatione* an idealized prospect of things unseen. Apart from this general atmosphere, we may remark two points of relatively specific similarity. One is the conventional sentiment of contrasting the possibility of a Golden Age "over there" with the Age of Iron elsewhere (cp. *DNC*, 37–67). But Chapman's gesture in this direction (lines 30–2) is merely an

10 *Amintae gaudia*, v, 82–7.
11 Chapman's poem originally prefaced Lawrence Keymis, *A relation of the second voyage to Guiana* (London, Thomas Dawson, 1596). For a more accessible text, see e.g., Swinburne's edition of *The works of George Chapman: poems and minor translations* (London 1875), pp. 50–2.
12 See Sir Walter Ralegh, *The discoverie of the large and bewtiful empyre of Guiana*, ed. V. T. Harlow (1928).

incident in his display of the bait of real gold which he repeatedly dangles before his readers:

> *Then most admired sovereign, let your breath*
> *Go forth upon the waters, and create*
> *A golden world in this our iron age.*

The second point of similarity is the picture of Guiana trying to catch England's attention and asking to be allowed to become her subject. This vividly recalls Parmenius' fantasy of North America reaching out her hand and, with dejected crown (*submisso diademate*), begging to be liberated by England (*DNC*, 242–47). Chapman writes (lines 18–24):

> *Guiana, whose rich feet are mines of gold,*
> *Whose forehead knocks against the roof of stars,*
> *Stands on her tip-toes at fair England looking,*
> *Kissing her hand, bowing her mighty breast,*
> *And every sign of all submission making,*
> *To be her sister, and the daughter both*
> *Of our most sacred maid; ...*

These observations do not, of course, amount to evidence that Chapman and Watson had actually read Parmenius. But it is not impossible that it was after encountering the Hungarian's treatment of his American theme at first or second hand that Chapman, the eminent translator of the classics, came to regard such material as a suitable medium for flexing the young muscles of fledgling vernacular verse. For his poem was, as Buxton remarks, "one of the few poems written about those enterprises overseas which we should have supposed so well worth the writing."[13]

As Hakluyt was read in the century following, so also (we may presume) were Parmenius' principal poem and Newfoundland letter, preserved in the collection of *Principal navigations*. We cannot assume, however, that the independent 1582 editions of his poems continued to be known. Hakluyt himself did not become the subject of detailed academic inquiry until the eighteenth century, but it is significant that, when he did, Parmenius is picked out as one of the prizes of his collection. In his important notice of Hakluyt in 1757, William Oldys remarked on the "heroic poem" of the "learned and ingenious Stephanus Parmenius of Buda", and

---

13 Buxton, *Sidney* (1964), p. 222.

mentioned his Newfoundland letter and subsequent death at sea.[14] If Parmenius was to the taste of one eighteenth-century scholar, he may well have been so to others, but we have not found evidence of this in England. It is in post-revolutionary America, when he has become part of a transatlantic inheritance, that Parmenius is eventually revived.

For two hundred years no one seems to have paid any particular attention to the young Hungarian scholar. His revival as a historical figure is in a peculiar degree associated with the Massachusetts Historical Society. The indefatigable Abiel Holmes, minister of the First Congregational Church at Cambridge, was attracted by the Parmenius poem as it appeared in Hakluyt. From the information contained in the *Principal navigations* he put together a brief "Memoir of Stephen Parmenius" and proceeded to translate his Gilbert poem and its epistle. He offered these to the Massachusetts Historical Society for its *Collections* on 30 October 1804,[15] and they were duly printed that same year in volume IX, pp. 49–75.

The memoir contains most of the few items we have about Parmenius, and the verse translation, quaint though it sounds to present-day ears, fairly represents the sense and spirit of the original. It is not without the occasional gap and misunderstanding,[16] but it contains a number of sonorous lines which do full justice to Parmenius' Latin. Despite his disclaimer that "no freedom has been intentionally used with the original, excepting to deprive queen Elizabeth of her poetical divinity", Holmes's version is somewhat looser than the present one aims to be, in so far as it often reproduces the general meaning of a passage without attempting to reflect its verbal structure at all precisely. It should be added that this is at least partly a consequence of his wanting to produce a line-for-line rendering of an inflected language in a non-inflected one, and (more importantly, perhaps) of thus trying to turn six metric feet of Latin into five of English. However, such is Holmes's ingenuity that he very nearly succeeds in this numerical design, requiring only some 344 lines as against the 319 of his text. We include in the notes some extracts from his translation to illustrate these features. Holmes appended a few useful footnotes, mainly about the people and figures to whom Parmenius alludes, to complete an edition and study which constitute the only significant advances made in the nineteenth century.

Winsor was not able, in the eighties,[17] to do more than refer to Holmes's version and to Hakluyt, apparently not having seen a copy of the 1582 edition of the

14 William Oldys, in *Biographia Britannica*, IV (1757), 2465.
15 Massachusetts Historical Society, *Proceedings, 1791–1835* (1879), p. 166.
16 See *DNC*, notes to ll. 2 (title page), 15 (Preface), 27 (Preface), 45, 50, 91, 142, 168, 179, 210, 220.
17 Justin Winsor, *Narrative and critical history of America*, III (Boston, 1889), 171, 187.

71

poem. Henry Deane, however, by printing "A particuler discourse" for the first time in 1877 (under the title *Discourse on western planting*),[18] at last made available the "bedfelowe" reference.

For a long time, however, American scholars did not have easy access to the original printings of Parmenius' writings. Thus Sabin, listing in 1870 the British Museum copy of the *De navigatione*, put it under "Budeius, S.P."[19] In 1907 the *Church catalogue* gave the first full description of a copy in America, that now in the Huntington Library.[20] It was the Massachusetts Historical Society again which gave the next impetus to the study of the poem, by circulating, in its *Americana* series in 1922, ten copies each of photostats of the British Museum and Huntington Library copies.[21] The *Paean* remained unnoticed on the shelves of the British Museum and of Eton College.

18 *Documentary history of Maine*, II (Cambridge, Mass., 1877), and separately. It was printed from the Phillipps Manuscript (the only surviving text); a new edition was included in E. G. R. Taylor, *The original writings and correspondence of the two Richard Hakluyts*, II (1935), 211–326, where the Parmenius passage (part of which is in Fig. 1) is to be found on pp. 230–1.
19 Joseph Sabin, *A dictionary of books relating to America*, III (New York, 1870).
20 George Watson Cole, ed., *A catalogue of books relating to the discovery and early history of ... America forming part of the library of E. D. Church*, I (1907), 288 (no. 127). In "Elizabethan Americana", *Bibliographical essays: A tribute to Wilberforce Eames* (Cam-bridge, Mass., 1924), pp. 166–67, Cole again describes the Church copy (by then in the Huntington Library), and notes that the British Museum copy is the only other one known to exist.
21 Massachusetts Historical Society, *Americana* series (photostats), no. 78 (British Museum copy), no. 78a (Huntington Library copy) (Boston 1922).

PART ONE

De Navigatione

illustris et magnanimi equitis aurati

HUMFREDI GILBERTI

ad deducendam in novum orbem coloniam suscepta,
Carmen ἐπιβατικὸν

STEPHANI PARMENII BUDEII

LONDINI

Apud Thomam Purfutium

Anno 1582

An Embarkation Poem

for the voyage projected by the celebrated and noble

SIR HUMPHREY GILBERT

Golden Knight, to take a colony to the New World

BY STEPHEN PARMENIUS OF BUDA

LONDON

Thomas Purfoote

1582

Ad eundem illustrem Equitem autoris praefatio

Reddenda est, quam fieri potest brevissime, in hoc vestibulo ratio facti mei et cur ita homo novus et exterus, in tanta literatissimorum hominum copia quibus Anglia beata est, versandum in hoc argumento mihi putaverim: ita enim tu, fortissime Gilberte, foetum hunc nostrum in lucem exire voluisti.

5   *In servitute et barbarie Turcica, Christianis tamen magno immortalis Dei beneficio parentibus, natus, aliquam etiam aetatis partem educatus, postquam doctissimorum hominum opera, quibus tum Pannoniae nostrae tum imprimis salvae adhuc earum re- liquiae florescunt, in literis adolevissem, more nostrorum hominum ad invisendas Christiani orbis Academias ablegatus fui. Qua in peregrinatione, non solum compluria*
10 *Musarum hospitia sed multas etiam sapienter institutas respublicas, multarum ec- clesiarum probatissimas administrationes introspeximus, iam ferme triennio ea in re posito. Fuerat haec nostra profectio ita a nobis comparata ut non tantum mores et urbes gentium videndum sed in familiaritatem, aut saltem notitiam, illustriorum hominum introeundum nobis putaremus.*

15   *Caeterum, ut hoc a nobis sine invidia dici possit, (certe enim taceri absque malicia nullo modo potest), non locus, non natio, non respublica ulla nobis aeque ac tua Britannia complacuit, quamcunque in partem eventum consilii mei considerem. Accedit quod praeter omnem expectationem meam, ab omnibus tuis civibus quibuscum aliqua consuetudo mihi contigit, tanta passim humanitate acceptus essem ut iam (sit hoc salva*
20 *pietate a me dictum) suavissimae Anglorum amicitiae ferme aboleverint desiderium et Pannoniarum et Budae meae, quibus patriae nomen debeo.*

   Quas ob caussas, cum saepenumero animus fuisset significationem aliquam nostrae huius voluntatis et existimationis edendi, accidit utique secundum sententiam ut, dum salu-

76

Author's preface to this celebrated knight

I feel bound to give, as briefly as possible in this introduction, the reason for
my writing; and to say why, when England is blessed with so many excellent
men of letters, it seemed to me that I, an unknown foreigner, had to apply
myself in such a way to this theme. For you, Sir Humphrey, wanted this
5 literary offspring of mine to be accompanied into the world by some such
account.

Although I was born in the servitude and barbarism of the Turkish
empire, my parents were, by the grace of God, Christians, and I was even
educated for some part of the time. After I had made some academic progress,
10 thanks to the efforts of my erudite teachers, such as have always been the
pride of my native Hungary (and are particularly so now, among her still
surviving relics), I was sent away to visit the universities of the Christian
world.

On these travels I saw not only many centres of culture but also a number
15 of wisely constituted states and the impeccable administration of many
branches of the Church, spending almost three years in the process. I had
conceived the object of this expedition to be not merely to have a look at the
cities and way of life of different peoples, but to make friends, or at least
acquaintance, with some of their eminent men.

20 But, in order that my mention of this may not provoke rivalry (for passing
over it in silence would certainly invite ill-feeling), let me say that no situation, no people, no state has pleased me so much as your country of Britain,
whatever aspect of my plan I consider. In addition, the warmth with which
I have been received at every turn, by the people with whom I have had any
25 dealings, has so exceeded all my expectations that now (and I say it with due
patriotism) the delightful friendship of the English has almost dispelled my
longing for Buda and the Hungary which I am bound to call my homeland.

As a result of this, I had often had the urge to publish some token of my
goodwill and respect; so it came about entirely in accordance with my in-
30 clinations that, while I was concerned with paying tribute to, and getting to

77

tandis et cognoscendis excellentibus viris Londini operam do, ornatissimus ac doctissimus
25 *amicus meus Richardus Hacletius ad te me deduxerit, explicato mihi praeclarissimo tuo*
de ducenda propediem colonia in novum orbem instituto. Quae dum aguntur, agnoscere
potui ego illud corpus et animum tuum sempiterna posteritatis commemoratione dignum; et
agnovi profecto, eaque tali ac tanta observantia prosequi caepi ut, cum paullo post plura de
tuis virtutibus et rebus gestis passim audissem, tempus longe accommodatissimum existi-
30 *marem esse quo aliqua parte officii studiique nostri, erga te et tuam gentem, perfungerer.*
Hoc est primum ovum unde nostrum ἐπιβατικὸν *originem ducit. Reliquum est ut*
eas et redeas quam prosperrime, vir nobilissime, et benevolentia tua, autoritate ac nomine,
tueare studium nostrum.

Vale.

know, eminent people in London, my distinguished and learned friend Richard Hakluyt took me along to you, having expounded to me your celebrated plan to lead a colonizing expedition to the New World in the near future. In the course of this, I was able to recognize that you are a man
35 of such stature and spirit as deserves to be remembered for ever by posterity; not only did I recognize it indeed, but I also began to study my subject so keenly that when, a little later, I had heard from various sources more about your qualities and achievements, I decided that much the most suitable time had come for me to discharge some part of my obligation and intention to-
40 wards you and your countrymen. This is the seed from which my *Embarka-tion* poem grew.

Finally, noble sir, may all good fortune bless your voyages both out and back; and may you look kindly, as one who has position and reputation, on this work of mine.
45   God speed!

Ad Thamesin

Amnis, inoffensa qui tam requiete beatus
    Antipodum quaeris iam tibi in orbe locum,
Nunc tibi principium meritae, pro tempore, laudis
    Fecimus, et raucae carmina prima tubae.
5 Tum, cum reddideris modo quam dimittimus Argo,
    Ornatu perages gaudia festa novo.

To the Thames

O waters so unruffled
    And blessed with peaceful grace,
You seek a destination
    Upon Earth's further face.
5 I now begin the praises
    Befitting such a time
By sounding first this fanfare
    Of unmelodious rhyme.
Then, when you bring back safely
10   The ship we put to sea,
Fresh laurels will adorn you
    In high festivity.

De Navigatione

Quae nova tam subito mutati gratia coeli?
    Unde graves nimbi vitreas tenuantur in auras,
    Diffugiunt nebulae, puroque nitentior ortu
    Illustrat terras clementiaque aequora Titan?
5 *Nimirum posuere Noti, meliorque resurgit*
    Eurus, et in ventos solvuntur vela secundos,
    Vela quibus gentis decus immortale Britannae
    Tendit ad ignotum nostris maioribus orbem
    Vix notis Gilbertus aquis.
                      Ecquando licebit
10 *Ordiri heroas laudes et facta nepotum*
    Attonitis memoranda animis, si caepta silendum est
    Illa quibus nostri priscis aetatibus audent
    Conferri et certare dies? Quibus obvia plano
    Iamdudum Fortuna solo, quibus omne per undas
15 *Nereidum genus exultat, faustoque tridenti*
    Ipse pater Nereus placabile temperat aequor.
    Et passim Oceano curvi delphines ab imo
    In summos saliunt fluctus, quasi terga pararent
    In quibus evectae sulcent freta prospera puppes.
20 *Et, quasi diluvium tempestatesque, minatur*
    Follibus inflatis inimica in vela physeter.
    Et favet Aegaeon, et qui Neptunia Proteus

An Embarkation Poem

WHAT STRANGE NEW RADIANCE IS THIS THAT SHINES
    So suddenly in heaven's changing face?
    How is it that the heavy clouds dissolve
    Into light breezes, mists disperse, and so
5 The sun can shine more brightly, since his path
    Is cleared, on land and on the gentle sea?
    The South wind drops, and now the milder East
    Blows once again. To this fair breeze unfurl
    The sails which England's Humphrey Gilbert sets
10 Towards a world our fathers did not know
    In seas they scarcely saw.
                  But when shall we
    Ever recount what their descendants did,
    What epic praise they merit (stories fit
    To fall on startled ears), if one must leave
15 Untold those things that make our present days
    Presume to vie and be compared with times
    Long past? For now Good Fortune walks the land
    In open view, and all the Nereid tribe
    Are prancing gleefully about the waves
20 While father Nereus soothes the docile deep
    With his propitious wand. Now here and there
    The Dolphins spring from off the ocean bed
    To break the surface, just as though their backs
    Were offered to the ships to carry them
25 Through kindly waters: whales with bulging cheeks
    Threaten the hostile sails, and imitate
    The rainy downpour of a stormy gale.
    But spirits of the sea provide support:
    And so does Proteus, guarding Neptune's herds

Armenta ac turpes alit imo in gurgite phocas.
Atque idem modo ab antiqua virtute celebrat
25 Sceptra Chaledonidum, seclis modo fata futuris
Pandit et ad seros canit eventura minores.
   Ut pacis bellique bonis notissima vasto
Insula in Oceano, magni decus Anglia mundi,
Postquam opibus dives, populo numerosa frequenti,
30 Tot celebris factis toto caput extulit orbe?
Non incauta sui, ne quando immensa potestas
Pondere sit ruitura suo, nova moenia natis
Quaerat, et in longum extendat sua regna recessum:
Non aliter quam, cum ventis sublimibus aptae
35 In nidis crevere grues, proficiscitur ingens
De nostra ad tepidum tellure colonia Nilum.
   Euge, sacrum pectus: tibi per tot secula soli
Servata est regio nullis regnata Monarchis.
Et triplici quondam mundi natura notata
40 Margine, et audacem quarto dignata Columbum,
Iam quinta lustranda plaga tibi, iamque regenda
Imperio superest. Europam Asiamque relinque,
Et fortunatam (nimium nisi sole propinquo
Arderet) Libyen. Illis sua facta viasque
45 Terminet Alcides: abs te illustranda quiescit
Parte alia tellus, quam non Babylonia sceptra,
Non Macedum invictae vires, non Persica virtus
Attigit aut unquam Latiae feriere secures.
Non illo soboles Mahometi mugiit orbe:
50 Non vafer Hispanus, coelo superisque relictis,

30 And feeding in the lowest depths his flock
   Of slimy seals. And now he celebrates
   The ancient might of Scotland's royal throne,
   Now shows the destiny of years to come,
   Singing to generations yet unborn
35 What things the future holds.
                                    How should we tell
   (If silence must be kept) that now the pride
   Of all the world is England, set about
   By giant seas and known for noble men
   In peace and war; that she, so rich in wealth
40 And people, now has raised her head above
   All other lands by many famous deeds?
   Lest from its own huge weight this monument
   Might crash to earth, let her in providence
   Now find her children other settlements,
45 Stretching her kingdoms far afield: just like
   The cranes, which in their nests grow fit to brave
   The winds high up and then fly off in flocks
   Toward the warmer Nile.
                              Rejoice, great soul!
   A land unruled by kings has been preserved
50 For you through many centuries: for you
   The secret nature of the earth, which once
   Was drawn with threefold sides but honoured bold
   Columbus' memory with yet a fourth,
   Is now to be explored along a fifth,
55 Retained for you to conquer. Leave the lands
   Of Europe, Asia and of Africa
   (A place less sun would make more fortunate).
   Let Hercules be limited to these
   In his activity: for you there lies
60 In distant parts, another world to bring
   To light. A world which has not felt the weight
   Of Babylon, the Persians' might, nor known
   Victorious Macedon, and never was
   Subdued by Rome. Nor has the Moslem wail
65 Disturbed those regions: there no scheming hand
   Of Spain rejects the early church and God

Sacra Papae humano crudelia sanguine fecit.
Illic mortales hominumque ignota propago:
Sive illi nostrae veniant ab origine gentis,
Seu tandem a prisca Faunorum stirpe supersint
55   Antiqua geniti terra, sine legibus urbes
Sylvasque et pingues habitant civilibus agros
Et priscos referunt mores, vitamque sequuntur
Italiae antiquae et primi rude temporis aevum
Cum genitor nati fugiens Saturnus ob iram
60   In Latio posuit sedem, rudibusque regendos
In tenues vicos homines collegit ab agris.
Aurea in hoc primum populo caepisse feruntur
Secula, sicque homines vitam duxisse beati:
Ut, simul argenti percurrens tempora et aeris
65   Degener in durum chalybem vilesceret aetas,
Rursus in antiquum, de quo descenderat, aurum
(Sic perhibent vates) aevo vertente rediret.
    Fallor an est tempus, revolutoque orbe videntur
Aurea pacificae transmittere secula gentes?
70   Fallor enim, si quassatas tot cladibus urbes
Respicio et passim lacerantes regna tyrannos:
Si Mahometigenis Asiam Libyamque cruento
Marte premi, domitaque iugum cervice subire.
Iamque per Europae fines immane tribunal
75   Barbari adorari domini, Dacisque Pelasgisque
Aemathiisque omnique solo quod dividit Hebrus:
Et, quondam bello invictis, nunc Marte sinistro
Angustos fines parvamque tuentibus oram,
Pannoniae populis et prisca in gente Liburnis.
80   Tum vero in superos pugnas sine fine cieri

Himself, to make a Papal sacrifice
Barbaric with the blood of fellow men.
   An unknown race and people occupy
70 That land: are they, perhaps, from our same stock
Or do they boast an ancient ancestry
Derived from Pan, inheriting from times
Gone by a land of woods and fertile fields
And cities needing not the rule of law?
75 Perhaps they still preserve the way of life,
Customs and attitudes of early times
In Italy, when father Saturn fled
His angry son, made Latium his home,
And set up little hamlets, drawing in
80 The people out of rough-tilled countrysides.
The Golden Age began (or so they say)
In such communities, and thus men lived
In blessedness: but once corrupted years
Had cheapened them, through Silver, Bronze and dull
85 Hard Iron, time's wheel (the poets said) would turn
Full circle back to where it started, – Gold.
   Well, could it be that that great time has come,
That round the globe we see peace-loving men
Promote an Age of Gold? It cannot be,
90 Or so it seems, if I look back on all
The cities shaken by disastrous wars,
And kingdoms beaten down on many sides
By despots: African and Asian lands
Are crushed by brutal Muslim regiments
95 And bow submissive heads. In Europe too
The hateful rule of pagan mastery
Is now conceded by Rumania,
By Greece, by Macedon and all the land
Through which the ancient river Hebrus flows;
100 Also by citizens of Hungary
Who, never yet subdued in war, now guard
Her narrow boundaries against the threat
Of conquest, as within her ancient ground
Croatia does. Indeed, Italian priests
105 Provoke continual attacks against

Patribus Ausoniis: ardere in bella necesque
Sarmaticas gentes, et adhuc a caede recenti
Hispanum sancto Gallumque madere cruore.
Non sunt haec auri non sunt documenta, sed atrox
85 Ingenio referunt ferrum et, si dicere ferro
Deteriora mihi licet, intractabile saxum.

   At vero ad niveos alia si parte Britannos
Verto oculos animumque, quot, o pulcherrima tellus,
Testibus antiquo vitam traducis in auro!
90 Namque quod hoc summum colitur tibi numen honore
Quo superi, atque omnis geniorum casta iuventus
Illius ad sacra iussa vices obit, arguit aurum.
   Quod tam chara Deo tua sceptra gubernat Amazon
Quam Dea, cum nondum coelis Astraea petitis
95 Inter mortales regina erat, arguit aurum.
   Quod colit haud ullis inclusas moenibus urbes
Aurea libertas, et nescia ferre tyrannum
Securam aetatem tellus agit, arguit aurum.
   Quod regio, nullis iniuria gentibus, arma
100 Arma licet ferruginea rubicunda quiete
Finitimis metuenda gerit tamen, arguit aurum.
   Quod gladii, quod mucrones, quod pila, quod hastae
In rastros abiere, et bello assueta iuventus
Pacem et amicitias dulces colit, arguit aurum.
105   Denique, si fas est auro connectere laudes
Aeris et in pacis venerari tempore fortes,
   Quot natos bello heroas, quot ahenea nutris
Pectora! Sint testes procerum tot millia, testes
Mille duces, interque duces notissima mille
110 Illa cui assurgunt Musae, quam conscia Pallas
Laetior exaudit, – Gileberti gloria nostri.
Illius auxilium et socialia praelia amici

The Fathers; Russia has a burning thirst
For war and slaughter; recently the French
And Spaniards steeped their hands in holy blood.
Such deeds do not become a Golden Age,
110 But call to mind the baser Age of Iron,
Or rather, baser still if possible,
They share the character of Rock.
                                    And yet,
If I should turn my mind and eyes elsewhere
To Britain's shining people, what a host
115 Can witness there that you, delightful land,
Preserve the Golden Age in daily life!
For you still worship God with that same awe
As did the Fathers, all your blameless priests
Perform their office as His holy will
120 Directs, – an Age of Gold! Your mighty Queen
Is reigning, dear to God as Justice was
When holding sway as goddess over men
Before she sought the Heavens. Freedom's light
Suffuses cities unconfined by walls:
125 The earth is innocent of having borne
Dictators: times are safe. Unjust to none,
Her weapons still are feared by neighbour states
Although disuse has stained them red with rust.
And so her swords and daggers, lances, spears
130 Are turned to ploughshares and the warlike youth
Study the arts of peace and brotherhood.
Such blessings must recall the Golden Age.
Lastly, if we may join with praise of Gold
Such virtues as befit an Age of Bronze
135 To venerate the brave in times of peace,
How many valiant sons and dauntless hearts
This land has raised! A host of noble men
And scores of leaders stand as witnesses:
Among them, him to whom the Muses rise
140 In acclamation, him to whom the wise
Minerva gladly listens, – England's pride,
Great Humphrey Gilbert.
                                    His support of friends

89

Mirantur Belgae, et quamvis iniustus Iberus
Commemorat iustas acies, domitasque per oras
115 Martia victrices formidat Hibernia turmas.
Illum oppugnatae quassatis turribus arces,
Illum expugnatae perruptis moenibus urbes,
Fluminaque et portus capti, hostilique notatum
Sanguine submersae meminere sub aequore classes, –
120 Hic ubi per medios proiectus Sequana Celtas
Labitur, et nomen mox amissurus et undas.
Omnia si desint, quantum est, ingentibus ausis
Humani generis pro pace bonoque, pacisci
Tam varios casus, freta tanta, pericula tanta?
125 Linquere adhuc teneram prolem et dulcissima sacri
Oscula coniugii, numerantemque ordine longo
Aucheriam digitis in mollibus aequora mille
Formidanda modis: atque inter pauca relatos
Aucherios exempla suos, fratremque patremque
130 Qui dum pro patria laudem et virtute sequuntur,
Obsessi in muris soli portisque Caleti
Praeposuere mori quam, cum prodentibus urbem
Et decus Albionum, turpi superesse salute.
      Quodsi parva loquor, nec adhuc fortasse fatenda est
135 Aurea in hoc iterum gens vivere mundo,
Quid vetat ignotis ut possit surgere terris?
Auguror (et faveat dictis Deus) auguror annos
In quibus haud illo secus olim principe in urbes
Barbara plebs coeat quam cum nova saxa vocaret

In war amazed the Belgians, his pursuit
Of honest battle was recorded by
145 Dishonest Spain, and warlike Ireland shakes
Throughout her conquered shores in fear of his
Victorious army. Captured citadels
Remember him with trembling turrets, towns
Reduced by storm and left with broken walls,
150 Bridgeheads and harbours taken, sunken fleets
Stained with the blood of enemies: all these
Confirm his reputation, where the Seine
Which rises deep in France begins to lose
Her own identity and pour her waves
155 Into the open sea. If all should fail,
How dear a price it is, for great attempts
To benefit mankind and fashion peace,
To risk those many different fates, vast seas
And frequent dangers! Dear it is to leave
160 One's children still so young, to leave behind
A precious wife's much-loved embrace, to leave
The Lady Aucher counting out a list,
On gentle fingertips, of all the fears
And hazards of the sea. As instances
165 She might recall the fate of relatives,–
Father and brother lost: for they, intent
To bring to Fatherland and chivalry
Good reputation, when besieged alone
In Calais' gates and battlements, chose death,
170 Rather than stay alive along with those
Who would betray the town and England's name
In safe dishonour.
                              Little though this seems,
And not enough to justify the claim
That in our land there dwells a Golden Race,
175 Why should not one inhabit unknown parts?
But there will come a time, I prophesy
(And may Almighty God fulfil my words),
A time in which the pagan tribes may move
Together, under Gilbert's leadership
180 Into new cities: as when shapeless rocks,

140 *Amphion Thebas, Troiana ad moenia Phoebus:*
Atque ubi sic ultro iunctas sociaverit aedes,
Deinde dabit leges custoditurus easdem.
In quibus, ignari cives fraudumque dolique,
A solida assuescant potius virtute beari
145 *Quam genio et molli liquentia corpora vita*
In Venerem ignavam pinguemque immergere luxum:
Quam nummos, quam lucra sequi, quam propter honores
Vivere ad arbitrium stolidae mutabile plebis.
Non illic generi virtus opibusve premetur
150 *Libertas populi, non contra in deside vulgo*
Oppugnabit opes, civis sub nomine, pauper:
Quisque suo partem foelix in iure capesset.
Tum sua magna parens ingenti foenore tellus
Exiguo sudore dabit bona: cura iuventam
155 *Nulla adiget senio, nec sic labor ocia tollet*
Quominus e virtute petant sua commoda cives.
O mihi foelicem si fas conscendere puppim
Et tecum, patria (pietas ignosce) relicta,
Longinquum penetrare fretum, penetrare sorores
160 *Mecum una Aonias, illic exordia gentis*
Prima novae ad seros transmittere posse nepotes!
Sed me fata vetant, memoraturumque canora
Inclyta facta tuba ad clades miserabilis Istri
Invitum retrahunt: his, his me fata reservent.
165 *Non deerit vates, illo qui cantet in orbe*
Aut veteres populos aut nostro incognita coelo
Munera naturae, dum spreto Helicone manebit
Illa Aganippaeis sacrata Oxonia Musis.

Drawn by Amphion's lute, once rose as walls
For Thebes, or, when Apollo played, for Troy.
And after families are brought to live
Together, laws will be decreed and he
185 Will see them kept. Then people, innocent
Of crime and falsity, will rather wear
The crown of lasting purity than sink
Their minds and bodies into sinful lust
And base indulgence: nor will they seek wealth,
190 Nor yet for glory ride the fickle whim
Of senseless masses. Freedom and the use
Of talents will not be repressed by wealth,
Nor will the poor divert their strength in feuds
Against the rich, based on the claim that all
195 Are citizens. Each man will take the part
That duly falls to him. Then Mother Earth
Will yield to all, from little effort, rich
Provisions from her ample store of goods:
No cares will then oppress the youth with age,
200 And labouring will not deprive a man
Of time to make a living through his own
Abilities.
              Oh, would that I were free
To go aboard that happy ship, leave home
   (Forgive the impious thought), and penetrate
205 Those far-off seas: and that the Muses too
Could come with me and there compose for all
Posterity a song about the rise
Of this new race! But Fate denies me that:
And when I start a trumpet-call of verse
210 About some glorious deed, she summons me
To sing reluctantly of sad defeats
In Danube lands: the Fates must keep me back
For tasks like that. There will be bards enough
Out there to celebrate their ancestors,
215 Or nature's blessings not revealed to us,
As long as there remains that shrine of Art, –
Oxford, which now the Muses sanctify
In place of Helicon.

Dum loquor in viridi festinant gramine Nymphae,
170 *Impediuntque comas lauro et florentis olivae*
Frondibus armantur, dominatricemque frequentes
Oceani immensi longe venerantur Elisam.
Illa autem ad gelidum celsis de turribus amnem
Prospicit, et iamiam Tamesino in patre tuetur
175 *Paulatim obliquis Gilebertum albescere velis.*
Sic dea Peliaco spectasse e vertice Pallas
Fertur Iasonios comites, ad Phasidos undas
Vix bene dum notis committere carbasa ventis.
Diva fave, nutuque tuo suscepta parari
180 *Vela iuva: si sola geris dignissima totum*
Talibus auspiciis proferri sceptra per orbem.
Propterea quia sola tuos ita pace beasti
Tranquilla populos, ut iam te principe possint
Augere imperii fines: quia sola videris
185 *Quo nivea Charites, quo corpore Delia virgo*
Pingitur, et (iusto si sit pro teste vetustas)
Talibus audimus quondam de matribus ortos
Semideos homines. Tali est de sanguine magnus
Sive Hector genitus, sive Hectore maior Achilles.
190 *Duntaxat sine fraude ulla, sine crimine, possint*
Ulla tibi veterum conferri nomina matrum,
Quae sexum factis superas, quae patribus audes,
Nympha, diis dignas laudes aequare Latinis.
Mentior infoelix, nisi sic in corpore virtus
195 *Lucet formoso ceu, quae preciosior auro est,*

But, while I speak,
                    The Nymphs
Frisk in the meadows, weaving crowns
220 Of laurel round their heads and brandishing
Their flowering olive branches, as they crowd
Around and pay remote respects to her
Who holds dominion over boundless seas, –
The Queen, Elizabeth: and she looks out
225 From lofty battlements, towards the cold
Waters of Father Thames where now she sees
The sails of Humphrey Gilbert's ship begin
To billow. Thus they say Athene watched
From Pelion's tip as Jason's crew put out
230 Into the river Phasis, little knowing how
The winds would blow. Help him, great Majesty,
And with your blessing speed his spreading sails:
Since you alone command authority
Worthy of being carried over all
235 The world with such auspicious signs as these.
For you alone bestowed a tranquil peace
Upon your people, so they might extend
Their empire's range, with you as head.
And you alone appear with that same form
240 In which pure Graces and the virgin nymph
Diana are depicted: if indeed
The testimony of antiquity
Bears faithful witness.
                    Demigods were born,
The legend goes, from mothers such as you.
245 From such a line the mighty Hector came,
And mightier still, Achilles: if indeed
One can without disparagement compare
The mothers of the past with you, fair Nymph,
When you in your achievements far outstrip
250 All others of your sex, and dare to vie
Against the godlike ancestors of Rome
In the degree of praise which you deserve.
There is a soul, I must make bold to say,
That shines within your elegance of form,

Gemma tamen pariter placituro clauditur auro.
Mentior et taceo, nisi sola audiris ubique
Induperatorum timor aut amor, inter et omnes
Securam requiem peragis tutissima casus:
200 Dum reliqui reges, duro quasi carcere clausi,
Sollicitis lethi dapibus plenoque fruuntur
Terrificis monstris furtiva per ocia somno.
Mentior et taceo, solam nisi vivere cives
Aeternum cupiunt: quando nec verbere torvo
205 Nec caedis poenaeve thronum formidine firmas.
Sed tibi tot meritis maiestas parta, et inermis
Ad patulos residet custos clementia postes:
Ut, quot pene rei iustum meruere tribunal,
Tot veniam grato narrent sermone clientes.
210 Nec tamen admittis nisi quod iustumque piumque
Agnoscit probitas, et, quae potes omnia, solis
Legibus usurpas cautas sanctissima vires.
Nec mala formidas: siquidem quasi fune ligatur
Consilio fortuna tibi. Nullum impia terret
215 In castris Bellona tuis: quin pronus adorat
Gradivus tua iussa pater, sequiturque vocantem
Quacunque ingrederis grato victoria plausu.
Dumque fores aliis vitamque et regna tuetur
Ianitor externus, cingunt tua limina cives;
220   Dumque aliis sordet sapientia regibus, almo
Pegasidum tu fonte satur tot Apollinis artes
Aurea vaticina fundis quasi flumina lingua.
Nil nostri invenere dies, nil prisca vetustas
Prodidit, in linguis peragunt commercia nullis
225 Christiadum gentes, quas te, divina virago,
Iustius Aoniae possint iactare sorores.

255 Just like a jewel that is set in gold
   By which, although itself more precious still,
   It is confined, a double joy to man.
   And you alone can strike with fear or love
   The hearts of emperors, and make your safe
260 Untroubled way through all adversities:
   While other rulers lead a life of hard
   Imprisonment, their feasts disturbed by fears
   Of death, and dream at furtive leisure-times
   Of ghastly monsters. You the people want
265 To "Live for ever."
                              Your authority
   Does not depend on lashes, rods and threats
   Of punishment: your royalty derives
   From much beneficence, and Mercy stands
   To guard your open gates, without a sword.
270 So that for all the miscreants who have
   Deserved to come to justice, almost that
   Same number can report the welcome word
   Forgiveness. Nor is anything let pass
   That your integrity cannot approve
275 As good and just; and though your competence
   Is boundless, yet you faultlessly adopt
   Only what power comes within the law.
   You fear no evil; you secure your fate
   By bonds of policy. No ravaging
280 War-god spreads terror through your palaces,
   But rather Mars himself takes your commands,
   And victory attends your very word
   With loud acclaim, whatever move you make.
   And while, for other rulers, foreign guards
285 Watch gateways, life and throne, here subjects crowd
   Your porches; wisdom other kings despise,
   But you have drunk the Muses' spring so deep
   That artistry can flow in golden streams
   From your poetic tongue. The Muses boast
290 Of nothing in our new discoveries,
   Nor in the heritage of ancient times
   Nor any culture known to Christian trade,

Audiit haec mundus, cunctisque in finibus ardet
Imperio parere tuo: et quae forte recusat
Miratur vires regio tamen. Hinc tua sceptra
230 *Incurva Mahometigenae cervice salutant:*
Hinc tua pugnaces properant ad foedera Galli,
Dumque sibi metuit toties tibi victus Iberus,
Nescia Romano Germania Marte domari
Quaerit amicitias Britonum: procul oscula mittit
235 *Virgineis pedibus Latium, longeque remoti*
Pannones in tutos optant coalescere fines.
 Magnanimi iuvenes, et qui Gilebertia cunque
Signa comes sequeris consors vitaeque necisque,
Quando quidem audimur votisque vocata virago
240 *Annuit, eia age, rumpe moras, quantumque per auras*
Accelerare datur, properantibus utere velis!
Nonne vides, quae submisso diademate nuper
Obtulit invictis fascesque fidemque Britannis,
Nonne vides passis ut crinibus horrida dudum
245 *Porrigit ingentem lugubris America dextram?*
 Et, "Numquid lacrymas", inquit, "soror Anglia nostras
Respicis et dura nobiscum in sorte gemiscis?
An vero nescisse potes quae tempora quantis
Cladibus egerimus, postquam insatiabilis auri
250 *(Nam certe non ullus amor virtutis) Iberos*
In nostrum migrare solum (pietasve) coegit?
Ex illo, quae sacra prius vaesana litabam
Manibus infernis, sperans meliora tuumque
Discere posse Deum, iubeor mortalibus aras
255 *Erigere; et, mutas statuas truncosque precata,*

More justly than of you, great godlike Queen.
　　The world has heard these things, and every part
295 Longs to accept your rule, and even those
　　That are reluctant wonder at your strength.
　　So that the unsubdued Mahommedans
　　Salute your kingdom, warlike France must make
　　A hurried treaty, much-defeated Spain
300 Is terrified for her security,
　　And Germany, which even Caesar's force
　　Could not keep down, makes friendly overtures
　　To Britain: Rome itself would now salute
　　Your feet with kisses, while the distant parts
305 Of Hungary decide to federate
　　For safety's sake within one boundary.
　　　　High-minded youths, and all who congregate
　　To Gilbert's flag as his companions
　　To live or die beside him, – since our voice
310 Is heard and our heroic queen now grants
　　Our prayer, – come then without delay, and set
　　Your speeding sails to make as fast a course
　　As winds allow! You surely see that sad
　　America, who proffered recently
315 (With downcast crown) her rights and loyalty
　　To independent England, now holds out
　　Her ample hand (unkempt, and with her hair
　　Long since dishevelled).
　　　　　　　　　"Please do not ignore
　　My tears, fair sister," she implores, "but feel
320 For me in my misfortune. Are you not aware
　　What times and what disasters I have seen
　　After the Spaniards' endless appetite
　　For gold had spurred them on to infiltrate
　　My lands? (For certainly they were not moved
325 By any moral zeal or holiness.)
　　In consequence, though hoping to progress
　　From those wild rites with which I formerly
　　Appeased the shades of ancestors, and learn
　　About the God you worship, now instead
330 They make me raise altars to mortal men

Nescio quod demens Romanum numen adoro.
Cur trahor in terras? Si mens est lucida, puris
Cur Deus in coelis recta non quaeritur: aut, si
A nobis coelum petitur, cur saepe videmus
260 Igne, fame, ferro subigi quocunque reatu
Oenotriae sedis maiestas laesa labascit?
Non sic relligio, non sic (me iudice) gaudet
Defendi sua regna Deus: quodsi optimus ille est,
Quodsi cuncta potest et nullis indiget armis.
265 Mitto queri caedes exhaustaque moenia bello:
Mitto queri in viles tot libera corpora servos
Abiecta, immanique iugum Busiride dignum.
   "Te tantum fortuna animet tua, te tua virtus:
Si tibi tam plenis habitantur moenibus urbes
270 Ut, nisi in excelsum crescant coeloque minentur
Aedes aeriae, quanquam latissima, desit
Terra tamen populo: si tot tua flumina nigrant
Turrigeras arces imitatae mole carinae,
Quot non illa natant eadem tua flumina cygni:
275 Si tibi iam sub sole iacens penetratus utroque est
Mundus, utroque iacens paragrata est terra sub axe.
   "Ni frustra gelidum vectus Wilobeius ad arcton
Illa in gente iacet cui, dum sol circinat umbras,
Dimidio totus vix forsitan occidit anno.
280 Ni frustra, sub perpetuis aquilonibus ausi
Burrhoidae fratres Scythicum sulcare profundum,
Invenere solum et vasto nova littora flexu:
Ultra quae quales populi, quae natio terras
Incolat, (in vero nisi si quid fabula possit)
285 Nondum scire dedit reliquo mundi arbiter orbi.

And pray to silent idols or to trees,
In madness honouring I know not what
Catholic deity.
    "Why drag me down
Towards the earth? Why may not God be sought
335 Directly, if one's intellect is clear,
In heaven's light; or why, if God's the goal
For which we make, is our attempt suppressed
Before our eyes by devastation, fire
And sword, whenever Rome's authority
340 Is challenged and begins to slip? Our God
Does not rejoice, I think, to see His faith
And kingdom thus upheld: for He is good,
All-powerful, and has no need of force.
I will not here lament the massacres,
345 The towns laid waste by war, the many souls
Reduced to abject slavery and fates
Like those once meted out by merciless
Busiris.
   "Let nobility of heart
And Destiny give you your energy.
350 You have such teeming cities that, unless
You build them upwards so that houses scrape
The sky, your land, however broad, will not
Support your people. Ships you build as big
As castles, crowding many waterways
355 More densely than the swans. You have traversed
The whole wide world that lies beneath the sun,
Both East and West.
      "For Willoughby did not
Sail north in vain, to lie among a race
For whom the sun, encompassing the gloom,
360 Somehow brings all its light in half the year.
Nor vainly did the Borough brothers face
Constant north winds in crossing Scythian seas
To find dry land and widely sweeping shores:
Nor can the world's adventurers yet tell
365 The rest of us what race lives in the lands
Beyond, what men they are (unless in fact

Ni frustra, per Cimmerios sylvisque propinqua
Flumina Riphaeis, eoa profectus ad usque est
Moenia Gincisonus, Persasque et proxima Persis
Bactra et Bactrorum confines regibus Indos.

290 Ni frustra quaesivit iter, duraque bipenni
Illo Forbiserus reditum sibi in aequore fecit,
Horridum ubi semper pelagus giacieque perenni
Frigora nativos simulant immitia montes.
Ni frustra, quod mortali tot secla negarant,

295 Hac tuus immensum nuper Dracus ambiit orbem
Qua patri Oceano clausas circumdare terras
Concessit natura viam, mediaque meare
Tellure et duplici secludere littore mundos.
Iam si fortuna iam si virtute sequare

300 Digna tua, sunt monstra mihi, sunt vasta gigantum
Corpora, quae magno cecidisse sub Hercule non sit
Dedecus, Ogygius non quae aspernetur Iacchus.
Quae si indigna putas tantaque in pace beata
Aversare meos multo ut tibi sanguine fines

305 Invidiosa petas, est nobis terra propinqua
Et tantum bimari capiens discrimen in isthmo.
Hanc tibi iam dudum primi invenere Britanni,
Tum cum magnanimus nostra in regione Gabotus
Proximus a magno ostendit sua vela Columbo.

310 Haec neque vicina nimium frigescit ab arcto,
Sole nec immodico in steriles torretur arenas:
Frigus et aestatem iusto moderamine servat,
Sive leves auras (grati spiracula coeli)
Seu diae telluris opes et munera curas.

315 Pone age te digno tua sceptra in honore, meoque
Iunge salutarem propius cum littore dextram.

Some legend can). And Jenkinson went far
Through Russia, down the Volga's forest course
To eastern cities, Persia, nearby Balhk
370 And Indian neighbours of the Bactrian king.
And not for nothing Frobisher sought out
The Passage, making his return with hard
Pick‑axes back through oceans where the sea
Is always bristling and the ruthless cold
375 Seems to grow mountains out of endless ice.
Nor can it be in vain that Francis Drake,
Your noble hero, recently sailed round
The vast circumference of Earth (a feat
Denied to man by many centuries),
380 To show how father Neptune circumscribes
The continents, and wanders in between
To keep two worlds apart.
                              "If you now look
For further enterprises fit for your
Peculiar gifts and destiny, you'll find
385 Dragons and giants here that Hercules
Would not have thought beneath his dignity
Or Bacchus would not scorn. But if, though blessed
With peace, you reckon them unworthy, turn
Away and plan to occupy our lands
390 By bloodshed, covetously for yourselves, –
Consider what a country lies close by,
Across the narrow neck of land that keeps
Us separate, with sea on either side.
Discovered first for you by Englishmen
395 Some time ago, when spirited Cabot
Approached these regions, following the wake
Of great Columbus: not so near the pole
That ice abounds, nor parched by too much sun,
But nicely poised between the harsh extremes
400 Of climate, whether heaven's gracious breath,
The gentle breeze, is what you hanker for,
Or wealth and produce from the fruitful soil.
Come then, forget your claim to rule, and grasp
My shore more closely with your saving hand

103

Sit mihi fas aliquam per te sperare quietem,
Vicinoque bono laetum illucescere solem:
Quodsi consiliis superum fatisque negatum est
320 *Durare immensum magna infortunia tempus,*
Quodsi de immerita iustum est cervice revelli
Ignarum imperii dominum populique regendi,
Quodsi nulla unquam potuit superesse potestas
Ni pia flexilibus pareret clementia frenis
325 *Obsequium. A miti quaesita potentia Cyro*
Amissa est saevae soboli. Parcendo subegit
Tot reges Macedum virtus: tot postera sensim
Abscidit a parto tandem inclementia regno.
Et quod Romuleis crevit sub patribus olim
330 *Imperium, diri semper minuere Nerones.*

405 In fitting graciousness.
                    "So let me hope
     That peace will come through you, that happy light
     Will start to shine from such a partnership.
     For so it must, if Fate's immortal plan
     Forbids great misery to last too long:
410 If justice lets one rescue subject folk
     From mastery by those who have no skill
     In government or organizing men:
     And if no might prevails for long unless
     Some tolerance and flexibility
415 Breeds willing subjects.
                    "Cyrus' throne was won
     In clemency, but inhumanity
     Lost it to his successor. Macedon
     Subdued a widespread kingdom leniently,
     But later harshness broke it bit by bit
420 Away from what had been acquired before.
     So, even when paternal Romulus
     Has laid foundations for an empire's rise,
     The men like Nero come and tear it down."

COMMENTARY

TITLE PAGE

2, 4: *equitis aurati*. For other examples of the use of this style, see notes to ll. 277, 295.

5, 1: ἐπιβατικόν. For comment on P.'s use of Greek, see p. 25 above, *Paean* (the first note to "Ad illustrem ... Henricum Untonum"), and *NL*, note to l. 4. This adjective derives immediately from the noun meaning a person (apart from the sailors) who goes on board ship – especially one of the troops which a ship is transporting. The Church translator thus calls it a "marine" poem, but A.H. offers no rendering (see above, pp. 71–2). In his capacity as patron of embark-ations, Apollo was known by a similar title *Epibasios*; it was to him under this designation, according to Apollonius Rhodius, that the Argonauts made sacrifice when they set out (*Argonautica* i, 317 ff.; see note to *Ad Thamesin*, l. 5 below).

There was a genre of classical "send-off" poem called the *Propemptikon*, which Statius occasionally used. An example is *Silvae* iii, 2, addressed to one Maecius Celer who is going on a voyage. The usual sea-spirits etc. are extensively invoked to give him a calm passage, but the only verbal similarity with P. is remarked below, note to l. 239. On the revival of this form during the Renaissance, in the general context of Latin travel-poetry, see P. Van Tieghem, *La littérature latine de la Renaissance* (Paris 1944), pp. 93–95.

8, 7: *Thomam Purfutium*. Thomas Purfoote was a general printer and is not known to have been aligned with the Puritan elements in the church.

AUTORIS PRAEFATIO / AUTHOR'S PREFACE

1, 2: *mei et*. The 1582 text has a comma between these two words and one after *copia* (l. 2), but it has none after *tu* (l. 3) where one is clearly required. We have omitted the former two, on the grounds that they (like many other commas in that text) do more to impede the flow of the Latin than to clarify its sense, and have supplied the last (as also does *H.1600*) for the sake of consistency. In general, only those emendations of punctuation which are of more substance than this will be acknowledged.

4, 6: *voluisti*. P. implies that he wrote the poem first and then showed it to Gilbert, who desired that it should be published with an explicit disclaimer that it was not commissioned promotion material.

5, 7: *Turcica*. Born in the pashalik of Buda after 1541, and in the city of Buda.

5, 8: Christianis. It may well be that he is saying here that his parents were Protestant, not merely non-Muslim; see above, p. 5.

6, 9: educatus. It is not clear what educational facilities were available in Buda at the time, nor is it possible to suggest who P.'s "erudite teachers" may have been. We have commented above (pp. 5–6.) on whom he may have in mind when he speaks of his homeland's reputation for producing classical scholars (*quibus … florescunt*).

7, 11: Pannoniae. Though Roman *Pannonia* had a much wider extent than post-medieval Hungary, the name was frequently used at this time for Hungary alone.

7, 11: imprimis … reliquiae. There is some obscurity of expression here. We follow the Church translator in taking *salvae* to mean safe from oppression; and the idea that Hungary's learned men are especially (*imprimis*) conspicuous (*florescunt*) at a time of national ignominy or jeopardy is not incomprehensible. The awkwardness arises, at least partly, from P.'s making two contrasts at once: (i) that between past and present (*tum … tum …*), and (ii) that between *Pannonia* in general, on the one hand, and her *salvae … adhuc reliquiae*, on the other. (We are indebted to Mr T.C.W. Stinton for this analysis of the congestion.)

8, 9: adolevissem. The first inkling of P.'s post-classical penchant for the subjunctive (see note to l. 19 of the Preface). After *postquam* the indicative is much more usual, though the subjunctive does occur, rarely, in Cicero.

9, 12: Academias. The custom of sending young men on an educational tour of the universities was reinforced in the case of Hungarians by the desire to divorce the educated classes from Turkish influence. For discussion of the educational centres he is most likely to have visited, see above, pp. 6–7.

9, 12: ablegatus fui. Classically, the "present"-perfect tense *ablegatus sum* is to be expected.

10, 15: respublicas. As a Calvinist, he would probably have studied with a particular interest the commonwealths of Geneva and Zürich and, if interested in government as such, Venice; Merbury also commended Genoa and Lucca as worthy of attention. See above, pp. 6–7, 17–19.

10, 15: multarum. Since P. presumably does not intend *administrationes* to be taken as in apposition to *respublicas* and *hospitia*, his omission of a conjunction at the start of this new phrase produces an arguably gratuitous asyndeton.

11, 16: triennio. This and the Heidelberg reference are our only chronological clues to P.'s peregrination. Departure from Hungary for Heidelberg in 1579 would have brought him near the end of three years at the time of writing. (see above, p. 6)

12, 17: profectio. It would be easy to conclude that P. was sent on his travels to fit himself for the ministry if his own statement here did not suggest that his interests were primarily secular. And in lines 157–64 he speaks as if his mission is to write poetry (rather than to preach).

15, 20: ut hoc … possit. We take it that the sentiment here is: "Having said this [*hoc*], about sampling the different communities and people of Europe, let me say at once, – in order to forestall envious speculation [*invidia*] about which of them I preferred […], – that my preference is for Britain." But even so it is not immediately obvious how to render the contents of the brackets. We opine that P.'s point is that as much bad feeling would be engendered (in Britain) by *failing* to specify that country as would be aroused (among rejected rivals in Europe) by *doing* so.

In this way the subject of the bracketed clause stays the same as in its predecessor (i.e. *hoc*, – "this whole question", "this matter"), and the two passives *dici possit, taceri potest* are directly parallel. A.H. invests the aside with a certain psycho-dynamic *profondeur*, construing "for it [*sc.*, presumably, 'envy' – Ed.] cannot be suppressed without malice"; this reading involves making *invidia* (understood) the subject of *potest*.

17, *22*: *Britannia*. The attraction of England for P. was partly its unity in society, politics, and religion as it would appear to a foreigner. He was evidently attracted to the Church of England, all his contacts in which, apart from Hakluyt and Gilbert, seem to have been on the (mainly moderate) Puritan wing (see above, p. 9). It is also legitimate to assume that he was fascinated by the geographical and cosmographical studies to which Hakluyt had introduced him, and which were interesting a growing group of young men in England at the time.

19, *24*: *acceptus essem*. Another example of P.'s predilection for the subjunctive. Classi-cal writers regularly followed *accedit quod* with the indicative. Nor is it clear why P. should use the pluperfect tense: the perfect is to be expected here, with convenient echoes, in this context, of the Greek "perfect-with-effects-remaining".

22, *28*: *ob caussas*. Both the 1582 version and H.1600 read *ab*, not *ob*. This must be a misprint, since *ab* never takes the accusative, whereas, for example, *quam ob rem, quam ob causam* are common set phrases in classical Latin. It is easy to imagine the *o* being falsely assimilated to the long *a*'s on either side of it in *quas* and *caussas*. The spelling of the latter word is a classical variant of the much more frequent form *causa*. Certainly in printing *NL* Hakluyt uses the more common form. A.H. emends both the text and the spelling, reading *Quas ob causas*.

We cannot tell, of course, to what extent such departures from the most common classical spelling reflect P.'s own preferences as opposed to those of his printers. But there is an instance where one of the few words we have in P.'s own hand also occurs, differently spelled, in one of the printed texts (see *NL*, note to l. 45).

24, *31*: *excellentibus viris*. For a discussion of his known and conjectural contacts, see above, pp. 9–22. The surviving correspondence of the time appears to contain no more than one or two references to him.

25, *32*: *Hacletius*. H.1600 substitutes the more anglicized spelling *Hakluytus*. This intro-duction by Richard Hakluyt could have taken place at the end of 1581 or very early in 1582. For the similar treatment of other proper names, see notes to ll. 277, 288, 291, 308.

26, *33*: *in novum orbem*. Hakluyt, who had been lecturing on Ptolemy at Oxford (1577–9), would have been a vigorous dispenser of geographical knowledge to his protégé while compiling the *Divers voyages*. Much of the knowledge of English exploration which P. shows in the poem (ll. 39–40, 277–98, 307–9) would have been picked up orally from Hakluyt, the rest from books and manuscripts. The elder Richard Hakluyt also had, by this time, a considerable geographical collec-tion, to which P. may have had access.

26, *34*: *Quae dum aguntur*. If *quae* refers back specifically to Hakluyt's exposition of Gilbert's project, rather than to P.'s London visitings and/or to Gilbert's actual agitations and preparations, then P. may be indicating that he decided to write the poem after he had been told about the project and done some research on

Gilbert's career, but before he had met him in person. In that case the point would be that P. had only to *hear* about the man in order to be fired with admiration and curiosity. The translation deliberately leaves the question open.

27, 35: *corpus.* Although the word can be used more figuratively, this may be a concrete allusion to Gilbert's physical appearance. John Hooker wrote that he was "a man of higher stature than of the common sort, and of complexion cholerike" (R. Holinshed, *Chronicles,* II (1587), 132; Quinn, *Gilbert,* II, 431).

27, 36: *et agnovi ... eaque.* In order to indicate that this *et* is regarded as starting a new clause, we have strengthened the 1582 text's comma after *dignum* to a semicolon. Taken with the *-que* of *eaque* it forms a variant, rare in Cicero but frequent in later prose-writers, of the much more common *et ... et* construction. Thus, rather than linking *agnovi* retrospectively with *agnoscere potui*, in which there would be little point quite apart from the clumsiness produced, *et* contrasts it prospectively with *prosequi caepi.* The point then is that P. did not just stand in passive amazement, but went and did something constructive.

The by-no-means literal Church translation incorporates something of this idea: "... I was able to conclude that you were worthy of everlasting glory: and so well did I recognize this, and with such zeal did I attend to its fulfilment, that. ..." But A.H. makes nothing at all of *et agnovi profecto,* rendering "... worthy of the perpetual remembrance of posterity, and hence [*sc.* 'I' – Ed.] began to attend to them with such respect that ...". He retains an acute accent on the *a* of *eaque,* as he does on the *e* of *longe,* as if he took it to be the long *a* of another ablative in agreement with *observantia;* but his translation clearly treats *eaque* as neuter plural.

28, 36: *caepi.* This is a non-classical variant for *coepi.* Purfoote's conflated diphthong for *ae* looks in itself not unlike *oe;* but he had in fact a clearly different sign for the latter combination, which he had used in *foetum* above (*4*). *H.1600* emends to *coepi;* but A.H., who follows Hakluyt's text, reverts to the unorthodox form here in spite of his two silent "corrections" to *ab caussas* above (see note to l. 22).

We have emended the punctuation here. The 1582 text has a semicolon after *caepi* and then nothing till a comma after *virtutibus* (*29*).

28, 37: *paullo.* In *H.1600* this rather archaic spelling is emended to the more classical *paulo.*

30, 39: *perfungerer.* The discharge of obligations by the writing of a complimentary poem is peculiarly the notion of a humanist scholar. Thus the list of such dedications made to Leicester, whose patronage of the arts was extensive, runs to 94 items; see E. Rosenberg, *Leicester,* pp. 355–62.

32, 42: *eas et redeas.* The use of the second person implies that P. was not, at this stage, associating himself in practical terms with the projected expedition; cp. ll. 157–64 below, esp. 162. We do not know definitely what made him change his mind. Gilbert expected to leave soon after early June 1582 and, indeed, three vessels were to be equipped to sail from Southampton by 25 July, but hitches occurred and the whole project was deferred until 1583. P. cannot have known of this before his poem appeared (see above, pp. 42–3).

34, 45: *Vale. H.1600* reads *Vale pridie Kalen. Aprilis 1583;* i.e. 31 March 1583. Clearly from this and from the text he prints, Hakluyt is not using the 1582 edition of the poem. What he printed was either a second edition called for and issued in 1583 (shortly after 31 March) in view of the year's delay in Gilbert's voyage, or a revised version in manuscript, completed in March 1583, copies of which P. presented to Gilbert and Hakluyt. No copy of a second published edition is known to have survived.

AD THAMESIN / TO THE THAMES

Thamesin. When the poem was completed (in March or April of 1582) it was planned that the expedition should leave from the Thames, but, shortly afterwards, Gilbert made Southampton his base.

2, 4: *Antipodum ... locum.* The Thames already had its connection with the Antipodes, for Sir Francis Drake's *Golden Hind* was preserved at Deptford. The reference three lines below thus compares Gilbert as much to a second Drake as to a second Jason. See T. Watson, *Amintae gaudia* v, 97; quoted in n. to *DNC*, l. 277.

5, 10: *Argo.* The ship sailed by Jason on his legendary voyage to recover the "golden fleece" from Colchis. P. returns to the theme of the Argonauts below (176–78), but the poem makes it clear that Gilbert's expedition is seen as destined to recover not a mere golden fleece but a whole Golden Age. There is an accessible and readable synopsis of the many legends surrounding the Argonauts' voyage in R. Graves, *The Greek myths* (London, 2nd ed. 1960), II, 215–53.

DE NAVIGATIONE / AN EMBARKATION POEM

4, 5: *Titan.* The sun-god, son of Hyperion and grandson of that Titan whose descendants, the "Titans", disputed the command of heaven with Saturn and were thrown into the underworld (cp. *Paean*, 92). P.'s contemporary, Edmund Spenser, was one of those who adopted this periphrasis in English verse, for example at the beginning of his *Prothalamium* (1596). Indeed, the whole scene-setting in the first few lines of that poem, which is also addressed to the Thames, is not unlike P.'s introduction: "Calme was the day, and through the trembling ayre, / Sweete breathing *Zephyrus* did softly play / A gentle spirit, that lightly did delay / Hot *Titan's* beames, ..." The start of Spenser's second stanza, in addition, could be said to resemble P.'s lines 169–73; but these similarities are attributable, no doubt, to the conventions of a common pastoral Muse rather than to any individual contact between the two poets.

8, 10: *ignotum.* There seems to be no study (or at least no accessible one) of the reception and influence of the discovery of the Americas in Hungary.

10, 13: *heroas ... facta.* Embarking as he is on the theme of the possible return of the Golden Age, P. cannot avoid producing echoes of Virgil's so-called "messianic" fourth *Eclogue* which treats the same idea. Virgil had used almost identical words there when envisaging an account of heroic deeds being passed from generation to generation (ll. 26–27): *At simul heroum laudes et facta parentis / iam legere ... poteris.*

11, 14: *animis.* The 1582 text has a question-mark after *animis* but no capital "*s*" for *si* which follows. Since the if-clause forms a vital part of P.'s rhetorical question, we have postponed the question-mark until l. 13 at the point where the original had a colon.

14, 17: *Fortuna.* There are conflicting traditions from antiquity about whether this god-dess was daughter or mother of Jupiter.

16, 20: *Nereus.* The benevolent Grand Old Man of the sea in Greek mythology. His daughters, the Nereids, were beautiful sea-nymphs of whom Thetis and Galatea were the most famous. Like Proteus (see note to l. 22), Nereus could change him-self into various shapes.

20, 26: *minatur.* (*a*) If this is taken with *quasi*, then (i) the expected form would be the imperfect subjunctive not the present, and (ii) there would be no main verb.
(*b*) If it is taken as the main verb itself, then (i) the *quasi* phrase is left rather hang-ing in the air (perhaps with *pararet* supplied from *pararent* in line 18), and (ii) we must suppose the expression *minari in aliquem* to mean "to threaten somebody" – which is unclassical. P. seems to have lost the thread of, or over-condensed, his construction (cp. notes to ll. 7 (Preface), 34, 195, 249 and p. 26 above).

21, 25: *physeter.* (*a*) This word can mean many sorts of "blower", and in this context one might suppose that it signifies a wind-god, such as appear at the corners of maps and maritime drawings of the period, complete with puffed cheeks (*follibus inflatis*) or even actual bellows, and blasts of air. But better sense ensues from taking it to mean a spouting whale (so used by the elder Pliny). This gives point to *inimica*, because the whale might well be thought to resent ships that intruded on its preserves, and to regard them as hostile. It also gives more force to *quasi*, because the whale would not produce an actual gale or rainstorm but only some similar effect. Further, it preserves the unity of the fantasy by keeping it in the animal kingdom along with *delphines*, *armenta* and *phocae*.
(*b*) The first vowel of *physeter* was treated as long in classical times, in which case P.'s line does not scan. The word is a transliteration from the Greek, in which form the *upsilon* is unequivocally long.

22, 28: *Aegaeon.* A sea-god whose parents were, according to the story in Ovid (*Meta-morphoses* ii, 9), Pontus and Terra (Sea and Land).

22, 29: *Proteus.* Described by Homer (*Odyssey* iv, 542) as an "old man of the sea", he was said to herd the seals and to know all things, but to have the power of changing into different shapes to avoid questioning. However, according to the *Odyssey*, Menelaus consulted him at Pharos, off the Egyptian coast, and forced him to disclose what was happening to Odysseus on his return from Troy. Virgil describes a different consultation, in an extensive passage (*Georgics* iv, 387–527) which was obviously known to P.; cp. next two notes.

Renaissance latinists tended to treat Proteus as a kind of all-purpose sooth-sayer, putting the most unlikely presentiments into his mouth. Thus Sannazzaro, in his hexameter poem *De partu virginis* (1526) makes the river-god Jordan recount a prophecy by Proteus of the "Feeding of the five thousand". See J. Sparrow "Latin verse of the high Renaissance", in E.F. Jacob, *Italian Renaissance studies*, p. 385, and note to l. 24 below.

In the general context of combining contemporary Elizabethan events with classical mythology, we may note that Scipio Gentili, another protestant refugee from the continent (see above, p. 15), produced, in 1585, a poem in which Nereus foretells the future of Philip Sidney's new-born daughter; see J. Buxton, *Sir Philip Sidney* (1964), p. 158.

23, 29: *armenta ... phocas.* Neptune's mythical, sub-oceanic "herd" was described by
Virgil in an almost identical line (*Georgics* iv, 394–5): *Neptuno ..., immania
cuius | armenta et turpes pascit sub gurgite phocas.*

24, 31: *idem.* This seems at first sight to indicate that the subject of the new sentence is
still *Proteus*; but it appears, in fact, to have prospective force, with reference to the
ensuing *modo ... modo* construction, rather than retrospective. A.H. takes it thus.
Virgil, it is true, specifically credits Proteus, in the passage that P. clearly has at the
back of his mind here, with knowledge of the present, past and future (*Georgics* iv,
392–93): *novit namque omnia vates, | quae sint, quae fuerint, quae mox ventura trahantur.*
To judge from the following line, however, P. is evidently alluding, perhaps by
means of another slightly awkward conflation, to his better-known contemporary
George Buchanan (see above, p. 32), whose "History of Scotland" had been in the
press in 1581 and was published in 1582 (*Rerum Scoticarum historia*; Edinburgh,
Alexander Arbuthnot). Vautrollier had by this time established himself as a bookseller in Edinburgh, in addition to his having a London printing business, and
would be one source of information about the progress of Buchanan's history; but
P.'s main informants were Camden and Thomas Savile, who both despised
Buchanan's historical work (see next note). This work accounts for the reference
to past events in the former *modo* clause; but it is not so clear where Buchanan
disclosed the future, as claimed by the latter.

However, in so far as Buchanan turned his hand to tragic drama, occasional
poems and political disquisition in addition to history-writing and psalm-transla-
tion, his talents were certainly "protean" in a general sense. More specifically, there
was current in Renaissance philosophy the view that the very essence of human
nature lies in man's self-determined versatility and capacity to choose different
roles, as a result of which he has it in him to become more godlike. It had been
provocatively pioneered by Pico, in the first part of that *Oratio* of 1486 which
came to be known as *De hominis dignitate.* He had remarked in section 4 that man's
chameleon-like qualities were rightly symbolized by Proteus. For the place of such
neo-classical philosophy in the background to P.'s work, see p. 34 above.

25, 32: *sceptra Chaledonidum.* Buchanan himself had used the expression *Caledoniae (orae)
sceptra* to mean the throne or kingdom of Scotland in dedicating his Latin
version of the Psalms to Mary, Queen of Scots (see above, p. 31). The relevant
couplet is: *Nympha, Caledoniae quae nunc feliciter orae | missa per innumeros sceptra tueris
avos, | ... .*

P.'s phrase may allude specifically to the myth about a succession of forty "kings
of Scotland", supposedly traceable from the fourth century B.C. Hector Boece had
popularized this story, which gave the impression of a long line of Scottish civilization, comparable with that of Greece and Rome; and indeed a parallel may
perhaps be seen in the historically dubious "Alban Kings" of Roman tradition,
who conveniently filled the chronological gap between the sack of Troy and the
founding of Rome (cp. note to l. 329). Buchanan had somewhat uncritically
adopted Boece's formula into his own work, using it for propaganda purposes.
But the Scottish myth was exploded, to Buchanan's unconcealed indignation, by
the Welsh historian Humphrey Llwyd in his *Commentarioli ... fragmentum*
(Cologne 1572) which Ortelius published four years after Llwyd's death. It seems

that manuscript versions of much of Buchanan's history were circulating in England as early as 1573, but that publication was delayed by the need to take account
of the Welshman's uncomfortable arguments. The whole question has been
clarified recently by Professor H.R. TrevorRoper in "George Buchanan and the
ancient Scottish constitution", *English historical review*, Supplement iii (1966), esp.
pp. 24–39.

P.'s antiquarian friends, Camden and Thomas Savile, were both familiar with
the work of Boece and Llwyd; so it was no doubt from them that he got the
story. They were no admirers of Buchanan as an historian. In a draft of a letter to
Savile, Camden derides Buchanan's "refutable legends" (*fabulae refellendae*) and the
"effusions of the intemperate and washedout bard" (*quae poeta male sobrius et dilutius effundet*). Savile in turn rejoices in one letter that Camden has been able somewhere to "draw the teeth of the doddering old don" (*senescentem rhetorem exarmare*).
Brit. Mus., Additional MSS, 36294 f.6ᵛ and Camden, *Epistolae* (ed. T. Smith),
p. 11. In the light of this, it would seem that this passage about Proteus/Buchanan
(ll. 22–26) makes something of an academic joke of the idea of consigning the
eminent Scottish scholarpoet to the bottom of the sea along with the "slimy seals"
(23).

27, 36: *Ut ... extulit.* We take this construction to refer back to the (by now forgotten)
ecquando licebit ...? of line 9, understanding some verb of "saying" from *ordiri* (10).
This would account for the tense of *extulit* and the question mark after *orbe* (30;
see note to l. 30); for these two points conflict with the expectation that the new
paragraph continues what Proteus (Buchanan) is said to be "prophesying".
Further, England's alleged worlddominance (*toto ... orbe*) and her imperial
expansion (*nova moenia ... quaerat*, 32–33) clearly invite comparison (*audent | conferri
et certare*, 12–13) with the example of ancient Rome, and thereby take up the theme
of the *ecquando ...?* construction (9–31). Later in the poem, Gilbert is specifically
said to rival Hercules (44–51); and the Queen, the forbears of Hector and
Achilles (183–93).

We follow *H.1600*, as against the 1582 text, in setting in for a new paragraph;
cp. note to l. 30 below.

27, 38: *notissima ... | Insula.* By using these two words at these particular positions in the
line, P. raises an echo of Virgil's description of the island of *Tenedos*, in the
Aegean, off the coast of Troy (*Aeneid* ii, 27): *Est in conspectu Tenedos, notissima
fama | insula, ...* There is no substance, however, to the comparison of islands, for
the questionable fame of Tenedos was certainly no match for what P. attributes to
Britain.

28, 38: *Oceano.* If P. is visualizing here and in the preceding lines a map of the British
Isles on the seas round which classical seafigures are depicted (see note to l. 21),
it is not to be found in Gerard Mercator's world map (1569) or Abraham Ortelius (*Theatrum*, 1570 etc.) which are the more obvious sources; so it may be
entirely a product of his imagination. But if we are right about the approach by
way of a map, we can think of P. looking down on a map of Great Britain and
seeing first Scotland (the map in Ortelius is horizontal, with Scotland shown as
large as England, and so possibly in his mind), remembering something of what
he had read or heard of its history (see note to l. 25). Then he goes on to the

destiny, not so much of Great Britain, as of England and to the inklings about the future which the sight of the country on the map brings to mind.

It is tempting to think that he may be looking forward to unity between the two kingdoms; but in 1582 Mary Queen of Scots was still a prisoner in England, James VI had not emerged as an independent factor in politics, and Queen Elizabeth was much too touchy to allow even an oblique reference to the succession to remain in print. P. clearly wished his poem to be seen by the Queen (see ll. 169–226, 239–40), and Hakluyt would not have allowed him to make an allusion which he knew would give offence. The reference to *fata ... eventura* ("the destiny of years to come", ll. 25, 26) probably does not, therefore, have this political significance.

29, 40: *numerosa*. Demographic studies of sixteenth-century population in England have not yet replaced intelligent guesses. Professor Joel Hurstfield's is: "Since the middle of the fifteenth century the fall in population, which had been going on for a century, had been arrested and soon numbers were rising. Even so, it is doubtful whether on the eve of Elizabeth's accession there were more than three or four million Englishmen, or more than five at the end of the reign." (*The Elizabethan nation*, 1964, p. 13.) What is clear is that Richard Hakluyt thought that the number of Englishmen was increasing and that under-employment was growing (Taylor, *Hakluyts*, II, 233–39, 319).

30, 41: *orbe?* *H.1600* reads a semicolon where the 1582 text had a question mark. The latter is bound to seem wrong unless the sentence is linked back to the *ecquando ...?* construction (9–13) as we suggest; see note to l. 27. When editing the text, Hakluyt presumably did not make this connection (and hence did not start a new paragraph at line 27).

34, 45: *Non aliter*. P. has a trick of disappointing the reader's expectation of a Homeric simile. For here (as in lines 194–6, where the Queen's soul is likened to a jewel set in precious metal) one anticipates the antithetical construction "just as when *p*, then *q*; even so when *x*, then *y*": but one is presented with the content of the first half in the form of the second – "even so does a flock of cranes set out" (cp. notes to ll. 7 (Preface), 20.). Variants of this ornithological image were fairly common among classical writers: cp. Euripides, *Helen* 1478–82 and Homer, *Iliad* iii, 1–6. Perhaps P. was familiar also with Aristotle's passage about cranes in *Historia animalium* (viii, 75–76); cp. also *Turner on birds*, ed. A.H. Evans (1903), pp. 94–95.

A later poet, Pope, was to turn this simile on its head, writing: "Who bade the stork, Columbus-like, explore / Heavens not his own, and worlds unknown before?" (*Essay on Man* III, 105.)

36, 47: *colonia*. Varro uses this word for a "swarm" (of bees: *De re rustica* iii, 16), but there seems to be no surviving classical precedent for applying it to a flock of birds, as P. does.

Inflated as it sounds in translation, the simile merely restates Hakluyt's view that England was overpopulated and that she needed a territory commensurate with her stature as a nation. Eulogy of the Roman empire, recollection of Continental territories now lost, commercial and industrial developments (especially the demand for new markets), the pressure of a restless and greedy class of gentry, all enter into the dream (or chimera) of imperial greatness. We should remember that as P. was composing this poem, Hakluyt was writing in his epistle to the *Divers voyages* (Sig. Iʳ⁻ᵛ): "I conceive great hope, that the time approcheth and nowe is, that we of England may share and part stakes (if wee will our selves) both with the Spaniarde and the Porttingale in part of America, and other regions as yet undiscovered ... Wee reade that the Bees, when they grow to be too many in their own hives at home, are wont to bee led out by their Captaines to swarme abroad and seeke themselves a new dwelling place . . . Let us learne wisdome of these smal weake and unreasonable creatures." He developed these sentiments greatly in his "A particuler discourse" for Queen Elizabeth in 1584.

38, 49: *servata*. The claim that God had "reserved" North America for colonization and development by Britain is argued in some detail by Edward Hayes (see above, pp. 21–2). He cites as evidence the failure of Spanish and French attempts to establish settlements in that continent.

40, 53: *quarto ... / ... quinta*. The reception in England of the concept of the fourth part of the earth (the Americas) is told by F. T. McCann, *English discovery of America to 1585* (New York 1952), pp. 24–55. The notion of the fifth part, North America, in isolation, is a fancy not related to current geographical notions. Below (ll. 245, 303–6) P. treats the Americas, poetically, as a unit.

42, 55: *relinque*. The exhortation to exclude Europe, Asia and Africa from the English orbit, in favour of America alone, shows P. yielding very far to rhetoric.

45, 58: *Alcides*. Hercules is so called for he was step-grandson of Alcaeus. Gilbert is urged to leave behind the area of Hercules' legendary activity and, in effect, to supersede him by adding conquests in the Atlantic regions beyond the "Pillars of Hercules" (i.e. the straits of Gibraltar) to his previous achievements on European soil. P. refers to the latter below (112–21). A.H. apparently takes *Alcides* to mean the "Pillars" themselves and renders, "Alcides / Their deeds and bounds may fix ..." But there seems to be no classical precedent for this use of the name.

Another foreign visitor who was to give verbal encouragement to imperial expansion was Giordano Bruno (see above, p. 25, n. 9), who arrived in England a few months before P. left it and who was lecturing in Oxford later the same year. In his *La cena de le ceneri* (1584), he wrote of Queen Elizabeth: "If her earthly territory were a true reflection of the width and grandeur of her spirit, this great Amphitrite would bring far horizons within her girdle and enlarge the circumference of her dominion to include not only Britain and Ireland but some new world, as vast as the universal frame, where her all-powerful hand should have full scope to raise a united monarchy." (Translated in Frances A. Yates, "Queen Elizabeth as Astraea", Warburg and Courtauld Institutes, *Journal*, x, 1947, 80.)

49, 67: *mugiit*. The onomatopoeic verb *mugire* usually means "to low" or "to bellow", and thus reflects some disrespect for the Muslems on the part of P. Perhaps he has in mind specifically the sound made by the muezzin in the call to prayer, and the herdlike response of the faithful.

50, 66: *Non vafer Hispanus*. P. is again assuming that Gilbert's America (North America) and that occupied by the Spaniards were physically separated.

50, 66: *superisque*. We conjecture that P., in his use of *superi*, which classically means, for the most part, just "the gods" or "divine powers", is drawing on a rather non-specific conflation of neo-Platonic and Protestant theology to refer to the early Fathers of the Church, apostles, saints etc.; but we have not traced any exact precedent for this usage. There are even some indications that interest in such eclecticism was particularly acute in that part of Europe where P. had been brought up; see *New Cambridge modern history*, II (1958), 206. For the sixteenth-century Christian, those who are "up above" presumably include members of the "Church Triumphant" – those who have "gone before in the faith" (with this latter metaphor cp. the classical use of the comparative form *superior* to mean "previous", as in *NL*, 2).

Much neo-classical philosophizing of the Renaissance exploited the idea of "grades" or "levels" of existence corresponding to the quality of the soul. Ficino and the renewed interest in Plotinus have been mentioned above (p. 34); and Pico, for instance, thought that man had considerable self-determination and scope for moving towards the "higher forms", as against Ficino who emphasized man's central status. Thus in sections 6 and 7 of *De hominis dignitate* Pico argues man's capacity to become a "heavenly being" or "an angel", an important means to this end being purification (sections 9–12). This idea would obviously be attractive to those Puritans who did not hold too strictly the Calvinist doctrines of "election" and "predestination"; and the theme of spiritual purity recurs below (l. 91), as does that of upward striving (257–61). For discussion of Pico's teaching, see E. Cassirer *et al.*, *Renaissance philosophy of man* (Chicago 1948), pp. 215–54.

The medieval Church had taken for granted, of course, some hierarchical stratification of the spirit world. The accepted scheme seems to have corresponded fairly closely to the angelology of pseudo-Dionysius, but P. will have had little sympathy with such traditions; cp. notes to ll. 258, 259. See E.M.W. Tillyard, *The Elizabethan world picture* (London 1943), esp. chh. 4 and 5; and C.S. Lewis, *The discarded image* (Cambridge, Eng., 1964), ch. 4.

It might seem that *superi* could mean here, and later in l. 319, simply the Christian God in the singular (the plural form perhaps connoting the Persons of the Trinity), and the Church translator accordingly has "... forsaking Heaven and God ..."; but it cannot be so rendered when it recurs in ll. 80 and 91 (see notes to ll. 80, 91). A.H., however, treats the two words *coelum* and *superi* as a hendiadys for the single idea of "God", translating: "Nor subtil Spaniard, first his God renouncing, / Offered the Holy Father human blood. / " A.H.'s characteristic compression can be noted in the second line also.

To take *superi* here as we have done avoids this redundancy by specifying both God and his erstwhile representatives on earth, and also gives additional point to *relictis*: for contemporary Protestant reformers insisted that the Roman Church had deserted, abandoned, "left behind" the original apostolic teaching and tradition. P. goes on to say (90–2), however (if we have interpreted him correctly), that England's preservation of these doctrines and observances is one indication that she enjoys a Golden Age.

51, 67: *Papae*. We take this as dative rather than genitive. In the latter case it would mean that the Spaniard had made Roman Catholic ceremonies (*sacra Papae*) cruel by imposing them with bloodshed. It appears, however, that P. had no sympathy for them in the first place, and regarded them as essentially pagan and idolatrous.

Cp. the complaint which he puts into America's mouth (254–6) that she is instructed, by the Spaniards, to set up "altars to mortal men, and pray to silent idols or to trees" (*mortalibus aras / erigere; ...*). For an exactly parallel construction meaning to perform rites to a deity, see Propertius, *Carmina* iv, 9, 43.

51, 68: *crudelia ... fecit.* We can see here the influence of Bartolomé de las Casas, *Brevíssima relación de la destrucción de las Indias* (Seville 1552), translated into Dutch (*Seer cort verhael destructie van d'Indien*, Brussels or Antwerp 1578) and French (*Tyrannies et cruatez des Espagnols* (Antwerp 1579; repr. Rouen 1580 and Paris 1582) as anti-Spanish propaganda. An English translation was being made by a certain M. S. (not otherwise identified) and was to appear as *The Spanish colonie* (William Broome, 1583: S.T.C. 4739). P. could have seen a manuscript copy of the latter or have read a foreign version from Hakluyt's library (no doubt too he heard of the tract verbally from Hakluyt).

54, 72: *Faunorum.* In Roman tradition the *Fauni* were spirits of the countryside, and the idea of a single deity Faunus, identified with the Greek Pan, developed from them.

55, 71: *geniti.* How far was P. aware of the problem of the origins of the American Indians? In current doctrine, they must have been descended from survivors of Noah's flood, in which case a story for their loss and rediscovery had to be worked out. Here P. seems to be merely exercising his poetical fancy. Yet classical fancies and Christian diffusionist theories were, potentially, in conflict. Thus William Bourne, in *A booke called The treasure for traveilers* (1578), discusses the problem from the orthodox Christian standpoint, which did not differ greatly between Protestant and Catholic. Bourne (sig. 5E2ʳ) says: "I have harde some vayne and foolish arguments thereof, why there shoulde be people there, never knowen before, except there were any more Adams then one, or any more Noyes [Noahs], then one. So we may see by experience, how apt a number of people are to fal into errours, using most vayne and contentious arguments in those matters that are past their capacities, which is a great offence before God, and also to the evill Ensample unto the world. ... For it is no small errour for us to fal into, for to think that there was ani more Adams in the world then one, for that it is utterly against all the Canonicall Scriptures: and also ... to say that there were saved any more people after the deluge or flood, more than Noy and his family, that was in the Arke with him, as it is manyfestly declared in Genesis."

Bourne's comment is an interesting indication that the discovery of America had already complicated the Christian story of human history. Bourne put forward the view that America was a remnant of lost Atlantis, cut off, with its inhabitants, from the Old World a long time before, between the Flood and the birth of Christ. It is not clear that P. was aware of this line of argument.

57, 75: *priscos .../... antiquae.* For Virgil's description of what these mythical times were like, when "golden Saturn used to conduct this way of life on earth" and before the rule of Jupiter took over, see *Georgics* ii, 495–540.

59, 77: *fugiens Saturnus.* Saturn is said to have been an early king in Latium and to have founded a citadel on the Capitoline hill. His reign was regarded as the Age of Gold (see following note). His son Picus was, according to Virgil (*Aeneid* vii, 48), father of Faunus (see note to l. 54); but the son who threatened him, and from whom he was fleeing, was Jupiter. Thus Virgil, whom P. was no doubt deliberately echoing, has (*Aeneid* viii, 319 f.): *Primus ab aetherio venit Saturnus Olympo | arma Iovis fugiens ...*

62, *81*: *Aurea*. The legend about the sequence of ages is to be found, for example, in the early Greek poet Hesiod (*Works and days* i, 109–210) writing in the eighth century B.C., and there is an extensive Latin treatment of the theme by Ovid (*Metamorphoses* i, 89–162). In the Golden Age, under Cronus (or his Roman counterpart, Saturn; see previous n.), there was no labour, injustice, or conflict and the earth gave its produce plentifully of its own accord. Then, in the Silver Age, men became impious and had to be destroyed by Zeus (Jupiter). In the following period, when everything was made of bronze, men destroyed each other. The Heroic Age, which came next, was better than its predecessor and was the time of the Trojan wars. The final Iron Age, the worst of all, was regarded as the present one.

P.'s scheme is rather different, and the idea that the Golden Age might return is not to be found in the earlier classical expositions. However, the notion of historical cycles, of one sort or another, was current by the end of the fourth century B.C., and some such conception of a "second coming" occurs in Virgil's so-called "messianic" fourth *Eclogue* (see below, note to l. 94).

68, *88*: *revolutoque orbe*. P. moves, from the idea of the "wheel of time" turning back, to that of turning a geographical globe and considering the various countries that fall under one's eye. Thus the prefix of *transmittere* (69) has the force of "across" the earth from one country to another. If *revoluto ... orbe* were taken to mean just "on the other side of the earth" (i.e. in America), then some of the point of the prefix and of the subsequent political tour would be lost.

73, *95*: *iugum ... subire*. The personnel of an army defeated by the Romans were often made to pass under a yoke, fixed between two spears and parallel to the ground, in a gesture of submission. Hence this phrase comes to mean simply to "submit" or "be conquered." For Julius Caesar's use of the ceremony, see, for instance, his *De bello Gallico* i, 12.

75, *97*: *Dacisque ...|... Hebrus*. The inhabitants affected by the spread of Turkish power were the Dacians (Transylvanians and, as we should say, Rumanians as well), the Aemathians (Macedonians), the Pelasgian (Greeks), the Liburnians (occupants of the part of Illyricum between Istria and Dalmatia – Slavonians) and the Pannonians (Hungarians). The river Hebrus in Thrace is now the Maritza.

75, *98*: *Pelasgisque*. According to a rare but classical practice, P. elides the final "-*que*" against the initial vowel of the next line.

77, *103*: *Marte sinistro*. Literally "in unfavourable (ill-fated) war." Propertius uses the adjective in this sense in a similar military context, when referring to the disastrous defeat of the Roman army by Hannibal at Cannae (216 B.C.): *pugnamque sinistram | Cannensem* (*Carmina* iii, 3, 9). On Hungary's hapless military position at this time, see note to l. 163 below.

79, *100*: *Pannoniae*. Although he may also refer to Transylvanian autonomy, P. probably means Hungary as comprising the small Austrian sector alone. Mention of Croatia (*Liburni*) in the same line suggests that P. may be alluding specifically to the future Ferdinand i's policy, dating from mid-century, of encouraging Christian refugees from Turkish domination to settle along the border of Austrian Hungary and of allowing them certain privileges as frontier-guardians (cp. previous line, *angustos fines ... tuentibus*). The Croat and Windisch 'marches' developed from this arrangement. See *New Cambridge modern history*, vol. III (ed. R.B. Wernham, 1968), pp. 360–62.

80, *106*: *in superos*. Cp. note to l. 50 above. The phrase cannot refer here to the gods of pagan polytheism, but *superi* must still represent something (people, organization, group) that is in some sense divine or sacred; and it must presumably be given a meaning in this line which is consistent with that of l. 50 and can be retained in 91. The same sense would not necessarily have to be kept in 319 also, because, apart from its being some distance away, the word is there put into the mouth of "pagan" America.

The Church translator takes P. to be meaning Roman priests in conflict with God; but this involves rendering *superi* differently in l. 91, where it must be *summum ... numen* which refers to the Christian divinity. The context (e.g. 51, 90–92) and P.'s general attitude (cp. 249–63) suggest the idea of Roman Catholic authorities distorting or destroying the "true" essence of Christian teaching; but this interpretation has the disadvantage of making *pugnas* into the somewhat meta- phorical battles of doctrinal dispute (e.g. the papal Bull of 1520 against Luther), which then contrast with the very concrete conflicts mentioned in the lines before and after. But such disputes did, of course, issue in military engagements, such as that of 1531 at Kappel, in which Zwingli was killed.

Alternatively, it might be suggested that P. has in mind actual feuds and skir- mishes between Church and State; and that the contrast is between secular "superiors" (*patres*) and spiritual ones (*superi*). "*Patres conscripti*" was, after all, the regular form of address to the assembled Senate at Rome. To suppose that the idea is "church-versus-state" would involve a different meaning for *superi* here from that given in the surrounding context: the word can hardly mean the general clergy in l. 91, and certainly not in 50.

81, *104*: *Ausoniis*. *Ausones* was an old name, perhaps Greek, for the inhabitants of lower Italy. *Ausonia* then came to be used to refer to Italy as a whole. P. is thus viewing the activities of the Counter-Reformation papacy from the Protestant standpoint.

82, *106*: *Sarmaticas*. P. refers here to the long war between Poland (with its Catholic Hungarian king Stephen Bathory) and Russia (under Ivan IV). It was to end later in 1582.

82, *107*: *caede recenti*. Cp. *Paean*, 43.

83, *108*: *Hispanum ... Gallumque*. There had been a continuous record of "recent slaughter" by the Spanish in the Netherlands, which had lately (March 1582) culminated in the attempted assassination of William the Silent who championed the Protestants; see p. 13 above and Appendix III. The reference to France may be specifically to the St Bartholomew's Day massacre of 1572.

89, *116*: *auro*. We substitute an exclamation mark for the pointless question mark in the 1582 text and *H.1600*; cp. notes to ll. 30, 108. The *quot* here (88), as in 107 below, is surely exclamatory rather than interrogative.

91, *118*: *Quo superi*. Cp. notes to ll. 50, 80 above. Understand *colebant*, from *colitur* in the previous line. It is perhaps more natural to understand the passive form *cole- bantur*, i.e. "... this honour, with which so-and-so were worshipped"; but there

are presumably no previous deities etc. whose worship P. would want to hold up as a model for the Christians' worship of their God. To do so would surely be theologically injudicious, even if P.'s point is that the *one*, true God is accorded all the honour etc. which was classically shared by *all* the gods of Olympus. Yet this is the sense which A.H. appears to take, for in his version the whole phrase *hoc ... honore / quo superi* is rendered "as divine". If one assumes, however, that the *active* verb-form is implied, it becomes clear that P. is pursuing the point that in England the Protestant reformers have reverted to uncorrupted, pristine traditions of religious observance (cp. his use of the words *niveus* and *castus*, ll. 87, 91) and are in this way preserving the *antiquum aurum* (89) of the Christian world.
   The Church translator also takes *superus* to mean "elder" this time, in spite of not having done so before. He does not reproduce the syntax of the Latin at all closely, but it can be seen that he takes the whole of 91–92 as one clause introduced by *quo*, whose joint subjects are *superi* and *casta iuventus*. This construction avoids supplying some part of *coleo* with *superi*, but it makes the singular verb-form *obit* (92) very incongruous and cannot be right. He has: "The worship of the Al- mighty and the reverence with which the elder and the chaste youth perform this [? "His" – Ed.] sacred commandment, that is a sign of the Golden Age."

91, 118: *omnis geniorum casta iuventus*. Who are (literally) "the whole pure youthful group of spirits"? The theme of "purity", which has been introduced by *niveus* (line 87), suggests that P. refers specifically to "the Puritans". His friend Thomas Savile used the Greek equivalent of *castus* (καθαρός) in a letter to Camden about a victimized Puritan; see p. 15 above. At any rate, even if the allusion is not so precise, it seems that, consistently with notes to ll. 50 and 80, the sentence must have something to do with the leaders of the (Reformed, Protestant) church performing their sacramental duties (and preaching the faith etc.) in holiness and purity in Britain; there is a contrast with the *vafer Hispanus* (50) who makes *sacra Papae ... crudelia*, and with the purveyors of idolatry mentioned later, 248–56. The *genii* are then "spiritual agents" or "reforming spirits", such as the Protestant martyrs Ridley, Hooper, and Latimer (the spiritual descendants of Wycliffe). They are called *castus* because they are doctrinally "pure", uncorrupted by Rome, and free from theological vice and religious malpractice.
   P. uses this same combination of words (*genii, iuventus, iussa*) in the *Paean*, 19–20; in that context, incidentally, *iuventus* does not seem to have any necessarily "youthful" connotations for P. Since he is there paraphrasing the passage ren- dered in R.S.V. as "who makest the winds thy messengers, fire and flame thy ministers" (v. 4), it might be thought that he is referring to angels here also: but it is not easy to see what he could sensibly be saying about them. In both poems, neo-platonic ideas about a "hierarchy of being" are in the background. We sug- gest, as argued above, that P. has in mind here mortal "ministers", servants of God on earth. The phrase *vices obire* (meaning "to fulfil one's allotted functions", "perform one's duties") may have the implications of "taking turns", almost like the runners in a relay race (– a Pauline touch); in which case there would be a veiled refer- ence to the "apostolic succession" of the ministry. This doctrine was a contem- porary bone of contention between Catholics and Protestants. It is even possible that this whole notion of playing earthly roles (*vices obire*) in accordance with

heavenly instructions (*illius ad sacra iussa*) owes something to pseudo-Dionysius (cp. note to l. 50): for he had taught that the Celestial Hierarchy was revealed to man so that the ecclesiastical hierarchy on earth might imitate "their divine service and Office" (Lewis, *Discarded image*, p. 74).

The idea of the leaders and martyrs of the early Church being reborn in Britain, to the admiration of the rest of Europe, is elaborated in another poem of the times, which Holland includes at the beginning of the British section of his *Herωologia*. The relevant lines are: *Multa reviviscunt Britannae lumina gentis,* | ... *atque renascuntur Patres, vigilesque Sionis* | *martyrio clari, variis virtutibus aucti;* | *hos videt, hos Europa stupet, pars optima mundi.*

A.H. appears to take *casta iuventus* to refer to the youth of the land in general, and to ignore the problematical *geniorum* altogether. His version of 90–92 is: "For, that the sovreign Deity by thee / Is worshipp'd as divine, and thy chaste youth / Regard his sacred mandates, argues gold."

93, *121*: *chara*. Lewis and Short (*A Latin dictionary*, p. 295) specifically condemn this spelling of forms of the adjective *carus*, as being unclassical.

93, *122*: *tua sceptra*. By scanning the "*a*" of *tua* short before "*sc*" (as also in 229, 315), P. treats that pair of letters as forming a softer combination than most consonant-pairs (which would normally lengthen the vowel), and more like one of which the second letter is "r" or "l" – such pairs regularly being metrically equivocal. This treatment of *sc* was not unknown classically, but was perhaps becoming more frequent in the sixteenth century under the influence of Italian (see above, p. 26, n. 17).

93, *120*: *Amazon*. By referring thus to Queen Elizabeth, P. stresses the military power at her command. The Amazons were a legendary race of women-warriors said to have lived near the Black Sea during the Heroic Age (see note to l. 62).

94, *121*: *Astraea*. The legend was that, in the Golden Age, Zeus' daughter Astraea lived among men, but that, when they became wicked in later ages, she withdrew to the sky as the star Virgo. Ovid describes it thus (*Metamorphoses* i, 149–50): *Victa iacet pietas, et virgo caede madentes* | *ultima caelestum terras Astraea reliquit.*

In Virgil's picture of the return of the Golden Age, the first sign mentioned is her reappearance on earth (*Eclogues* iv, 6): *Iam redit et Virgo, redeunt Saturnia regna.* Thus a tradition developed in the sixteenth century of using Astraea as a symbol for Queen Elizabeth; see Frances A. Yates, "Queen Elizabeth as Astraea". For the varied practice of eulogizing the virgin queen, see E.C. Wilson, *England's Eliza* (1939), and notes to ll. 176, 185, 215, 220, 223, 226.

96, *124*: *haud ... moenibus*. Ovid specifically says that in the Golden Age cities had no defences (*Metamorphoses* i, 97): *Nondum praecipites cingebant oppida fossae.* Virgil attri-butes the existence of defensive walls in the returned Golden Age to the survival of some degree of "original sin," which will also compel men still to make sea-voyages and till the land for crops (*Eclogues* iv, 31–3): *Pauca tamen suberunt priscae vestigia fraudis,* | *quae temptare Thetim ratibus, quae cingere muris* | *oppida, quae iubeant telluri infindere sulcos.* We may note the irony that P., while eulogizing a projected Atlantic voyage, draws on a classical legend which explicitly taught that sea-faring was a product of the impious and sinful Iron Age. Ovid also says that no such expeditions were made in the Golden Age (*Metamorphoses* i, 94–6), and repeats (132–34) that it was only when the *nefas* of the Iron Age came in that they began: *Vela dabant ventis nec adhuc bene noverat illos / navita, quaeque prius steterant in montibus altis, / fluctibus ignotis exsultavere carinae ...*

101, *132: arguit aurum.* The peaceful isolation of England, and her consequent freedom from fortification and military activity (in the south, at least), are contrasted with parts of the Continent. But P. exaggerates, because a serious military campaign was still in progress in Ireland, the Scottish border fortresses were manned, Hawkins was greatly enlarging the striking power of the Queen's ships, and the prevailing raids on Spanish shipping were gradually growing into the scale of a maritime war. These aspects were not evident to P., who was as yet familiar only with Oxford and London.

However, his quandary becomes apparent a few lines below (105–6) where, after attributing a Golden Age to England, he realizes that her eminence, and Gilbert's alleged greatness, rest at least partly on military prowess which is a feature of the inferior Bronze Age.

102, *129: gladii ... hastae.* The absence of weapons and of soldiering were features of the Golden Age mentioned by both Ovid (*Metamorphoses* i, 99–100) and Virgil (*Georgics* ii, 539–40).

107, *136: ahenea.* H.1600 reads *ad haenea,* which is not Latin. It would seem that some intermediary, not recognizing the less frequent spelling of *aeneus,* has tried in that text to produce a reading that looked more plausibly Latin but has ended with a piece of nonsense. Perhaps it is no more than a proof-reading slip: but for Hak-luyt's apparent fallibility as a Latinist, see *NL*, notes to ll. 12, 26, 27.

108, *137: Pectora.* Punctuation emended as indicated in note to l. 89.

111, *141: gloria.* Gilbert's eminence was, after all, a minor one. Although P. no doubt got some of Gilbert's history from his own mouth, and more from Hakluyt's, he could have followed his career from works of Thomas Churchyard in print: Newhaven (Le Havre) 1563 (sig. H1^r), Kilkenny (Sig. E4^r), Munster 1569 (sig. Q1^r–R1^v), Flushing 1572 (K4^r–4^v), and *A generall rehearsall of warres* (Edward White, 1579: S.T.C. 5235), and the 1578 American preparations in *A discourse of the Queenes Majesties entertainement ...* (H. Bynneman, 1578: S.T.C. 5226).

113, *143: Belgae ... Iberus.* Gilbert had led a force of 1100 volunteers in the Nether-lands between July and November 1572 and had been involved in several engage-ments, though rather minor ones, with the Spaniards (cp. Quinn, *Gilbert,* I, 215). The idea of defeated peoples "admiring" or "wondering at" their conqueror may have been borrowed intentionally from Horace, who pictures submissive nations looking up to Augustus (*Odes* iv, 14, 41–4 and *passim*): e.g., *Te Cantaber non ante domabilis / Medusque et Indus, te profugus Scythes / miratur,* .... Ironically, how-ever, in another passage of Horace (*Odes* iii, 5, 2–4) it is Britain herself who has been added to the empire of Augustus: ... *praesens divus habebitur / Augustus adjectis Britannis / imperio ....* Cp. p. 25 above.

For elaboration of the image, cp. ll. 227–36 below.

115, *145: Hibernia.* Gilbert had served in Ireland between June 1566 and January 1570, first as captain of an infantry company, and later as colonel of the English forces in Munster, being knighted by Sir Henry Sidney in January 1570 (cp. Quinn, *Gilbert,* I, 3–4).

116, *148: Illum ... / ... urbes.* This exactly balanced repetition is more characteristic of

Hebrew verse than of Latin. Cp. *Paean*, 41–42 and 118–21, where P. is clearly
imitating the psalmist's device.

120, *152: Sequana.* Gilbert's earliest military service had been at Le Havre between
October 1562 and August 1563, in the humble position of captain of a company
of infantry (cp. Quinn, *Gilbert*, I, 3–4). In this catalogue of Gilbert's services
(112–21), P.'s exaggeration borders on the ludicrous.

127, *162: Aucheriam.* These *Aucherii* are members of Gilbert's wife's family, the Auchers.
Gilbert married Anne, eldest daughter of Sir Anthony Aucher, of Otterden,
Kent, who had died at the siege of Calais in 1558 (E. Hasted, *History of Kent*,
2nd ed., V (1798), 536, VI, 476–7, cp. Quinn, *Gilbert*, I, 25–6). The Gilberts
had six sons and one daughter, four sons being mentioned in a document of
February 1581.

128, *164: atque .../... patremque.* We follow *H.1600*, as against the 1582 text which
reads: *et si quid avusque paterque / Aucherii moveant, exempla propinqua docentem:.* This
is the first discrepancy of content between the two texts, and we assume that the
revisions are by P.'s own hand (see above, pp. 26f., 42f.). If so, he seems here to be
correcting a previous error in genealogy, "brother and father" now taking the place
of "grandfather and father"; as if he has discovered, contrary to what he previously understood, that it was Anne Aucher's brother, not grandfather, who had
been killed at Calais with her father (see previous note). Anne was named as Sir
Anthony's heir on 16 November 1559 (*Calendar of patent rolls, 1558–9*, p. 20).

131, *169: Caleti.* After the surrender of the outer forts of Sandgate, Risbank, and Newn-
ham Bridge, the captains retired to the town of Calais. The French advanced on
the town, taking the castle without resistance, launching their attack from there.
"But by the prowes and hardy courage of syr Anthony Ager [i.e. Aucher – Ed.]
knight and Marshal of the town with his souldiers they were repulsed and driven
back agayne into the Castell gate for their suretie, least it should have recovered
against them as it was once attempted by Sir Anthony Ager, who there with his
sonne and heyre, and a Pursivaunt at Armes called Calice with divers other to
the number of xv. or xvi. Englishmen lost their lives" (Grafton's *Chronicle*, 1569,
p. 1335). Suggestions of treachery current at the time (cp. *prodentibus*, 132) probably arose from the desertion of the outer forts. P. may be referring to the capture
by the French of the English captains after Calais was surrendered; cp. *Tudor tracts*,
ed. A.F. Pollard (from E. Arber, *An English garner*), 1903, pp. 290–4, 312–17.

The operation was celebrated in Latin verse by George Buchanan (see notes to
ll. 24, 25). Originally entitled *De Caleto recepta carmen*, when published by Robert
Stephen in 1558, his poem appears as the first item of *Miscellaneorum* in Ruddi-
man's complete edition (1725) under the title *Ad invictissimum Franciae regem
Henricum II post victos Caletes.* Other poems *De Caleto* are to be found in Paradin,
De motibus Galliae (Lyons 1558).

136, *175: ignotis.* This idealistic expectation of a lost Golden Age among the primitive
societies of newly discovered lands paved the way for the later myth of the noble
savage, but there is some discrepancy in P.'s thought. If their primitive life was
ideal, why should the American Indians be urbanized (*in urbes /... coeat*, 138–9)?
The humanist idealizing the past, and the Protestant wishing to Christianize and
Europeanize the primitives, are surely here at odds!

140, *181*: *Amphion Thebas*. Amphion was a son of Zeus, and his mother was descended from the ancient ruling family of Thebes which sprang from the dragon's teeth sown, at Athene's instruction, by Cadmus. With his twin brother Zethus, Amphion became ruler of Thebes and built its walls. He was such an accomplished harpist that the stones were drawn into place by his playing. P. might have found the allusion in Statius (*Thebaid* i, 9–10).

140, *182*: *Troiana ... Phoebus*. According to Ovid's story (*Heroides* xvi, 180), Apollo built the walls of Troy in the same way as Amphion built those of Thebes.

142, *184*: *dabit leges*. Gilbert had power to make laws, under his patent, for lands he occupied. For his use of that authority in Newfoundland in 1583, see above, pp. 19, 53, *NL* 23–5 and Appendix 1.

A.H.'s splendid version of the immediately following lines (143–48) runs: "By these the citizens, in frauds unskilled, / May learn from virtue to derive their bliss, / Rather than seek it in voluptuous ease, / And riot in the luxuries of life; / Rather than gain pursue, and for renown / Live at the will of a capricious mob /."

148, *191*: *arbitrium ... plebis*. P. reflects the Tudor view (shared by the Hakluyts) that democracy was bad in itself, but that the poor were, by the fact of their poverty, subversive of propertied society and monarchical rule (cp. 149–50). In his *A briefe discourse of royall monarchie* (1581), Charles Merbury showed his strongly anti-democratic spirit (pp. 9, 11, 34, 43–44) and said that the common people, as "they have more authoritie are for the most parte more insolent, and more disposed unto rebellion". P. would have read him too, and may have been influenced by his views on statecraft. Indeed, if Merbury and P. had met in Italy, we might suppose that the influence was mutual (see above, p. 17).

Gilbert himself was busy at this time concocting an elaborate hierarchical constitution for the colonies he proposed to establish in America. It was to be feudal in structure with himself as lord paramount (cp. Quinn, *Gilbert*, I, 59–60; III, 266–78).

150, *193*: *non .../... pauper*. In a passage which may be compared with P.'s ll. 147–152, Lucretius also had commented that civil discord follows the striving for social position: *De rerum natura* iii, 59–73. Virgil had held it a happy feature of pastoral life that the countryman neither bemoans his poverty nor envies those who are better off (*Georgics* ii, 498–99): *... neque ille / aut doluit miserans inopem aut invidit habenti*.

A similar picture, of the absence of civil disquiet from the Rome of Augustus, was drawn by Horace (*Odes* iv, 15, 17–20): *Custode rerum Caesare non furor / civilis aut vis exiget otium, / non ira quae procudit enses / et miseras inimicat urbes /* (cp. *exiget otium* with P.'s *ocia tollet*, line 155). Both Ovid and Virgil said that the desire for possessions (*amor habendi*) was a feature of the decadent ages that followed the Golden: Ovid, *Metamorphoses* i, 131; Virgil, *Aeneid* viii, 327. Cp. note to l. 249 below.

Edmund Spenser (cp. note to l. 4) was to develop in English poetry this conventional sentiment, that the pastoral life is characterized by freedom, security, reliable prosperity, and absence of conflict, in his *Faerie Queene* of 1597 (vi, 9, stanzas 19–21).

153, *196*: *sua magna parens .../... dabit*. This was precisely the kind of propaganda

which might bring Gilbert extensive support for his enterprise, but it was misˏ
leading and dangerous. Nothing was less true than that settlers in North America
might expect unlimited returns with minimum effort. From the literary point of
view, however, P. is merely echoing his models; Ovid, *Metamorphoses* i, 101–12;
Virgil, *Eclogues* iv, 39–40.

155, 201: *ocia*. Elizabethan spelling of *otia*, as in l. 202 below; see p. 26 above. The
phrase *otium cum dignitate* was a slogan indicating the classical Roman ideal of
leisure without decadence: cp. Ovid, *Metamorphoses* i, 100.

158, 204: *pietas ignosce*. Literally, "O Piety, forgive [*sc.* 'me']!"

160, 205: *Aonias*. The Muses are designated "Aonian Sisters" because they were said to
live on Mt. Helicon in Boeotia, and a poetic name for this area of Greece is
Aonia.

163, 211: *clades ... Istri*. Literally, "defeats of the sad Danube," because *Ister* (or, more
classically, *Hister*) refers to the lower part of that river. The adjective *miserabilis* is
applied to the river rather than to the defeats, according to the regular classical
device of "transferred epithet" or "hypallage" – unless the river is thought of as
being sad about what has happened on its banks. The reference is especially to
the disastrous engagement at Mohács in 1526, where the Hungarian army lost
some twoˏthirds of its men in a vain attempt to resist the Turkish invasion under
Sulaiman. On the death of the puppet governor whom Sulaiman had put in
charge of the annexed territory (1540), there was further bloodshed in Danubian
regions as Ferdinand I, the Habsburg king of "free" Hungary, tried unsuccessˏ
fully to retake the conquered part. Such conflicts continued to flare up from time
to time until an unfavourable peace was concluded in 1562. But Ferdinand's
successor provoked another decade of intermittent "Danube disasters" in 1566.
See *Cambridge modern history*, III, 1904, ch. iv.

This last transdanubian campaign of the Turks was recorded by the Italian
historian Bizarri in his *Pannonicum bellum*, a Latin version of which was produced
at Basle in 1573. Christianus Schesaeus, whom Leonhardus Uncius mentions in
his preface (see next note), had also written in Latin of the *Ruinae Pannonicae*
(1571). See I. Gál's recent essay, "Sir Philip Sidney's guidebook to Hungary",
Hungarian studies in English, IV (1969).

164, 212: *me*. This phrase *his ... reservent* seems to indicate that P.'s ambition at the
time of writing was to return home and compose a national epic about Hungary's
unequal struggle against the Turk. We do not know precisely what made him
change his mind and join Gilbert's expedition after all (see above, p. 44).

If he had accomplished this literary design, P. would not have been the first
Hungarian to bewail his homeland's tragedies in Latin verse. When sheltering
from the plague in Padua (p. 7), Leonhardus Uncius had employed his enˏ
forced solitude in writing no less than seven books of poems about the fortunes of
Hungary (*Poematum libri septem de rebus Ungaricis*); they were published at Cracow
in the year that P. was at Heidelberg (1579). See E. Veress, *Fontes rerum Hunˏ
garicarum*, I, 215 and note to l. 236 below.

168, 217: *Aganippaeis*. On Mt. Helicon (see note to l. 160) there were two sacred
springs, Hippocrene and Aganippe: hence this adjective for the Muses. Philip
Sidney gently mocks at such conventional periphrases for "artistic inspiration" in

his sonnet beginning: "I never drank of Aganippe well / Nor ever did in shade of Tempe sit, /..."

168, 217: *Oxonia*. P.'s picture of Oxford as the world centre for classical scholarship at the time is overdrawn. The university's reputation was not commensurate with that of, say, Padua, Florence, or even Paris. See R. Weiss, *The spread of Italian humanism* (London 1964), ch. 7; and for a glimpse of Giordano Bruno's assessment, see above, p. 25. All the same, there were competent Latin poets in action at Oxford then, some of whom might have been equal to the theme of the New World: see above, p. 36.

According to John Hooker, Gilbert had spent some time at Oxford in his youth, but no record of his college or of his achievement appears to have survived (cp. R. Holinshed, *Chronicles*, II (1587), 132–3: Quinn, *Gilbert*, I, 2; II, 452).

172, 224: *Elisam*. P. is continuing to assume that Gilbert would sail from the Thames and so might be observed by the Queen from her favourite palace at Greenwich. He may have seen Christopher Hall's journal of Frobisher's 1576 voyage (which Hakluyt was to reprint in *Principall navigations*, 1589), p. 615, describing Frobisher's departure from the Thames: "The 8. day being Friday, about 12. of the clocke we wayed at Detford, and set saile all three of us, and bare downe by the Court, where we shotte off our ordinance, and made the best shewe wee could; Her Majestie beholding the same commended it, and bade us farewell with shaking her hand at us out of the windowe." For Thomas Watson's later reference, in Latin verse, to the Queen at Greenwich, see above, p. 68.

176, 229: *Peliaco*. Mt. Pelion was a wooded mountain near the coast of Thessaly; now called Zagora. It was supposed that the Centaurs lived round about it.

176, 228: *Pallas*. P. compares the Queen with the patron deity of Athens (Athene, Minerva), who was also goddess of wisdom. There was a tradition that she helped Jason to build the *Argo*, by setting into the prow a piece of wood from the speaking oaks in the grove at Dodona (Apollodorus, *Bibliotheca* i, 9; 16–27). But it was Hera, the wife of Zeus, who was Jason's main protectress, according to both Homer (*Odyssey* xii, 69) and Pindar (*Pythians* iv).

In his *Lusiads*, Camões (see above, p. 3) makes Venus the champion of the Portuguese on their expeditions. In *canto* II (esp. stanzas 44 and 45) Jupiter foretells to her the future greatness and conquests of that nation, and of da Gama in particular, saying that they will outstrip the heroes of classical antiquity: see *The Lusiads*, trans. W.C. Atkinson (London 1952), pp. 64 ff. For P.'s use of similar devices, cp. ll. 22–26, 44–46, 299–302.

177, 230: *Phasidos undas*. The introductory elegiacs ("Ad Thamesin") have already alluded to Jason and his Argonauts (see note to l. 5). Phasis is a river in Colchis which flows into the Black Sea; it is now called Rioni. Ovid had himself ended a line with these two words early in his account of the legend (*Metamorphoses* vii, 6).

179, 231: *Diva*. By using this adjective of the Queen, P. may be alluding to the Roman practice of conferring "divinity" upon emperors after their death. Thus Julius Caesar was pronounced "*divus Iulius*"; and see note to l. 113 above for Horace's use. Cp. Statius, *Silvae* i, 3, 4.

In the introduction to his edition, A.H. objected strongly on theological grounds to P.'s imitation of this device. He says that in his translation "... No freedom has been intentionally used with the original, excepting to deprive queen Elizabeth of her poetical divinity. Poets and painters have great licence by pre-scription, but it had a pagan origin, and Christians ought to contribute nothing towards perpetuating their idolatory." He also rebukes Buchanan, in passing, for describing Henry VIII as "equal to the immortal gods" – *dis immortalibus aequum* (*Miscellaneorum*, 15).

180, *232: Vela iuva.* P. would know that the Queen had given no direct support for the expedition, and accordingly adds his mite of supplication to her to do so. We may note that *H.1600* omits the later lines (237–41) in which she is said, over-optimistically, to have given it her blessing (see note to l. 239). Perhaps, when the revision was being made, royal support looked even less likely; but she did, in fact, send good wishes and a token to Gilbert at his next intended departure in March 1583 (cp. Quinn, *Gilbert*, II, 348; pp. 204–5 below).

183, *238: possint | ... fines.* Reading with *H.1600*, as against the 1582 text which has *possit | Imperii modus augeri.* This is the first modification which is purely stylistic and does not affect the content. It avoids the jingle of a long "i" as the first half of both second and fourth foot, and the active (rather than the passive) voice lends direct-ness to the expression.

185, *240: Charites.* There were usually taken to be three of these goddesses, who personify loveliness or grace, and their names are given as Aglaia, Euphrosyne, and Thalia.

185, *241: Delia.* The woodland goddess Diana (the Greeks' Artemis) is so called because she, and her brother Apollo, were supposed to have been born at Delos, one of the Aegean islands. There is a poem of Catullus (*Carmina*, 34) describing her major functions. Thomas Watson (see pp. 68–70), who himself refers to the Queen as Diana, explicitly remarks that some call her "Delian" and others "Sybilline": *Delia quae dicta est aliis, aliisque Sybilla* (*Amintae gaudia* v, 32, 64).

186, *242: vetustas.* The Church translator confuses this with *venustas.* There seems to be no question of a variant reading.

195, *255: ceu ...| ... auro.* Another of P.'s over-compressed similes: cp. notes to ll. 7 (Preface), 20, 34, 249. Here, delaying the subject (*gemma*) and omitting a con-junction like *quanquam* distorts and truncates the construction. Expanded, it might read: *ceu gemma quae, quanquam pretiosior auro est, auro tamen ... clauditur.*

201, *263: Sollicitis ...| ... somno.* Another feature of pastoral life which, according to Virgil also, characterized the Golden Age was the absence of political anxiety and fear of intrigue: see *Georgics* ii, 495–8. In transferring the idea to the Elizabethan scene, however, P. again exaggerates; the Queen had frequently had cause to fear Catholic and Spanish plots.

A.H.'s sonorous version of ll. 200–2 runs: "... While other princes as in prison pent / Partake their dainties charged with deadly fear, / And sleep, at furtive moments, terror-filled."

204, *265: Aeternum.* The inverted commas in the translation serve to hint that P. may be alluding to the greeting "O King, live for ever." And A.H. suggests that he may specifically have in mind some lines of Statius where Julius Caesar is addressed with the words *Teque ...| aeternum sibi Roma cupit* (*Thebaid* i, 22–4); the reference is corrected, according to the *Oxford classical text*, from that given by A.H.

210, *275: iustumque piumque /... probitas.* This insistence on the moral rectitude character-izing Elizabeth's reign, as well as the themes of peace and security from potential enemies, closely resemble features which Horace attributes to the Rome of Augus-tus (*Odes* iv, 5, *passim*). Thus, *nullis polluitur casta domus stupris, / mos et lex macu-losum edomuit nefas, / ...* (ll. 21–2) may be compared with P.'s ll. 210–12 and 143–46. Augustus did, in fact, introduce (in 18 B.C. and A.D. 9) specific legisla-tion aimed at reforming "public morals".

For the possibility that this theme in P. specifically reflects Puritanism, see note to l. 91 above.

215, *280: Bellona ... /... Gradivus.* Both refer to war deities of the Romans. Bellona was a goddess whose temple stood outside the walls at Rome and was used for receiving foreign ambassadors. Gradivus was a surname of the god Mars; its etymology is not certain. Virgil uses the phrase *Gradivus pater* in *Aeneid* iii, 35.

215, *281: adorat /... tua iussa.* This picture of the god Mars being subservient to Eliza-beth in the guise of Diana recalls the classical myth of Mars overpowered by Venus (or, more particularly, by a combined Venus-Diana figure). During the Renaissance, that image enjoyed a considerable vogue, throughout different regions of the arts (e.g. Cossa and Veronese in painting, Ficino and Pico in aesthetics), as representing, in the context of "discord", "concord" and "harmony", the interaction between forces of peace and love on the one hand and strife and death on the other. For discussion of various examples and the theory behind them, see E. Wind, *Pagan mysteries in the Renaissance* (2nd ed. London, 1967), pp. 85–96. And for other instances of this *Venus-Virgo* conflation, which can be traced to Virgil (*Aeneid* i, 314–20), being applied specifically to Elizabeth, see Wind, pp. 77–8.

Thomas Watson also makes the point that the Queen is peace-loving but feared by her enemies for her power; see p. 68, and cp. ll. 99–101 above.

219, *284: Ianitor externus*; i.e. foreign mercenaries. Although their use was common in Europe, Elizabeth did not employ them directly. Professor Gavin Townend sug-gests that the phrase alludes specifically to Swiss Guards at the Vatican.

219, *285: cives.* In his celebrated Funeral Speech, Pericles had said that allowing every-one unopposed access to the city and its affairs was one of the laudable character-istics of the Athenian way of life (Thucydides ii, 39).

220, *286: sordet.* A.H. translates "imparts / A niggard portion," as if the verb could mean "to give a poor supply" or "be mean towards". Such a usage would make a good contrast here with *tot ... artes /... fundis* (221–2), but it seems to have no classical precedent. We take it in the sense it has in, e.g., Virgil's *quoniam sordent tibi munera nostra* (*Eclogues* ii, 44). The contrast, then, is not so much that other rulers have little talent and Elizabeth has a lot, but rather that whereas they despise and reject learning etc., she fosters and partakes of it.

220, *286: regibus, ... /... satur.* Following *H.1600*, against the 1582 text which reads *Dumque aliis ducibus sordet sapientia, sacro / Pegasidum tu iuncta choro,* ..... . This is the main example of the revised version putting, for stylistic reasons, the same sense into different words.

(*a*) *regibus* for *ducibus*: this perhaps avoids the unwanted military connotation of *dux*; but the main point is that by putting the noun towards the end of the line P.

128

separates it from its qualifying adjective (*aliis*), thus giving the verse better balance and internal cohesion.

(*b*) *almo* for *sacro*: for the sake of the metre the final word now has to begin with a vowel or "h". The choice of *almus* in the context of imagery about the arts, learning etc., may allude to the designation of universities, colleges, etc., as *alma mater*.

(*c*) *Pegasidum*: the Muses' connection with Pegasus (the winged horse of Perseus) is that their spring, Hippocrene (see note to l. 168), was said to have been produced by a stamp of the hoof of Pegasus.

(*d*) *fonte satur* for *iuncta choro*: the change of metaphor represents another variation on the theme of springs and rivers on the Muses' mountain, thus preserving a unity of imagery. Pope was to use the same image in his famous line "Drink deep, or taste not the Pierian spring" (*Essay on criticism*, 216), Pieria being a region of Mt. Olympus whence the Muses were said to have migrated to Mt. Helicon.

221, *288*: *artes*. P.'s compliments to the Queen on her learning and patronage of writers may well have been sincere, for the list of dedications compiled by E.C. Wilson is impressive: *England's Eliza* (Cambridge, Mass., 1939), pp. 411–58. Although there is the view, expressed for example by Professor L. Stone in *The crisis of the aristocracy* (Oxford 1965), p. 703, that history has made too much of Elizabeth's alleged patronage of the literary arts, there can be no doubt that in the musical field, at any rate, she fostered the genius of Tallis and Byrd to a material extent. For she granted them, in 1575, a joint monopoly over the space of twenty-one years for the printing of music and music-paper. The Letters Patent which she issued for the purpose are said to be the earliest known examples of their kind in England. In that same year the two composers produced their famous combined work *Cantiones sacrae*, a compilation of 34 motets to which they each contributed half. See for example G. Reese, *Music in the Renaissance* (revised ed.; New York 1959), pp. 784–85.

Attesting to the Queen's Latinity, Professor J. Hurstfield retails the story of her replying spontaneously in the same language to a Polish ambassador who had made an unexpectedly hostile speech in Latin; *Elizabeth I and the unity of England* (London 1960), pp. 176–7. And a more eminent European scholar than P., Giordano Bruno (see note to l. 45), also saw fit to compliment her on her literacy, writing: "I leave it to the world to judge what place she takes among all other princes for her knowledge of the arts and sciences, and for her fluency in all the tongues." See *La cena de le ceneri* (1584), translated in Frances A. Yates, "Queen Elizabeth as Astraea", p. 80).

223, *289*: *Nil ...///... sorores*. These four lines do not appear in the 1582 text. In the somewhat contorted construction, P. apparently expresses the idea that Elizabeth, by virtue of her artistic prowess and patronage, is as great a credit to the Muses as any product of any civilization anywhere at any time. Cp. Horace's sentiment that Augustus is the greatest gift that the gods ever bestowed upon the world, not excluding the Golden Age (*Odes* iv, 2, 37–40): *.../ quo nihil maius meliusve terris / fata donavere bonique divi / nec dabunt, quamvis redeant in aurum / tempora priscum*. See p. 25 above.

If we understand him, P. specifically wants to reinforce the conviction, only recently dawning under the encouragement of men like Leicester and Philip Sidney, that the English could, contrary to what had previously been thought, produce a literature of international stature which might rival those of classical Greece and Rome and, in particular, that of contemporary Italy. Richard Carew, a Christ Church man whom P. may well have met when staying at that college, was writing his propaganda work on this subject, *The excellency of the English tongue*, toward the end of the century (though it was not printed till 1614): see J. Buxton, *Sir Philip Sidney*, pp. 8–17, 41. In the very same year that P. was writing, Richard Mulcaster published his *The first part of the elementarie*, where he defends (esp. in ch. 13) the literary stature, actual and potential, of English. One of his arguments appeals to the influence of England's widespread trade; cp. P.'s line 224. And, before Carew's monograph appeared, Puttenham had given the movement impetus with his *Arte of English poesie* of 1589, the second chapter of which is explicitly headed, "That there may be an art of our English poesie as well as there is of the Latine and Greeke".

224, *292: linguis*. P. seems to use *lingua* here to mean a cultural group (civilization, people) delineated by language. This would be a non-classical extension.

225, *293: te*. P. would have made his meaning clearer by using a *quam* construction after *iustius,* rather than the ablative of comparison. If this latter corresponds to the nominative of the pronoun (rather than to the accusative, parallel to *quas,* as we have taken it), then the sense is that Elizabeth has as much to be proud of as have the Muses themselves.

225, *293: divina virago*. The adjective displays again that untheological extravagance to which A.H. objected (see note to l. 179), but the noun might seem uncomplimentary. Professor Edgar Wind, at any rate, seems in no doubt that such adulation of Elizabeth did amount almost to a religious cult, and he provides another example of this same phrase being used to refer to her. "In view of the Italian sources of Elizabethan imagery, perhaps the question is not unjustified whether the worship of Queen Elizabeth as Diana was not also a cult of Venus in disguise. Among the portraits of the queen by Isaac Oliver there is one that bears ... an inscription which unmistakably refers to ... Virgil: *Virginis os habitumque geris, divina virago.*" The line of Virgil referred to is *Aeneid* i, 315; see E. Wind, *Pagan mysteries*, p. 77.

226, *289: Aoniae.* See note to l. 160.

228, *295: Imperio ... tuo.* Reading with *H.1600,* against the 1582 text's *Idcirco ... tibi.* The revised noun-adjective version binds the first half of the line together better, and lightens the rhythm by making the first foot a dactyl instead of a spondee. But it does not avoid the rather ungainly elision of a long vowel by a short one – *tu(o) et*; see above, p. 26 for P.'s use of this device.

229, *296: tua sceptra.* See note to l. 93 above.

230, *297: Mahometigenae.* Although William Harborne had brought back a flattering letter to the Queen from Murad III in 1579 and had acquired a useful privilege for English merchants in 1580, relations were by no means stable, as can be judged from M. Epstein, *The early history of the Levant Company* (1908), pp. 9–12; and Samuel C. Chew, *The Crescent and the Rose* (1937), pp. 152–3. Hakluyt had copies of both the Harborne documents by 1589 and printed them in *The princi-*

pall navigations, pp. 163–70. P. could perhaps have seen them in Hakluyt's hands, or in those of Hakluyt's cousin.

231, *298: Galli*. A French alliance was very much in the air up to the time of Anjou's departure from England in February 1582, and was thus still a possibility when P. was writing.

232, *299: Iberus*. This picture of Anglo-Spanish relationships was far from accurate. Spain was retaking the offensive vigorously in the Netherlands and was able, a little later in the year, to repulse the French and Portuguese (with some English transports) at the Azores.

233, *302: Nescia*. Germany is said to be "ignorant" of military domination by Rome because, although her tribes had been pushed back to the Rhine by Julius Caesar in 58 B.C., in the course of resisting subsequent Roman attempts to extend the frontier farther westward they had inflicted (under the leadership of Arminius) a severe defeat on the imperial army in A.D. 9.

   When Renaissance humanism reached her in the latter part of the 15th century, Germany proudly emphasized this historical independence of ancient Rome. As Professor Roberto Weiss puts it (*The spread of Italian humanism*, p. 95), "This national feeling became even stronger after Luther had broken with Rome. The German past was now openly set up against the Roman past. Arminius was hailed as the national German hero because he had been the first to show that the Romans were not invincible."

233, *301: Germania*. There were no friendly reactions from Germany and, in particular, none from the Emperor, Rudolf II. This and the Italian reference are to be regarded as either wishful thinking or poetic licence.

235, *304: Virgineis pedibus*. Presumably, "for the feet of the virgin [queen]."

235, *303: Latium*. It is hard to see how any part of Italy was seeking English friendship in 1582, since only hostile reactions were reported to the English administration (cp. *Calendar of state papers, foreign, 1581–2*, pp. 58, 571; *1582*, p. 52).

236, *305: Pannones*. Perhaps a reference to Stephen Báthory's design to unite what remained of Hungary with Poland, and eventually oust the Turk; but this had nothing to do with respect for Elizabeth. See *Cambridge modern history*, III (1904), 103. P.'s Hungarian contemporary, Leonhardus Uncius (cp. note to l. 164) had already (1579) put into Latin verse this idea of alliance under Báthory to set Hungary free. The dedicatory verses from his poems about Hungary include:
O utinam Savus et Dravus, Tybiscus et Ister, | pulchraque in excelsis Buda locata iugis, | Bathoreis sese dedant pulso hoste clientes, | libera Pannoneis possit ut esse fides.

237, *307: Magnanimi ...||||... velis*. H. 1600 omits these lines; cp. note to l. 180.

237, *308: Gilebertia ...| Signa*. In the spring of 1582 Gilbert has just revealed his elaborate project for settling North America, but we have little evidence of how he prepared it before June 1582 – by which time P.'s poem was complete. We would expect him to begin with his 1578 subscribers, who included many youngish courtiers and a few senior officials. Around them he would seem to have gathered a new band of young enthusiasts.

238, *308: consors ... necisque*. Cp. Ovid, *Heroides* iii, 47.

239, *310: audimur, ...| Annuit*. The Queen appears to have given general approval to the plan and to have made it known that she permitted Gilbert to set out, but early in 1583 she was to attempt to retract that permission. Perhaps that is why these lines were left out of the revised version. At any rate, P. here gives an impression of the flurry of early preparations for a 1582 voyage about which we have very little other evidence. See Quinn, *Gilbert*, I, 55-9, 82, and pp. 192-7 below.

For the same use of *audimur*, cp. Statius, *Silvae* iii, 2, 50.

240, *311: eia … moras*. Virgil uses this same set phrase in *Aeneid* iv, 569.

242, *313: Nonne vides*. H.1600 substitutes *Quinetiam*, which makes no sense because there would then be no construction. Clearly P. wished to abolish, in his revision, a repetition which he had originally thought rhetorically effective. It may be, therefore, that intending to alter the second instance (244), he inadvertently struck out the first; or that the compositor misread or misunderstood his correction. That revision would build something of a climax, by adding extra weight to *dudum* (244) and emphasizing the contrast with *nuper* (242). We owe this conjecture to Mr T.C.W. Stinton. But, rather than introduce an emendation which (though he may have meant it) P. did not in fact make, we retain the 1582 reading.

242, *315: submisso*. H.1600 adjoins the side-note "*Nova Albion*" to this line, indicating that the reference in this phrase is to Drake's annexation of California in 1579. Cp. Chapman's lines, quoted on p. 70 above.

245, *317: America*. P. had earlier distinguished Spanish America as the fourth part of the world and Gilbert's North American objective as the fifth (39-42). But now he has personified a single America, who is groaning under Spanish and Roman Catholic oppression.

246, *318: Numquid*. In setting out the speech of "America" as a new paragraph, and inserting quotation marks, we depart from the 1582 text which runs straight through from *Et* to *nostras* with no more punctuation than a pair of commas round *inquit*.

248, *320: An*. H.1600 is surely right thus to correct what had appeared in the 1582 text as *Au*. An interrogative particle is needed, and *au* is no more than an exclamation, rarely found in formal literature, such as "ah!" The absence of a comma after the 1582 reading also suggests that *an* was intended.

249, *322: postquam*. Both the 1582 text and H.1600 read a question-mark after *egerimus*, followed by no capital, commas after *auri* and *solum* (251), and a full stop at *coegit*. The lack of a capital and the presence of the stop indicate that the *postquam* is retrospective, and not prospective (to be taken up by *ex illo*, 252). We have added some commas to try to clarify the structure of what is, in effect, another of P.'s over-compressed constructions.

The clause *nam … virtutis* (250) is really in parenthesis, with *pietasve* (from 251) tacked on, and something like *eos coegisset* understood from *Iberos* and *coegit; amor* has to function outside the parenthesis as well as in. Any of these displacements or ellipses would be tolerable and effective by itself, but when they are multiplied within a clause (subordinate, at that) awkwardness tends to result; particularly when, as here, both the verb and its subject are concurrently affected (cp. notes to ll. 7 (Preface), 20, 21, 34, 195).

249, *323: insatiabilis auri /… amor*. Perhaps an allusion to Ovid's *amor sceleratus habendi* (*Metamorphoses* i, 131), which he had said was a feature of the decadent Age of Bronze; cp. also Virgil, *Aeneid* viii, 327, and note to l. 150 above. Camoens in his *Lusiads* (viii, 96) also has a homily against the power of gold; and he makes a similar, if indirect, attack on Spanish missionary motives, writing, "Even among those who are wholly dedicated to the service of God omnipotent, you will find countless examples where this enchanter has corrupted and misled, ..." (trans. W.C. Atkinson, pp. 197–8). Edward Hayes indicates (see above, p. 57) that financial interests were not absent from Gilbert's calculations when he changed his attitude toward Newfoundland after seeing it at first hand.

251, 325: *pietasve.* Contrary to what P. imputes to the Catholics, the missionary motive for colonization was very much in the minds of his own associates. The epistle to Florio's Jacques Cartier, *A shorte and briefe narration* (1580), sig. B2ᵛ, has as an English colonial objective, "to reduce those poore, rude and ignorant people to the true worship and service of God, and to teache them how to manure and till the ground" (cp. *NL,* note to l. 39). This was either written or inspired by Hakluyt, who also wrote in the epistle to his *Divers voyages* (sig. ¶2ᵛ) of the need for "the advauncement of the kingdome of Christ, and the enlargement of his glorious Gospell." Edward Hayes, in turn, was careful to preface his account of the Gilbert voyage (see above, p. 67) with protestations of lofty intent.

252, 326: *Ex illo.* Either referring back to *amor* (250), with *ex* meaning "as a result of" (cp. *NL,* ll. 48–9, *ex acerbata maris unda*); or, with *tempore* understood, taking up *postquam* from l. 249.

253, 326: *sperans meliora.* Protestant clergy, in particular, were very sensitive to Catholic gibes that they had achieved nothing in the missionary field. But Laurence Humfrey counter-attacked in his *Oratio* (1575, sig. C1ʳ⁻ᵛ) by accusing the Catholics of merely leading the Indians from one superstition into another: "Very many men, deprived of this light, had rushed on into darkness, superstition and a boundless morass of errors; so that at the present time the Indians and others, spellbound by the paraphernalia and incantations of Jesuits and Papists, have been converted from their traditional idol-worship to a new one, – albeit a most papal one."

P. would have known these references. He probably hoped to canvass missionary prospects in America, and his disappointment at not finding Indians in Newfoundland (cp. *NL,* ll. 31–32) may have stemmed partly from this.

258, 335: *recta.* A truly Protestant advocacy of the view, contrary to Catholic preference for a hierarchy of intercessors and mediators, that the individual believer may communicate "directly" with God. P. may even be harking back to the earlier teaching of Boethius, in *De consolatione philosophiae,* that prayer is a direct *commercium* between man and God. By introducing the notion of the "right mind" (*si mens est lucida*), P. implies a typically Protestant plea for a "rational" faith – as opposed to one apparently encumbered with dogmas and mysteries into which the intellect is discouraged from inquiring (cp. previous note). Perhaps there is an allusion also to the promise of the Beatitudes that purity of heart is a sufficient condition for "seeing God".

259, 337: *A nobis ... petitur.* The idea that *coelum* (God, "the Kingdom of Heaven", perhaps "salvation") could be sought for themselves by individual believers (*a nobis*), as opposed to being the perquisite of ecclesiastical authority (*maiestas,* 261), had been one of Luther's more provocative doctrines, known as the "priesthood of all believers". He expounded it in his *An appeal to the Christian nobility of the*

German nation (1520), and similar themes recur in his *Of the liberty of a Christian man* published in the same year. Lutheran teaching had been propagated in Hungary, during the 1530s by Mátyás Dévai Bíró; after his arrest in 1533, he had specifically affirmed, among a few particular theses, the priesthood of all believers. See *New Cambridge modern history*, II (1958), 199–209.

    Doutbless also at the back of P.'s mind, here again, are some general features of Renaissance neoplatonism (cp. p. 34, and notes to ll. 24, 50). The doctrine of levels of existence or metaphysical strata (allied to the perhaps more concrete medieval concept of the "Chain of Being") raised the question of transition from one level to another. Plotinus' description of the stratification involved seems to confuse two rather separate sorts of graduation (*Enneads* ii, 3); but when he discusses the soul's attempt to rise to higher levels, he speaks of the frustration encountered in being "dragged down again" in language rather similar to that used here by P. (cp. l. 257, *cur trahor in terras?*): see *Enneads* ii, 9, 2; and A.H. Armstrong, *The intelligible universe in Plotinus* (Cambridge, Eng., 1940), ch. 6. But it was Ficino, in the neoplatonic revival, who revised Plotinus' scheme and made the soul's upward striving a dominant motif in his "psychology", elaborating the theme that the human spirit has an innate orientation (*appetitus naturalis*) in that direction. In contrast with Pico's emphasis on purification as facilitating this ascent (cp. note to l. 50 above), Ficino stressed the role of the intellect (cp. P.'s *lucida mens*). Ficino's teaching on this topic is to be found especially in his *Five questions concerning the mind* (1476): see Cassirer *et al.*, *Renaissance philosophy of man*, pp. 185–212; and P.O. Kristeller, *The philosophy of Marsilio Ficino* (New York 1943), pp. 270–6.

261, 339: *Oenotriae.* Oenotria was a name given originally to the extreme southeastern part of Italy, but later used poetically of Italy in general and even of Rome in particular. P. has to scan the second syllable short for the sake of the metre, although strictly it is a long "o", transcribing the Greek *omega*.

267, 348: *Busiride.* Busiris was a legendary king of Egypt who sacrificed foreigners and was himself killed by Hercules. His name no doubt became a byword for savage persecution.

269, 350: *tam plenis.* For the two Hakluyts' view that the overpopulation of Britain required and justified overseas colonization, see notes to ll. 29, 36.

275, 356: *sub sole.* English enterprise in the East was signalized at this time especially by Drake's circumnavigation, and in the West by John Hawkins's voyages.

277, 357: *Wilobeius.* H. 1600 has side note "*Hugo Willobeius eques auratus.*" We read, with the 1582 text, a single "*l*" in the surname, because doubling it lengthens the metrical value of the first syllable and upsets the scansion.

    The Willoughby-Chancellor voyage to the Northeast in 1553 had led to Sir Hugh Willoughby's death on the Murmansk coast (hence *iacet*, 278), as well as to Chancellor's successful establishment of the maritime link with Muscovy. It is possible that P. had seen Clement Adams, *Nova Anglorum ad Moscovitas navigatio* (London 1554), which Hakluyt was to reprint in *The principall navigations* (1589), pp. 270–9. He had certainly discussed with Hakluyt the list of English travellers with which the latter prefaced the *Divers voyages*, and in which appear all those whom P. mentions by name.

The ensuing "catalogue of explorers" (ll. 277–98) may be compared with Thomas Watson's of 1592, which has been discussed above (p. 68). After the lines about Cabot, quoted there, Watson turns to Chancellor: *Sed quae vela refert ex alto puppis eodem | et salsas diffindit aquas foelice carina, | Cancellerus eam coelo clemente reducit | in solitos portus, haud pauca pericula passam | et vario longos emensam marmore tractus. | (80) Si tua nymbosum se pupula vertet in Austrum, | qua figit nobis adversas incola plantas, | ecce novos, . . .* Then follows the passage about Wyndham, quoted on p. 69 above; and Watson concludes with references to Willoughby, Frobisher, Drake, and Cavendish: *Axe sub opposito gelidam qui sustinet Arcton, | dum salis arva secat Wylobaeus et os Aquilonis | (90) impavidus subit, ut terras populosque latentes | inveniat charisque addat commercia cunis, – | en ubi tanta viri virtus in fluctibus haeret | Arzinae; proh fata! coit firmata pruinis | unda, gravique ratis glacierum mole fatiscit. | (95) Haec Furbisseri est, quam Meta Incognita pinum | miratur, metuitque tamen refugitque procantem. | Ille Dracus, lacero qui ditia pondera ligno | imponit Thamesi. Quae pandit serica ventis, | Candicii corbita polum prosperit utrumque.*

280, 361: *Ni frustra ...||||... orbi.* H.1600 omits these lines and puts 290–3 in their place, adding the sidenote *"Martinus Frobisherus eques auratus."* For possible reasons for the omission, see above, p. 42. It is not apparent why the lines about Frobisher were displaced. Seeing that to mention him between Willoughby and Jenkinson spoils both the geographical and the chronological sequence, we have restored him to where he was in the 1582 text.

281, 361: *Burrhoidae fratres.* The brothers Stephen and William Borough were the most expert navigators concerned with the Muscovy Company voyages. They served with Chancellor in 1553, and Stephen, accompanied by William, led the first systematic search for the Northeast Passage in 1556–7. Both took part in subsequent expeditions. They were included in the younger Hakluyt's list of "certaine late travaylers" in *Divers voyages* (1582), sig. 2^r, and either of the Hakluyts could have told P. more about them; he might even have met William Borough in London (but see p. 42 above).

281, 362: *Scythicum ... profundum.* The Boroughs were trying to sail round Scythia, the northern Asia of the Romans (cp. Quinn, *Gilbert*, I, 142, 144, 153). On the theoretical problems of the northern passages P. had available in print Sir Humphrey Gilbert's own small book, *A discourse of a discoverie for a new passage to Cataia* (1576) and a treatise by Richard Willes (in his *The history of travayle* (1577), ff. 230–6). He could also have got a summary of English achievements in George Best's accounts of the Frobisher voyages, *A true discourse of the late voyages of discoverie* (H. Bynneman, 1578). This has a preliminary survey of earlier voyages, which Hakluyt left out when he included much of Best's account in *The principal navigations* (1598–1600).

284, 367: *quid.* Literally, "in any way", "to any extent"; the grammatically free translation tries to avoid awkwardness.

286, 368: *Cimmerios.* The Cimmerii had lived around the Sea of Azov in Roman times.

287, 368: *Riphaeis.* The Rhiphaean "mountanes" are depicted in Jenkinson's own map, reproduced by Ortelius (*The theatre of the earth* (1601), sig. 2A1^v). They are "in the North part of Scythia, where snow lyeth continually". But no particular forests are represented in the area, to account for P.'s *sylvisque* (286).

288, 367: *Gincisonus.* H.1600 reads *Ienkisonus* and adds the side-note *"Antonius Ienkin-sonius"*. The original form is the more Latin-looking (cp. *Hacletius*, note to l. 25 (Preface)), and since the spelling may have been altered by Hakluyt, to tally more with his side-note, rather than by P. himself, we retain it.

For the Anthony Jenkinson voyages of 1557–72 there were only a few scraps in print (in Willes, *History of travayle*), so it is likely that P. heard of them mainly from the Hakluyts. They may have shown him some journals of the voyages which the younger man was to print in 1589.

288, 369: *Persis.* Jenkinson's visit to Persia took place in 1562–3.

289, 370: *Bactra.* In Roman times the chief city of Bactria, now called Balkh; it lies some 150 miles due south of Samarkand.

289, 370: *Indos.* Jenkinson's nearest approach to India was at Bokhara in 1558–9.

291, 371: *Forbiserus.* Anglicized to *Frobisherus* in H.1600. The displacement of the first vowel in the 1582 text may represent a deliberate attempt to Latinize by P., though the name was often spelled "Furbisher" in England at the time; cp. Watson's Latinization in note to l. 277 above (l. 96 of the quotation). On the Frobisher voyages (1576–8), P. could see in print George Best's work covering all three (see note to l. 281 above), Dionyse Settle on the second (*A true reporte of the laste voyage by Captaine Frobisher*, H. Middleton, 1577) and Thomas Ellis on the third (*A true report of the third and last voyage into Meta Incognita*, T. Dawson, 1578). T. Churchyard, *A prayse, and reporte of Maister Martyne Forboishers voyage to Meta Incognita* (London, for Andrew Maunsell, 1578) is another account of the second voyage.

294, 379: *mortali ... negarant.* Reading with H.1600, as against the 1582 text which has *vix ulli ... dederunt* ("have given to scarcely onyone"). The first part of the revision improves the rhythm by avoiding two successive monosyllables; and, although *vix ulli* is really a litotes for *nemini*, it removes the note of dubiety from the claim that Drake's voyage was the first of its kind (which it was not, of course, for Magellan's expedition had anticipated him in 1519–22). The change in the verb improves the sequence of tenses by substituting pluperfect for perfect.

295, 376: *Dracus.* H.1600 has side-note *"Franciscus Dracus eques auratus"*. This, with that in *Divers voyages* (sig. 3ʳ), is among the earlier printed references to Drake's voyage, about which publicity in England seems to have been held back by the Queen; see Quinn and Skelton's edition (1965) of the 1589 *Principall navigations*, p. xxxi. There are, however, some rather general references to Drake's discoveries in a tract by Nicholas Breton called *A discourse in commendation of Maister Frauncis Drake* (1581). See H.P. Kraus, *Sir Francis Drake* (1970), pp. 82, 197

299, 384: *fortuna ... virtute.* Referring back to l. 268.

300, 385: *monstra.* In the course of the Twelve Labours imposed on him by Eurystheus, Hercules (see 301, and cp. 45) had to overcome various monsters. They included the Nemean Lion, the Hydra, and the Erymanthian Boar.

300, 385: *gigantum.* A reference to the "giants" of Tierra del Fuego, of which Drake's men had tales to tell.

302, 389: *Ogygius ... Iacchus.* Iacchus was a deity celebrated, in company with Demeter and Persephone, at the Eleusinian Mysteries. He was identified with Dionysus, god of vegetation, wine and artistic inspiration (the Roman Bacchus). There was a legend that, in the course of defeating those who refused to recognize his deity and persecuted him, he performed many heroic and miraculous feats. Euripides' play the *Bacchae* concerns the tragic revenge wrought by Dionysus at Thebes when his worship was initially rejected there. In classical tradition Dionysus had become especially honoured at Thebes; some authorities make him grandson of Cadmus, founder of the citadel there. Ogyges was another legendary founder and early king of that city, so that the epithet *Ogygius* comes to mean "Theban"; used of Bacchus by Ovid in *Heroides* x, 48.

306, *392: isthmo.* The Verrazzanian maps show the sea of Verrazzano as an arm of the Pacific separated from the Atlantic only by an isthmus in the Carolinas/Virginia area. In *Divers voyages*, Hakluyt printed Michael Lok's map which shows the isthmus strikingly; this map was used to illustrate Verrazzano's letter which Hakluyt translated from Ramusio's Italian text, and no doubt P. had seen the letter.

308, *395: Gabotus.* H.1600 reads *CABOTUS*. Hakluyt had discovered and printed the 1496 patent to John Cabot and his sons (*Divers voyages*, sig. ¶3ᵛ, A2ʳ⁻ᵛ), but he still gave the main credit to Sebastian, as does P.; cp. Thomas Watson's comment, discussed on p. 68 above.

309, *397: Columbo.* How (John) Cabot is now thought to have followed Columbus is discussed in D.B. Quinn, "The argument for the English discovery of America between 1480 and 1494", *Geographical Journal*, CXXVII (1961), 279–85; and J.A. Williamson, *The Cabot voyages* (1962), *passim*.

312, *400: iusto moderamine.* America draws attention to her balanced climate, which contrasts with that of North Africa mentioned above (43–4). The whole purpose of Hakluyt's *Divers voyages* was to create such an impression of North America as P. puts into verse. In particular, the notes on colonization (by the elder Richard Hakluyt, though not ascribed to him; sig. K1–3ᵛ) emphasized that the colony "is to bee chosen in temperate climate". This is apparently P.'s immediate source.

315, *403: tua sceptra.* See note to l. 93 above.

319, *408: Quodsi.* It is unclear from the 1582 text whether this is meant to be two words here, and also in 321, 323. Since it is clearly printed as one in 263, 264 we have maintained consistency.

319, *408: superum.* Since it is "pagan" America speaking here, we need not suppose that *superi* means anything other than "the gods" in this instance, especially as it is coupled with the "Fates"; cp. notes to ll. 50, 80, 91 above.

322, *412: imperii . . . populique regendi.* This combination of words echoes a famous line from the memorandum about foreign policy which Virgil puts into the mouth of Anchises (*Aeneid* vi, 851–3). Indeed P.'s whole homily on government and empire-building is reminiscent, in its advocacy of firmness tempered with clemency, of that passage: *Tu regere imperio populos, Romane, memento | (hae tibi erunt artes) pacisque imponere morem, | parcere subiectis et debellare superbos.* The same motif, combined with the idea (which P. is just about to introduce) that indiscriminate power destroys itself, occurs in Horace (*Odes* iii, 4, 65–7): *Vis consili expers mole ruit sua: | vim temperatam di quoque provehunt | in maius; . . . .* See p. 25 above.

325, *415: Cyro.* Cyrus the Great was founder of the Persian Empire at the middle of the sixth century B.C. In the course of his conquests he overthrew Astyages, king of Media, and Croesus, king of Lydia. He captured Babylon in 539 B.C.

327, 417: *Macedum.* King Philip of Macedon (*c.* 382–336 B.C.) and his even more famous son Alexander the Great (356–323 B.C.) respectively founded and extended the Macedonian empire. It eventually included even part of India. When Alexander died, Perdiccas was appointed regent of the empire and many regions were allotted to individual generals to govern. As a result of the internal struggle for power that followed, the empire began to break up and finally disintegrated in 306 B.C.

329, 421: *Romuleis.* Romulus, the legendary founder of Rome in the eighth century B.C., was said to have killed his twin-brother Remus in a quarrel that arose soon after they had decided to build a settlement between them. The twins were sons (by Mars, the war-god) of Rhea Silvia, herself a daughter of the penultimate Alban king; cp. note to l. 25.

330, 423: *Nerones.* The notorious emperor Nero ruled A.D. 54–68. A brutal and eccentric man, by all accounts, he had his mother and his wife Octavia put to death in order to pave the way for marriage with Poppaea Sabina. He promoted contests of music and drama, and even went so far as to appear publicly in them himself. Such exhibitions (not to mention his crimes) were regarded as detrimental to the image of his office and of Rome. Contrary to what P. suggests, however, the Roman empire survived in some form for a further three-and-a-half centuries.

PART TWO

Paean

STEPHANI PARMENII BUDEII

ad psalmum Davidis CIV conformatus
et, gratiarum loco,
post prosperam ex suis Pannoniis in Angliam peregrinationem,
Deo optimo et ter maximo servatori consecratus

LONDINI

Excudebat Thomas Vautroullerius Typographus

1582

Thanksgiving Hymn

BY STEPHEN PARMENIUS OF BUDA

modelled on Psalm of David 104
and dedicated to
the Good Lord and Almighty Saviour
in gratitude for a safe journey from Hungary to England

LONDON
Printed by Thomas Vautrollier
1582

Ad Illustrem et Nobilissimum Genere, Virtute ac Doctrina

Henricum Untonum προσφώνησις

> *Victor ab adverso quondam qui Marte redibat,*
> *Aut de navifragae vortice sospes aquae,*
> *Vel spolia in templis vel vestimenta locabat,*
> *Tutius hoc starent quod monimenta loco.*
> 5 *Tale aliquid quisquam nostrum paeana vocarit:*
> *Illo iam positum munus ab usque die*
> *Cum sumus emensi quicquid terraeque marisque*
> *Inter Pannonios Albionasque iacet.*
> *Excipe, magnanimis Britonum sate patribus heros,*
> 10 *Subque tuo poni nomine posse sine.*
> *Si tanto pendere tholo mea dona licebit,*
> *A sera metuent posteritate nihil.*

Address to Henry Unton

famous for his noble ancestry, personal qualities and wide learning

When men returned from battle
　　With hard-won victory
Or safe survived the currents
　　Of ship-destroying sea,
5　They used to leave their trophies
　　Or garments in some shrine,
To keep them there more safely,
　　And constitute a sign.

Perhaps you'll say my poem
10　Is something just the same,
A grateful composition
　　To mark the day I came
Across the many waters
　　And boundaries that lie
15 Between the shores of England
　　And my own Hungary.

I pray you then, accept it,
　　To grace it with a name
That boasts a long tradition
20　Of great heroic fame:
For if I may entrust them
　　To such a noble knight
My verses need fear nothing
　　From time's far-reaching flight.

143

Paean

NUNC AGE, PARS NOSTRI MELIOR, SEU SPIRITUS AURAM
Seu mihi mens alacres vitam diffundis in artus,
Dicamus bona verba: age grata voce loquamur
Res gestas et facta Dei pulcherrima nostri.
5   *Quandoquidem valde egregio dudum ille paratu*
Inclitus evasit: sic illum gloria circum
Induit, et multo maiestas ambit honore.
Aut quid nobilius, quid magnificentius, illo
Aurea purpureo quem lux illustrat amictu,
10 *Quem radiis subtile iubar, cui regia coelum*
Pendula convexo tanquam cortina cubili?
Quae, quanquam igne rubet iugi flammisque coruscat,
In gyrum lustratur aquis, et massa resultans
Sideribus liquido pellucida diffluit amni.
15 *Idque opus est, pater alme, tuum: tu in nubibus altis,*
Et mediis in fulminibus multoque tonitru,
Ignipedes moderaris equos, totoque profectus
Aethere praepetibus volucer spaciaris in auris.

Paean

C OME, BETTER SELF, AND LET US NOW COMPOSE
   Fine phrases; whether, as their soul, you give
   My limbs their breath, or, being intellect,
   You permeate them all with life to make
5 Them active. Come, and let us tell aloud
   In thankful verse our God's accomplishments
   And works of finest beauty.
                 Since He rose
   In view some time ago, illustrious
   And quite unmatched in all His finery,
10 So glory cloaks Him round and majesty
   Encircles Him about with all the show
   Of honour due. What nobler sight is there,
   What more magnificent to see, than one
   Whom shining rays light up as if he wore
15 A scarlet robe? – on whom transparent beams
   Of sunlight fall; who makes the very sky
   His palace, like a canopy which hangs
   Over an arching bed. A palace which,
   Although it glows with unremitting fire
20 And flames that shimmer, yet is lapped about
   By water where its massive form sweeps down
   And leaves the stars, dispersing in clear streams
   Translucently: and this has all been made
   By your kind hands, O Father.
                  You direct
25 Your team of fiery-footed horses through
   The clouds above, through many lightening-storms
   And claps o thunder, setting out to range
   On headlong winds across the whole wide sky.

Ergo et quae peragit tua regia iussa iuventus
20 Sunt immortales genii, sunt labe carentes,
Sunt animi volucres: illi, tua quando voluntas,
In rapidos abeunt flammis crepitantibus ignes.
    Atque etiam magnae huic terrae, cum mobilis olim
Stare loco nondum sciret, tua summa potestas
25 Fundamenta dedit solidoque coercuit orbe.
Illud erat tempus quando circumfluus humor
Abdiderat montes, medioque in viscere clausam
Undique tellurem vasta impediebat abysso.
Tu simul ac subito signum terrore dedisti,
30 Iussaque fulmineum crepuerunt nubila murmur:
Dividuum fugit pelagus, terraque relicta
Aethera Nereides formidavere tonantem.
Tunc etiam apparere solum, caeloque minari
Aerii montes, gelidae subsidere valles
35 Imperio cepere tuo, subitoque resultu
Arida de liquido caput extulit aequore tellus
Quae ne vaesanis iterum madefiat ab undis,
Terminus est undis: est quo Neptunus in alveo
Littora fluctisono nequicquam exerceat aestu.
40   Iamque quod e parvis ingentia flumina tophis,
Quod tumidi veniant mediis de montibus amnes
Et medii lateant tumidis sub montibus amnes,
Hoc opus omne tuum est. Bibit hinc de caede cruenta
Bestia, veloces illic implentur onagri:
45 Inde pecus levat omne sitim, levat ales et altis
Frondibus assuetae volucres, circumque supraque
Flumina suavisono mulcent modulamine coelum.

Therefore the ministers who carry out
30 Your royal will consist of deathless souls
And fleeting spirits, ones who have escaped
Corruption: they disperse in darting flames
And crackling fire when you dictate. You laid
The very earth's foundations long ago,
35 Your might confined its mass within a firm
And stable circle when it had before
Shifted about, not knowing how to keep
Its place. For them an all-embracing flood
Covered the hills and swallowed up the earth,
40 Impeding it on every side within
Its huge abyss.
                But when you gave the sign, –
A sudden awesome signal setting up
A stormy roar that echoed your commands
With menace, – then the waters rushed apart
45 And on the liberated land the nymphs
Trembled in fear beneath the rumbling sky.
Then landscape, too, began to show itself
At your instruction, mountains rose
To threaten heaven, sheltered valleys sank,
50 And thus, with one convulsive shrug, the dry
Land-masses raised their heads above the waves:
And, lest they might be swamped again by wild
Sea-waters, boundaries were set to them
Such that old Neptune holds his ground and plagues
55 The coasts with noisy breakers harmlessly.
Your work has made the giant rivers spring
From little rocks, and swelling rivulets
Flow from the heart of hills, or even lurk
Unseen inside them. Beasts of prey may leave
60 Their gory kill to drink from one such stream
While swift wild asses use another: there
A whole herd slakes its thirst, in company
With many birds, both larger kinds and those
Accustomed to the treetops bordering
65 The riverside, from which they charm the sky
With singing. These things also represent

147

Idque opus omne tuum est: et iam fortasse per agros
Tota Ceres primis praeceps moreretur in herbis,
50 *Ni bene maturos resolutis nubibus imbres*
Montes et bibuli caperent tua munera campi.
Ergo quod aetherii satur est aspergine roris
Magna parens tellus: quod praebet terga colono,
Pabula iumentis, epulas mortalibus, herbas
55 *Afflictae vel ferro hominum vel peste saluti,*
Hoc opus omne tuum est.

Abs te proficiscitur uno
Quod securum animi parvo de stipite nectar
Luxuriant vites, et vitibus arbor amica
Exhilaraturum frontem desudat olivum;
60 *Quod toties saturi ambrosia et Cerealibus offis*
Pascimur, et vitam seros agitamus in annos:
Quod de nubigenis, quos tu pluis, imbribus arbor
Ebria deposito toties flaccore virescit.
Hinc Libano sua forma, suus decor annuus, et quam
65 *Tu sator ingenti posuisti in vertice sylvam,*
Crescit odorato speciosa cacumine cedrus.
Sunt illic quae vere novo, sub frondibus altis,
Aedificent volucres genitiva cubilia nidos.
Illic procera sublimis in abiete sedem
70 *Collocat oblongo promissa Ciconia rostro.*
Nec desit vastis suus incola montibus: illic
Aut pavidi latitant lepores, aut aspera tergo
Spicula laesuros histrix iaculatur in hostes.
Parva loquor: iuvat e terris succedere coelo.
75 *Huc ubi mirando vaga sidera vortice torques;*

Your handiwork.
               The tender sprouting crops
Of spring might fade and die throughout
Our fields at present, but for rains released
70 By timely clouds upon the hills and sent
As welcome gifts of drink to thirsty plains.
In this way, too, your work ensures for us
That mother earth is well supplied with dew
And heaven's moisture, lets us cultivate
75 Her back and so provides domestic herds
With food, and men with banquets and, – to use
If health should be impaired by injury
Or sickness, – herbs. To you we owe the vines,
Whose slender branches copiously supply
80 Heart-warming juice, and also olive-trees, –
A friendly host to grapes, – which yield an oil
To gladden human faces. We refresh
Ourselves so often with the food of gods,
And eat bread made from wheat, that life can be
85 Pursued to ripe old age; so often trees,
No longer limp, grow green by soaking up
The cloud-borne showers rained on them by you.
In this way Lebanon is handsomely
Decked out each year: for shapely cedars grace
90 Her scented summit where you planted seeds
Along her massive crest to raise a wood.
Here come such birds as build their nests each spring
Under the topmost leaves to breed their young:
To this place too the long-beaked stork sets out,
95 Coming to make her home high up among
The lofty firs. And open hills support
Inhabitants: for either timid hares
Lie low in them, or else the porcupine
Rattles her pointed quills at enemies
100 Who threaten harm.
               But these are little things
Of which I speak. The time has come to leave
The earth and raise our eyes to heaven where
You spin the roving stars in their immense

Huc ubi fraterna Diana redintegra luce
Mensibus ingentem brevibus discriminat annum;
Huc ubi deprimitur certoque revertitur ortu
Sol, oculus mundi, – sol, qui simulatque iugales
80 Merserit Oceano lucemque negaverit orbi,
Iam subit obscurae tempestas horrida noctis.
    Caedica iam suasu vaesani bellua ventris
In pecudes caeca grassatur nocte minores:
Iam magnum auditur Massyla per avia murmur,
85 Magnanimum quando soboles excita leonum
Rugit et immeritum sitit iracunda cruorem.
Verum idem roseos iterum simulatque iugales
Reddit ab Oceano lucemque recolligit orbi,
In sua Marmarici redeunt spelaea leones:
90 Securusque animi iam rusticus arma vicissim
Tollit, et hinc rastros hinc iugera grata fatigat,
Donec equos undis Titan mersurus in iisdem
Dimidium claudat tenebroso vespere mundum.
    Terrarum nitidique sator pulcherrime coeli,
95 Totque bonorum aeterne parens! Quis enim illa videndo,
Quis, pater, attonitus non te adm'retur et alto
Pectore tot meritis merito stupefactus adoret?
Si, quocunque adverto oculos, occurris ubique
Formosus, dives, sapiens, longaevus, bonorum
100 Plenus et in vita solus felice beatus.
    Nam quantae hic telluris opes: quae copia rerum?
Quanta soli semper post parvam foenera sortem?
Quanto illic longum spacio quam margine latum
Porrigitur pelagus? Non illi animantia desunt

Orbits, and where the moon marks out long years
105 In shorter months, reflecting borrowed light;
To where the sun, that universal eye,
Rises and sinks in turn dependably –
That sun who, when he dips his wheel below
The far horizon, cutting off his light
110 From earth, gives way to eery hours of night.
And then in darkest gloom do savage beasts,
Prompted by hunger's rage, make havoc through
The helpless flocks: then, too, a roar is heard
To ring throughout the wastes of Africa
115 In which majestic lions rouse themselves
And growl and thirst for undeserving blood.
However, when this very sun once more
Recalls his shining steeds from Ocean's sea,
And summons up another day of light,
120 Then Egypt's lions slink back to their caves
And countrymen feel safe again, take up
Their tools and work by turns with rake and plough
Until the sun, about to plunge his team
Again in that same stream, envelopes half
125 The world in evening gloom.
                                        Eternal God
And glorious Creator, who has made
The earth, the shining sky and so much else
Of beauty, – how could anyone at sight
Of them not marvel in astonishment
130 And worship you, the Father, with his heart
And soul, in all the admiration due
To such great benefits? For you are seen
On every side, wherever I may turn
My eyes; in beauty, wisdom, length of days,
135 In wealth, respect and unique happiness
Of life. For who can tell how great are earth's
Resources, what reserves of things there are?
How rich an interest can well-tilled soil
Keep giving on such little capital?
140 And yet how far the seas extend, how wide
They reach away from land! And they contain

105 *Maxima cum minimis: illi monstrisque ferisque*
Terribiles habitantur aquae, magnoque recessu
Innumeris semper populosum est foetibus aequor.
Velivolis spumat summum mare puppibus: imo
Deformes ponunt immania corpora ceti.

110   *Omnia te passim venerantur, ut omnia passim*
Opportuna tuo capiant alimonia iussu.
Nam quoties animis iam deficientibus aurem
Advertis, bene habent: quoties effundis, abundant
Deliciae et pleno ditissima copia cornu.

115 *Idem difficili quoties tua munera vultu*
Avertis, macilenta fame et moerore fatiscunt
Omnia, et informis rerum natura laborat.
Quod si animam et diae tollis spiracula mentis,
Protinus imbuitur cognato pulvere corpus:

120 *Quod si animam et diae reddis spiracula mentis*
Protinus emergit redivivo e pulvere corpus,
Effoetusque novis iuvenescit honoribus orbis.
   Nunc ergo, aeterni pulcherrima gloria patris,
Aeternum celebranda mane! Laetatur et ille

125 *Dum meminit quod fecit opus: dum respicit alto*
Aut formidantes terras, aut verbere magno
Emissura leves tangit fastigia fumos.
Illi ego, dum vivos inter pars ulla manebo,
Assiduum paeana canam, studioque perenni

130 *Immortale pio fundam de pectore carmen.*
Iucundum carmen quod, cum bonus audiat ille,
Audiat ille lubens: sed et ipse, quod audiat ille,
Plena voluptatis capiam solacia vivae.

Both huge and tiny creatures: monsters lurk
With other savage beasts in some more dark
And gruesome waters, while a long way off
145 The ocean teems with countless living things
Of minute size. Its surfaces are ploughed
By vessels under sail, while down below
The monstrous whales lay their ungainly bulk.
    All things throughout the world hold you in awe,
150 So that they may receive timely support
At your command. For when you turn your ear
To souls in need, they prosper; rich supplies
And luxuries abound whenever you
Dispense them. So, when you implacably
155 Withhold your gifts, a miserable world
Grows thin with hunger, fades, and nature's realm
Struggles in chaos. Why? – because if you
Remove the soul, that spark of your divine
Intelligence, then bodies are at once
160 Reduced to dust, from which they came;
But if you should restore those elements,
The living body will emerge again
From animated dust, and all the world,
That was worn out, receive fresh energy
165 And new adornments.
                    Let the majesty
And beauty which the Father has displayed
Stay to be celebrated endlessly:
And He is glad as He recalls the work
His hands have done, looks down on trembling lands,
170 Or strikes the hill-tops such a heavy blow
That they begin to smoke. So then, as long
As I remain a living force among
Creation, I will sing an earnest hymn
Of praise to Him, and with an endless zeal
175 Pour out undying songs with faithful voice:
A joyful song, which when He hears in all
His goodness He may hear contentedly,
And I shall find much comfort, much delight
In His attentiveness. But let the ranks

> At vos, o homines turba execranda prophani,
> 135 Ilicet e vivis steriles vanescite in umbras.
> Sed mihi mortales qui spiritus incolit artus,
> Factorem memorato suum mecumque vocato, –
> "Salve summe Deum, salve immortalis, aveque
> Coelicolum pater; et, nostrum dignatus honorem,
> 140 Tantum te dignas mitissimus aspice laudes."

180 Of hateful pagans leave the living world
For that of empty shadows; let the soul
That lives within this mortal frame invoke
Its Maker, praising him with me: "Hail King
Of Kings, Eternal God, hail Thou who art
185 Father of Heaven! May you think this show
Of honour not unworthy, and regard
Benignly praise which only you deserve."

1, 1: *Paean.* The *paean* was one type of Greek "choral lyric", a verse-form which became incorporated into the classical drama. Originating as a song of invocation or thanksgiving to Apollo, it was especially cultivated at Sparta. Some fragments of paeans by Pindar, who claimed descent from Spartan nobility, are extant. The classical Latin poets did not widely adopt the form, and P.'s verses bear no resemblance in metre or composition to the Greek model. In designating them a "paean", he merely calls attention to the spirit in which they were written.

3, 3: *ad psalmum.* For the general practice of producing such Latin versions of the psalms, see above, pp. 31-2. The question of what text P. may have been working from is also discussed there; but, in spite of circumstantial evidence for the special relevance of the Zürich Latin Bible (hereafter referred to as "Z."), it will appear from comparing various word-usages that P.'s vocabulary is often closer to that of the Roman Psalter ("R.Ps.") or Buchanan ("B.") than to Z.'s. See below, notes to ll. 47, 136, and Table of Comparative Vocabulary, p. 164.

3, 3: *conformatus.* The structural relation between the verses of the psalm and the lines of P.'s poem is as follows: verse (i), lines 1–7; (ii), 8–11; (iii), 12–18; (iv), 19–22; (v), 23–25; (vi), 26–28; (vii), 29–32; (viii), 33–36; (ix), 37–39; (x), 40–43; (xi), 43–45; (xii), 45–47; (xiii, xiv), 48–55; (xv), 56–61; (xvi), 62–66; (xvii), 67–70; (xviii), 71–73; (xix, xx), 74–83; (xxi), 84–86; (xxii), 87–89; (xxiii), 90–93; (xxiv), 94–102; (xxv), 103–7; (xxvi), 108–9; (xxvii), 110–11; (xxviii), 112–14; (xxix), 116–19; (xxx), 120–22; (xxxi), 123–25; (xxxii), 125–27; (xxxiii), 128–30; (xxxiv), 131–33; (xxxv), 134–40.

5, 6: *peregrinationem.* P.'s itinerary is discussed above, pp. 6–7.

6, 5: *ter maximo.* Literally "three times the greatest", but *ter* with a superlative was a common idiom for "very much the most ..." In this Christian context there may be an allusion to the Trinity. Cp. the triple invocation which characterizes the *Trisagion,* an ancient Christian hymn in which God is addressed three times (*tris*) as "holy" (*hagios*). It is also possible, however, that P. is translating the Greek title *trismegistos,* which was given to Hermes by the Gnostics of the third century A.D. who identified that deity with the Egyptian Thoth. Since Hermes was classically the patron god of travellers, this allusion would be particularly fitting for P.'s purpose.

Interest in the Hermetic tradition of establishing parallels and fusions between elements of Christian and pagan theology had been revived by the Renaissance neoplatonists. P. is likely to have encountered these ideas in his travels or his reading, and they do seem to have influenced some passages of *DNC*; see pp. 34/5 above, and notes to ll. 1, 19 below. The concept of the Holy Trinity was a particularly rich source for such speculation, as may be seen from Professor Edgar Wind's discussion in *Pagan mysteries of the Renaissance*, pp. 241–55.

8, 8: *Vautroullerius*. For the choice of Vautrollier, and his experience in printing this sort of material, see above, pp. 31/2.

AD ILLUSTREM ... HENRICUM UNTONUM / ADDRESS TO HENRY UNTON

προσφώνησις. P.'s precedent for using this word in a Latin context is Cicero himself, who writes to Atticus (13, xii, 3) that Varro has promised to make such a "dedication" to him (Cicero). He caustically wonders how long it will take to materialize. On this dedication to Henry Unton, see p. 30 above.

8, 16: *Pannonios Albionasque*. (*a*) P. uses the form for "people of Hungary" rather than "land of Hungary", because the latter would have produced the unwanted jingle of two successive "-as" endings. See note to l. 122 for his failing to avoid such an assonance elsewhere.

(*b*) Although *Albion* was an ancient name for Britain (cp. *DNC*, 133 and note to l. 242) the form *Albionae* does not occur classically. P. takes the "o" to be short, but we may note that in the declension of *Albion*, at any rate, the "o" is lengthened when a syllable is added.

11, 22: *tholo*. Literally, " ... if it will be allowed to hang my offerings from so great a dome", referring back to the classical practice, described by P. in the first few lines, of hanging votive gifts in temples. Thus Statius makes Tydeus say: . . . *figamque superbis / arma tholis, quaeque ipse meo quaesita revexi / sanguine* (*Thebaid* ii, 733–34).

PAEAN

1, 2: *seu spiritus .../ seu ... mens*. In this apparently casual disjunction, for which there is no precedent in the original psalm, P. touches on a vast topic of Renaissance philosophical controversy, only to pass over it. We have commented briefly above on some of the strands in contemporary speculation about the constitution and status of the human soul; cp. pp. 34/5 and *DNC*, notes to ll. 24, 50, 259. To the modern reader it may seem that P. is making no more than a familiar and conventional distinction between "soul" or "spirit", on the one hand, and "mind" or "intellect" on the other. Even if this were so, the distinction is made in a climate of theological opinion which cannot have failed to colour it, and the main contributors to which are worth tracing. But it is evidently not as simple as this, in fact, because the "intellectual" wing of the comparison is said to diffuse "life" (*vitam*) throughout the body's limbs, and therefore to fulfil a biological role which is not conventionally associated with intellect. And if *aura* is to be taken as "breath of life" (consistently with the derivation of *spiritus* from a verb meaning "to breathe"), then the "spiritual" part also is being treated as having a biological function. But the whole New Testament metaphor of the Holy Spirit as "breath of God" would no doubt come into this picture, the word *aura* corresponding exactly to the Greek *pneuma* used in that context.

Other treatments of the theme, which contributed to the contemporary climate of opinion mentioned above, may be noted by reference to their main exponents. Towards the end of the fifteenth century, renewed interest, especially at Padua, in the *De anima* reopened Aristotle's discussion of the unity of the "intellective soul" and culminated in Pomponazzi's reconsideration of the whole question, in the light of the original text and of subsequent interpretations by Aquinas, Averroes, Alexander of Aphrodisias and others. Naturally there is much concern with what we should now call the "body-mind" relationship; this is to be found in books 4 and 8 of his major work *De immortalitate animae* (Bologna 1516). But the most relevant book for our purposes is the first, where he argues that, corresponding to the three modes of cognition of which man is capable, he has three souls (variously dependent upon bodily functions) – the "vegetative", the "sensitive", and the "intellective". According to the internal balance between these soul-types, there will be three sorts of men, those few who have subjugated the vegetative and sensitive elements being "numbered with the gods". It is to these that the psalmist refers, says Pomponazzi, in the phrase "Thou hast made him but a little lower than the angels" (Psalm VIII, 6). P. seems to have some such elevated, and yet not unhuman, souls in mind when he uses in *DNC* the words *superi, iuventus* and *genii*; cp. esp. *DNC*, note to l. 91. As a general reference to Pomponazzi, see E. Cassirer, *et al.* (edd.), *Renaissance philosophy of man*, pp. 257–381.

Plotinus, with his Platonic background, has a rather confused discussion of man's "higher soul" and "double" nature in *Enneads* ii, 3, 9; but more striking is the contribution of that other great Platonist, Marsilio Ficino, whose commentaries and translations of the 1460s had made the later works of Plato more widely familiar. We comment elsewhere (esp. *DNC*, notes to ll. 50, 259) on the way in which his ontological hierarchy and doctrine of the soul's *appetitus naturalis* seem to influence P.'s expression now and again. But it is his stress on the difference between the soul's two functions of "will" (*voluntas*) and "intellect" (*intelligentia*), argued in the *De mente* of 1476, which is relevant here. The idea is that since the human soul occupies a middle place in the "orders of Being", coming third out of five, it strives both to make intellectual contact with members of the level immediately above itself and to enjoy, by means of the will, things of the immediately lower order; Ficino also uses *mens* for this "highest part" of the soul (cp. P.'s *pars ... melior*). And he devotes a section of his *De mente* to the relation between intelligence and will, on the one hand, and *vita* on the other. See E. Cassirer, *op. cit.*, pp. 198, 185–212; P.O. Kristeller, *The philosophy of Marsilio Ficino*, pp. 270–76; F.A. Yates, *The art of memory* (London 1966) pp. 151–7.

In spite of this lively Renaissance interest in the topic, it may be thought that the closest parallel is to be found in the non-Christian Epicurean tradition which Lucretius had expounded in the third book of *De rerum natura* (see p. 34 above). There we find his notoriously slippery distinction between *animus* and *anima*. The former seems to be treated as a part, or subsystem, of the latter; and the latter, though "spread abroad throughout the body", is subject to the authority of the former (which "we also call" *mens*) and which is relatively localized. *Animus* is therefore more concerned with intellectual control, and *anima* with sensation and emotion. However, the cause of life (*vita*) remaining in the body is neither of these directly, but the "seeds" (atoms) of air and heat (cp. *aura* in P.).

2, 3: *mens*. In the original text this is shortened to *mēs.* because the decorated initial of *Nunc* (1) makes ll. 2–4 start an inch inset from the left-hand margin and thus leaves too little space.

3, 5: *Dicamus*. For the same reason as above (previous note), this appears in the original as *Dicam'*.

9, 15: *amictu*. (*a*) The original reads a question-mark after this word, with another after *iubar* (10) not followed by a capital.

(*b*) The choice of word here agrees with Z., V. and R.P. against B.: see Table, p. 164.

11, 18: *convexo*. The bed in the simile would be curved in the sense of being vaulted or arched-in, in fact almost concave rather than convex. The word is applied in this way by Virgil to overhanging branches, etc.: *Classem in convexo nemorum sub rupe cavata / occulit* (*Aeneid* i, 310–12). Cp. also Ovid's *ignea convexi vis ... caeli / emicuit* (*Metamorphoses* i, 26–7).

11, 17: *cortina*. Although Ennius uses the word for the "vault of heaven" (according to Varro, *De lingua Latina*, 7) and *massa* (13) suggests a rather more solid fabric, the adjective *pendula* leaves little doubt that P. means a hanging curtain and not an inverted bowl (*cortina* can also mean "cauldron"). P. is here paraphrasing the psalmist's image of a solidly built room with an overhead canopy: "... who hast stretched out the heavens like a tent, who hast laid the beams of thy chambers on the waters" (R.S.V.). P.'s choice of a classically rare word here agrees only with Z., and the corresponding words in V., R.Ps. and B. also differ among themselves. This is the only instance of P.'s usage agreeing with Z. against all three other sources considered; P. would have been very unlikely to use this particular word here if he had been drawing only on those other versions. The other texts are more explicit than P. about the two separate parts of the structure envisaged, and his picture is comparatively unclear. For example, B. has: *Tu tibi pro velo nitidi tentoria coeli / et liquidas curvo suspendis fornice lymphas.*

12, 18: *Quae*. This may take up either *cortina* or *regia* (10), the structure of the simile not being entirely clear. At any rate, the two parallel clauses *Quae .../... aquis* and *massa .../ amni* serve to elaborate the "canopy" simile. This sort of balanced repetition is a feature, of course, of the poetic style of the Hebrew original (which P. echoes again in 41–2, 118–21, and 131–2).

13, 21: *massa*. Apparently in quasi-apposition to *cortina* with *pellucida* (14) having almost adverbial force. The idea seems to be that, at the extremes of its downward sweep (*in gyrum*), the "canopy" of heaven merges invisibly or transparently (*pellucida*) with the sea which surrounds the earth (*oceanus*, according to the classical cosmography). Perhaps the analogy is what happens "where the rainbow ends".

Just as A.H. censured P. for perpetuating in his verse certain aspects of pagan theology (*DNC*, notes to ll. 180, 225), so Richard Hakluyt might have been unhappy with this promulgation of cosmographical falsehood in the name of religion.

18, 27: *spaciaris*. See p. 26 above for comment on this sort of spelling. Other non-classical instances in *Paean* are *spacio* (103) and *moeror* (116).

19, *29: iussa iuventus* / ... *genii.* See *DNC*, note to l. 91. The passage being para-
phrased here (19–22) is translated in R.S.V. as "Who makest the winds thy
messengers, fire and flame thy ministers." P. says that the band of attendants etc.
(*iuventus*) who carry out God's orders (*peragit* ... *iussa*) in heaven are "immortal
spirits". This suggests that the problematic lines in *DNC* (90–2), where the same
words are involved, refer to those earthly "ministers" who are indeed spiritual (*genii*)
but not *immortales* in the same sense as the angels.

Both passages should probably be seen against the background of that neo-
classical theologizing which was so much a part of Renaissance humanist culture;
cp. note to l. 1 above.

25, *36: solidoque coercuit orbe.* If any further evidence were needed that P. was familiar
with Ovid's account, in *Metamorphoses* i, of the creation of the world and the pre-
history of mankind, it is provided by certain verbal coincidences in this *Paean* (cp.
DNC, notes to ll. 62, 94, 96). Thus Ovid has ... *circumfluus humor / ultima
possedit solidumque coercuit orbem* (30–1). P.'s very next line (26) ends in the same
way as does Ovid's l. 30; cp. also note to l. 34 below.

The picture which P. draws in lines 26–28 has some features in common with
that of Lucretius in *De rerum natura* (see p. 34 above). But the latter speaks of the
world originally being surrounded by *aether*, not *humor*, and there is no such correspondence of language as between P. and Ovid. Lucretius writes, *Sic igitur tum
se levis ac diffusilis aether / corpore concreto circumdatus undique flexit, / et late diffusus in
omnes undique partes / omnia sic avido complexu cetera saepsit* (v, 467–70).

34, *49: subsidere valles.* Cp. Ovid, *Metamorphoses* i, 43: *Iussit et extendi campos, subsidere
valles*; and Lucretius, *De rerum natura* v, 492f.: *Sidebant campi, crescebant montibus
altis / ascensus.*

41, *58: tumidi* ... *de montibus amnes.* Cp. note to l. 12.

43, *60: cruenta.* The final vowel here may be read as either long or short. The absence
of an accent in the original text is nothing to go by: the final "*a*" of *grata* (3),
though long, is not accented, while that of *Iussaque* (46), though short, is.

Taking it as long, in agreement with *caede* (as in the translation), prevents the
line from ending rather weakly with two short vowels and also allows to *de* the
force of "coming from". It also preserves an echo of a passage from Virgil where
Aeneas speaks of needing to wash in a river because he has just come away from
so much warfare and recent slaughter. Virgil's parallel phrase *caede recenti* occupies
the same place in the line as P.'s *caede cruenta*, and a force similar to that of *de* is
supplied by the prefix of *digredior*. The passage reads, *Me bello e tanto digressum et
caede recenti / attrectare nefas, donec me flumine vivo / abluero* (*Aeneid* ii, 718–20). Cp.
DNC, 82.

Reading the "*a*" of *cruenta* short, with *bestia*, produces the vivid picture of a
"blood spattered" animal coming to drink: cp. Virgil, *Aeneid* ix, 341 (quoted
below, note to l. 82). But when used in this sense classically there is usually a
plain ablative for the source of blood.

44, *61: Bestia* ... *onagri.* P.'s usage here coincides with that of both V. and R.Ps.
against B.: see Table, p. 164 below. The first impression of Z. nonsensically read
feras at this point, but subsequent printings corrected the slip.

45, *63: ales et* ... / ... *volucres.* P. expands (perhaps for the sake of the visual pun *ales* ...

altis) on the original Hebrew, which R.S.V. translates as "the birds of the air" and which other Latin versions except Z. render simply *volucres*.

45, 64: *altis / Frondibus assuetae*. Cp. *DNC*, 34–5: ... *ventis sublimibus aptae /* ... (*grues*).

47, 65: *mulcent*. P. follows B. in using this word in his expansion of the phrase "They sing among the branches" (R.S.V.): B. reads *Per virides passim ramos sua tecta volucres / concelebrant, mulcentque vagis loca sola querelis /*.

54, 75: *iumentis*. P.'s usage here agrees with V. and R.Ps. against Z. and B., who both have *pecus*; see Table, p. 164.

56, 78: *est*. The colon which the original reads at this point is the only mark stronger than a comma which that text has between the beginning of 52 and the end of 61.

57, 83: *nectar*. Nectar and ambrosia (see line 60) were the legendary nourishment of the Olympian gods. Perhaps there is a veiled reference here to the spiritual food of the Sacrament of the Last Supper. The doctrinal dispute over "transubstantiation" in this context had been a burning controversy among the reformers.

68, 92: *volucres*. P.'s usage here agrees only with R.Ps. against other versions, among which V. appears to specify "sparrows"; see p. 164.

68, 92: *genitiva cubilia*. P. seems to have hit on a wrong word here: by classical standards, *genitivus* (a variant of *genetivus* condemned by Lewis and Short) does not have the meaning he intends. Aside from its purely grammatical sense, it usually meant something like "innate" or "congenital", rather than "fertile" or "productive" as required here. In a classical idiom, therefore, P. should have used *genialis* or *genitalis*: a common phrase for the "marriage-bed" was *genialis lectus*, and Virgil refers to farmers sowing *genitalia semina* (*Georgics* ii, 324). But in mediaeval usage the respective roles of these three adjectives had shifted considerably, and *genitivus* had taken on more nearly the significance which P. gives it here. Thus the thirteenth century chronicler Matthew Paris of St Albans refers to a particularly unfruitful and disease-ridden year as *chronicarum infirmitatum genitivus*; see R.A. Browne, *British Latin selections* (Oxford 1954), pp. 96–8, 142.

Shakespeare was to adopt, some quarter-century later, the same circumlocution for "nests" in *Macbeth* (i, 6): "procreant beds"; the bird in question there is the "temple-haunting martlet".

70, 94: *Ciconia*. So the other versions except V., whose usage here is a transliteration of the Greek word for "stork" found in the Septuagint at this point. The Latin form is not classical and seems not to occur outside the Vulgate. See p. 164.

72, 97: *pavidi ... lepores*. The "timid hares" take the place of what the R.S.V. (verse xviii) translates as "wild goats". As can be seen from the Table (p. 164), other sources except Buchanan specify some kind of goat or deer, and it seems to be the Scotsman who first stresses the idea of timidity. He indeed mentions no particular animal at this point, but uses the adjective *timidus* and leaves the reader to supply, from the context, some noun for "animals". P. seems to have taken his cue from B., without checking against Z. or R.Ps. (which agree here), and gone off on a different zoological track.

73, 98: *histrix*. More classically spelled *hystrix*, this is another transliteration from Greek. Hebrew scholars are in doubt about exactly what animal is designated by the original at this point, and the Septuagint is also ambiguous. The word used in R.Ps. (another Greek transliteration) appears not to be classical, and V.'s is unscannable in hexameters. Both Z. and R.Ps. refer to some mouse-like creature; P. is closer to B. (and, unusually, to V.) in specifying an animal with spikes or quills.

74, *102: succedere coelo.* When Virgil ends a line thus in *Georgics* (iv, 227), the context is an allusion to the Stoic theory of souls going up to heaven after death; cp. note to l. 120 below.

82, *112: suasu vaesani.* The juxtaposition of these two words produces an echo of Virgil's description (*Aeneid* ix, 339–41) of a hungry lion ravaging a sheep-fold: *Impastus ceu plena leo per ovilia turbans | (suadet enim vesana fames) manditque trahitque | molle pecus, mutumque metu, fremit ore cruento.*

85, *115: soboles ... leonum.* Here P. agrees with B. alone in not using *catulus*, which would easily scan; see Table, p. 164.

90, *121: securusque animi.* Cp. l. 57 above.

90, *122: arma.* This military metaphor of the farmer's implements as "weapons" is to be found in Virgil (*Georgics* i, 160) who may have had it from Hesiod. The imagery was to be expanded in English verse by, for instance, Gray (*Elegy written in a country churchyard*, lines 57–58): "Some village Hampden that with dauntless breast / The little tyrant of his fields withstood ..."

109, *148: ceti.* An instance of P.'s word coinciding with B.'s alone. It is another transliteration from Greek, which accounts for the nom.plur. usually being spelled *cete* (as B. has it) and not as here. Thus Virgil speaks of *immania cete* (*Aeneid* v, 822).

114, *152: copia cornu.* There was a legend that a nymph fed the infant Zeus on goat's milk and that afterwards he gave her the horn of the goat, having bestowed on it the power of producing anything its owner wished. This was the *cornucopiae* or "horn of plenty", which became a frequent symbol of fruitfulness and abundance. Another version of the original myth is that the goat herself, Amalthea, suckled Zeus; see Ovid, *Metamorphoses* ix, 88.

117, *156: rerum natura.* At the time when P. wrote, Lucretius' great poem *De rerum natura* was only recently being recovered from oblivion. See p. 34, and note to l. 1 above.

120, *154: diae ... spiracula mentis.* The idea that man, and to some extent animals, are animated by a spark of the divine mind was popularized by Stoicism, a Graeco-Roman school of "philosophy" which was respected in Christendom. It was founded by Zeno of Citium (*floruit c.* 315 B.C.). The views of the Renaissance Platonists and Aristotelians on this topic of a "world-soul" (*anima, mens*; l. 120) infusing the whole of creation were very much in the air when P. was writing; cp. note to l. 1 above.

122, *163: honoribus orbis.* Assonances like this tend to be avoided in classical Latin verse except for special effect. Such an effect is gained, with the same syllable ("*or*"), by Virgil in his famous line about souls of the dead who are longing to be ferried across the river Styx: *Tendebantque manus ripae ulterioris amore* (*Aeneid* vi, 314). The suggestion of moaning and wailing in the sheer sound of the words is intensified by the "awkward" (and rather unusual for Virgil) elision, or fusion, of the final diphthong of *ripae* before *ulterioris*. (On the latter point see above, p. 26.)

130, *175: Immortale ... carmen.* One of the neatest of P.'s "golden" lines (so called because of the highly valued balance between adjectives and nouns), and strongly reminiscent of Virgil's *Ascraeumque cano Romana per oppida carmen* (*Georgics* ii, 176). Other such lines in the *Paean* are 36, 109; cp. 70, 81.

136, 181: *spiritus ... artus.* Cp. B.: ... *dum spiritus hos reget artus* /.

138, 184: *summe Deum.* The polytheistic implication here consorts ill with the imputa‑ tions of paganism that P. makes against the Roman Catholics in *DNC* 252–56. It is not to be found in the original psalm, though such survivals do, of course, occur elsewhere in the *O.T.* A.H. would have had something severe to say about P.'s imagery here (cp. note to l. 13 above).

140, 187: *Tantum.* We take *tantum* here to mean "only"; cp. *DNC*, 306. The sentiment seems to be: "only to you could such (extravagant) praise be accorded (without blasphemy), because you are the only one who merits it". B. also uses the word in this sense at this point: ... *tantum ille meas facilisque bonusque* / *accipiat voces* ...

TABLE OF COMPARATIVE VOCABULARY
(* indicates agreement with P.)

Verse	R.S.V.	Parmenius	Vulgate (V.)	Roman Psalter (R.Ps.)	Zürich (Z.)	Buchanan (B.)
2	garment	amictus, 9	*, vestimentum	*, pallium	*	tegmen
2	tent	cortina, 11	pellis	aulaeum	* ≠	tentoria
11	beast of the field	bestia, 44	*, agri	*	ferae	pecudes
11	wild asses	onager, 44	*	*	*	*
12	birds of the air	ales, 45–46 / volucres	— / *	— / *	— / aves	— / *
14	cattle	iumenta, 54	*	*	pecus	pecus
17	birds	volucres, 68	passeres	* ≠	aves	ales
17	stork	ciconia, 70	herodius	*	*	*
18	wild goats	pavidi / lepores, 72	cervus	ibex	ibex	timidi
18	badgers	histrix, 73	herinaceus	hyrax	mus / alpinus	echinus
20	beast of the forest	bellua, 82	bestiae / silvae	bestiae / silvae	ferae / sylvestres	fera
21	young lions	soboles / leonum, 85	catuli / leonum	catuli / leonum	catuli / leonis	leunculus / gens
26	Leviathan	ceti, 109	draco	Leviathan	balena	* ≠

P.'s vocabulary coincides more often with R.Ps. than with other versions; four of these agreements conflict with B., and four with Z. text. P. coincides uniquely with R.Ps., Z., and B. in three separate instances (marked ≠), but never agrees with V. against all other sources. Apart from exact verbal coincidences, there are two points (ll. 72, 73) where the idea expressed in P. is closer to that in B. than in the others. We have remarked in notes to ll. 47 and 136 two occasions when, in elaborating a phrase beyond what is in the original, P.'s wording closely resembles B.'s.

PART THREE

Stephen Parmenius to Richard Hakluyt
from the harbour of St John's, Newfoundland
6 August 1583

Ornatissimo viro, Magistro Richardo Hakluyto, Oxonii
in collegio Aedis Christi, Artium et Philosophiae Magistro,
amico et fratri suo

S ALVE. *Non statueram ad te scribere, cum in mentem veniret promissum litera-*
rum tuarum. Putabas te superiore iam Iunio nos subsecuturum. Itaque de meo statu ex
doctore Humfredo certiorem te fieri iusseram. Verum sic tibi non esset satisfactum.
Itaque scribam ad te iisdem fere verbis, quia nova meditari et συνονυμίζειν *mihi hoc*
5 *tempore non vacat.*

   Undecimo Iunii ex Anglia revera tandem et serio solvimus, portu et terra apud
Plemuthum simul relictis. Classis quinque navibus constabat: maxima, quam frater
Admiralii accommodaverat, ignotum quo consilio, statim tertio die a nobis se subduxit.
Reliqui perpetuo coniunctim navigavimus ad 23 Iulii, quo tempore magnis nebulis inter-
10 *cepto aspectu alii aliam viam tenuimus: nobis seorsim prima terra apparuit ad Calendas*
Augusti, ad gradum circiter 50, cum ultra 41 paucis ante diebus descendissemus spe
Australium ventorum, qui tamen nobis suo tempore nunquam spiravere. Insula est ea
quam vestri Penguin vocant, ab avium eiusdem nominis multitudine. Nos tamen nec
aves vidimus nec insulam accessimus, ventis alio vocantibus. Caeterum convenimus
15 *omnes in eundem locum, paulo ante portum in quem communi consilio omnibus veni-*
endum erat (idque intra duas horas) magna Dei benignitate et nostro gaudio.

   Locus situs est in Newfoundlandia, inter 47 et 48 gradum; divum Ioannem vocant.
Ipse Admiralius, propter multitudinem hominum et angustiam navis, paulo afflictiorem
comitatum habuit, et iam duos dysentericis doloribus amisit; de caeteris bona spes est. Ex
20 *nostris (nam ego me Mauricio Browno vere generoso iuveni me coniunxeram) duo*
etiam casu quodam submersi sunt. Caeteri salvi et longe firmiores. Ego nunquam
sanior.

   In hunc locum tertio Augusti appulimus: quinto autem ipse Admiralius has regiones
in suam et regni Angliae possessionem potestatemque vendicavit, latis quibusdam

To his distinguished friend and brother,
Mr Richard Hakluyt, Master of Arts and Philosophy,
Christ Church College, Oxford

GREETINGS. I was not intending to write to you at the time when
your promise of a letter came to mind. Last June you thought that you
would be following us, and I had therefore left word that you should be told
about my situation by Dr Humfrey: but this would not satisfy you. So
5 I shall write to you in almost the same words, because I have no leisure
at the moment for new ideas and different *façons de parler*.

In the end we actually set sail from England, belatedly, on June 11,
leaving port and dry land at Plymouth. The fleet consisted of five ships, the
biggest of which had been provided by the admiral's brother and separated
10 herself from us, for some unknown reason, on the third day. The rest of us
carried on sailing together until July 23, when visibility was obscured by
thick mist and we all took different courses.

We sighted the first land on our own on August 1, at about latitude 50°,
after we had gone down, a few days previously, beyond 41 degrees in the
15 hope of finding southerly winds, which however never blew for us at their
usual time. It was what your people call Penguin Island, owing to the
number of that sort of bird there. But we neither saw the birds nor reached
the island, because the winds were calling us elsewhere. And yet we all met
in the same place, a little way out of the harbour which had been planned as
20 our common destination (and that within two hours of each other), by the
great goodness of God and to our own delight. The spot is a place in Newfoundland, between latitudes 47° and 48°, which they call St John's.

The admiral himself has had somewhat the harder-hit company, because
of their large numbers and the cramped quarters of his ship, and he has
25 already lost two of them from dysentery: there is good hope for the rest. Of
our own men (for I attached myself to Maurice Browne, a young man of
high character), two were drowned in some accident: but the rest are safe
and a good deal more robust. I myself was never more healthy.

We put in to this place on August 3, and on the 5th the admiral took
30 these regions into the possession and authority of himself and of the realm of

25 *legibus de religione et obsequio Reginae Angliae. Reficimur hoc tempore paulo hilarius*
et lautius. Certe enim, et qualibus ventis usi simus et quam fessi esse potuerimus, tam
longi temporis ratio docuerit: proinde nihil nobis deerit. Nam extra Anglos, 20 circiter
naves Lusitanicas et Hispanicas nacti in hoc loco sumus: eae nobis impares non
patientur nos esurire. Angli, etsi satis firmi et a nobis tuti, authoritate regii diplomatis
30 *omni obsequio et humanitate prosequuntur.*

    Nunc narrandi erant mores, regiones, et populi. Caeterum quid narrem, mi Hakluyte,
quando praeter solitudinem nihil video? Piscium inexhausta copia: inde huc commeanti-
bus magnus quaestus. Vix hamus fundum attigit, illico insigni aliquo onustus est.
Terra universa montana et sylvestris. Arbores ut plurimum pinus: eae partim con-
35 *senuere, partim nunc adolescunt. Magna pars vetustate collapsa et aspectum terrae et*
iter euntium ita impedit ut nusquam progredi liceat. Herbae omnes procerae: sed raro a
nostris diversae. Natura videtur velle niti etiam ad generandum frumentum. Inveni
enim gramina, et spicas in similitudinem secales: et facile cultura et satione in usum
humanum assuefieri posse videntur. Rubi in sylvis, vel potius fraga arborescentia
40 *magna suavitate. Ursi circa tuguria nonnunquam apparent, et conficiuntur: sed albi sunt,*
ut mihi ex pellibus coniicere licuit, et minores quam nostri. Populus an ullus sit in hac
regione incertum est: nec ullum vidi qui testari posset. (Et quis quaeso posset, cum ad
longum progredi non liceat?) Nec minus ignotum est an aliquid metalli subsit montibus.
Causa eadem est, etsi aspectus eorum mineras latentes praese ferat.

45   *Nos Admiralio authores fuimus sylvas incendere, quo ad inspiciendam regionem*
spacium pateret: nec displicebat illi consilium, si non magnum incommodum allaturum
videretur. Confirmatum est enim ab idoneis hominibus, cum casu quopiam in alia nescio
qua statione id accidisset, septennium totum pisces non comparuisse, ex acerbata maris
unda ex terebynthina, quae conflagrantibus arboribus per rivulos defluebat.

50   *Coelum hoc anni tempore ita fervidum est ut nisi pisces, qui arefiunt ad solem, as-*
sidui invertantur, ab adustione defendi non possint. Hyeme quam frigidum sit, magnae

England, having passed certain laws about religion and obedience to the
Queen of England. At the moment we are regaling ourselves rather more
cheerfully and sumptuously. For you will surely have gathered, from considering the length of time we took, what sort of winds we have used and
35 how exhausted we were able to become. From now on we shall not go short
of anything, because apart from the English we have come across some
twenty Portuguese and Spanish ships in this place, and they, being no match
for us, will not allow us to go hungry. The English group, although strong
enough themselves and unthreatened by us, attend us with all deference and
40 kindness, respecting the authority of our letters patent from the Queen.

Now I ought to tell you about the customs, territories and inhabitants:
and yet what am I to say, my dear Hakluyt, when I see nothing but desola-
tion? There are inexhaustible supplies of fish, so that those who travel here
do good business. Scarcely has the hook touched the bottom before it is
45 loaded with some magnificent catch. The whole terrain is hilly and forested:
the trees are for the most part pine. Some of these are growing old and others
are just coming to maturity, but the majority have fallen with age, thus ob-
structing a good view of the land and the passage of travellers, so that no
advance can be made anywhere. All the grass is tall, but scarcely any differ-
50 ent from ours. Nature seems even to want to struggle towards producing
corn; for I found some blades and ears that resembled rye and they seem
capable of being adapted easily to cultivation and sowing in the service of
man. There are blackberries in the woods, or rather very sweet strawberries
growing on bushes. Bears sometimes appear round the shelters and are killed:
55 but they are white, so far as I have been able to make out from their skins,
and smaller than ours. I am not clear whether there are any inhabitants in this
area, nor have I met anyone who was in a position to say (and who could be,
I ask you, since it is impossible to travel any distance?). Nor do we know any
better whether there is any metal in the mountains; and for the same reason,
60 even though their appearance may indicate underlying minerals.

We made representations to the admiral to burn the forests down, so as
to clear an open space for surveying the area; nor was he averse to the idea,
if it had not seemed likely to bring a considerable disadvantage. For some
reliable people asserted that, when this had occurred by accident at some
65 other settlement post, no fish had been seen for seven whole years, because
the sea-water had been turned bitter by the turpentine that flowed down
from the trees burning along the rivers.

At this time of the year the weather is so hot that if the fish which are put
to dry in the sun were not regularly turned over they could not be prevented

moles glaciei in medio mari nos docuere. Relatum est a comitibus mense Maio sex-
decim totos dies interdum se inter tantam glaciem haesisse, ut 60. orgyas altae essent
insulae: quarum latera soli opposita cum liquescerent, libratione quadam universam
55 molem ita inversam ut quod ante pronum erat supinum evaderet, magno praesentium
discrimine, ut consentaneum est. Aer in terra mediocriter clarus est: ad orientem supra
mare perpetuae nebulae. Et in ipso mari circa Bancum (sic vocant locum ubi quadraginta leucis a terra fundus attingitur, et pisces capi incipiunt) nullus ferme dies absque
pluvia. Expeditis nostris necessitatibus in hoc loco, in Austrum (Deo iuvante) pro-
60 grediemur, tanto indies maiori spe quo plura de iis quas petimus regionibus commemorantur.

Haec de nostris. Cupio de vobis scire: sed metuo ne incassum. Imprimis autem,
quomodo Untonus meus absentiam meam ferat praeter modum intelligere velim: habebit
nostrum obsequium et officium paratum, quamdiu vixerimus. Revera autem spero hanc
65 nostram peregrinationem ipsius instituto usui futuram. Nunc restat ut me tuum putes,
et quidem ita tuum ut neminem magis. Iuvet dei filius labores nostros eatenus ut tu quoque
participare possis. Vale amicissime, suavissime, ornatissime Hakluyte; et nos ama.

In Newfundlandia apud portum Sancti Iohannis, 6. Augusti 1583.

Stephanus Parmenius Budeius,
70　　　　　　　　　　tuus.

70 from scorching. But the huge masses of ice out to sea have taught us how cold it is in winter. Some of our company have reported that in the month of May they were stuck for sixteen whole days on end in so much ice that some of the icebergs were sixty fathoms thick; and when their sides facing the sun melted, the entire mass was turned over, as it were on a sort of pivot, in such 75 a way that what had previously been facing upwards was then facing down, to the great danger of any people at hand, as you can well imagine. The atmosphere on land is moderately clear, but there is continuous fog over the sea toward the east. And on the sea itself around the Bank (which is what they call the place about forty miles off shore where the bottom can 80 be reached and they start catching fish) there is scarcely a day without rain.

When we have provided for all our requirements in this place we shall advance southwards, with God's help; and the more that is reported about the regions we are making for, the greater will our expectations be from day to day.

85 So much for us; now I want to hear about you. But I fear my wish may be in vain. But, above all, I would especially like to know how my patron Unton is taking my absence. He will have my ready respect and service as long as I live. I sincerely hope that this expedition of ours will be of some service to his own project. Now it remains that you should think me yours, 90 and so much yours that no one else is more so. May the Son of God prosper our efforts to such an extent that you also can take part. Goodbye, Hakluyt, my most delightful and distinguished friend: keep me in your affection.

Yours,
Stephen Parmenius of Buda

95 St John's Harbour, Newfoundland, 6 August 1583

To the worshipfull, Master Richard Hakluyt at Oxforde in Christchurche Master of Art, and Philosophie, his friend and brother

[THE HAKLUYT TRANSLATION, 1589]

I HAD NOT PURPOSED to write to you, when the promise of your letters came to my mind: You thought in June last to have followed us your selfe, and therefore I had left order that you should be advertised of my state, by Master Doctor Humfrey: but so you would not be satisfied: I will write there-
[5] fore to you almost in the same words, because I have no leasure at this time, to meditate new matters, and to vary or multiply words.

The 11. of June we set sayle at length from Englande in good earnest, and departed, leaving the haven and lande behinde us at Plymmouth: our Fleete consisted of five shippes: the greatest, which the Admirals brother had lent
[10] us, withdrew her selfe from us the third day, wee knowe not upon what oc-casion: with the rest wee sayled still together till the three and twentie of July: at which time our viewe of one another beeing intercepted by the great mistes, some of us sayled one way, and some another: to us alone the first lande appeared, the first of August, about the latitude of fiftye degrees, when
[15] as before wee had descended beyonde 41. degrees in hope of some Southerly windes, which notwithstanding never blewe to us, at any fitte time.

It is an Ilande which your men call Penguin, because of the multitude of birdes of the same name. Yet wee neither sawe any birdes, nor drewe neere to the lande, the windes serving for our course directed to another place, but
[20] wee mett all together at that place a little before the Haven, whereunto by common Counsell wee had determined to come, and that within the space of two houres by the great goodnesse of God, and to our great joy. The place is situated in Newfound lande, between fortie seven and fortie eight degrees, called by the name of Saint Johns: the Admirall him selfe by reason of the
[25] multitude of the men, and the smalnesse of his shippe, had his company somewhat sickly, and had all ready lost two of the same company, which died of the Flixe: of the rest wee conceive good hope. Of our company (for I joyned my selfe with Maurice Browne, a very proper Gentleman) two persons by a mischance were drowned, the rest are in safetie, and strong, and
[30] for myne owne part I was never more healthy. Wee arrived at this place the

third of August: and the fift the Admirall tooke possession of the Country, for himselfe and the kingdome of England: having made and published certaine Lawes, concerning religion, and obedience to the Queene of England: at this time our fare is somewhat better, and daintier, then it was before: [35] for in good sooth, the experience of so long time hath taught us what contrary windes wee have founde, and what great travell we may endure hereafter: and therefore we will take such order, that wee will want nothing, for we founde in this place, about twenty Portingale, and Spanishe shippes, besides the shippes of the Englishe: which being not able to matche us, [40] suffer us not to be hunger starved: the English although they were of them selves strong ynough, and safe from our force, yet seeing our aucthoritie, by the Queenes letters patentes, they shewed us all manner of dutie and humanitie.

The manner of this Countrey, and people remayne nowe to bee spoken [45] of. But what shall I say, my good Hakluyt, when I see nothing but a very wildernesse? of fishe here is incredible abundance, whereby great gayne growes to them, that travell to these partes: the hooke is no sooner throwne out, but it is eftsoones drawne up with some goodly fishe: the whole lande is full of hilles and woodes. The trees for the most part are Pynes and of them [50] some are very olde, and some yong: a great part of them beeing fallen by reason of their age, doth so hynder the sighte of the Lande, and stoppe the way of those that seeke to travell, that they can goe no whither: all the grasse here is long, and tall, and little differeth from ours. It seemeth also that the nature of this soyle is fitt for corne: for I founde certayne blades and eares in a [55] manner bearded, so that it appeareth that by manuring and sowing, they may easelie bee framed for the use of man: here are in the woodes bushe berries, or rather strawe berries growing up like trees, of great sweetenesse. Beares also appeare about the fishers stages of the Countrie, and are sometimes killed, but they seeme to be white, as I conjectured by their skinnes, and [60] somewhat lesse then ours. Whether there bee any people in this Countrey I know not, neither have I seene any to witnesse it. And to say trueth who can, when as it is not possible to passe any whither: In like sort it is unknowne, whether any mettals lye under the hilles: the cause is all one, although the very colour and hue of the hilles seeme to have some mynes in [65] them, we moved the Admirall to set the woods a fire, that so we might have space, and entrance to take view of the Countrey, which motion did nothing displease him, were it not for feare of great inconvenience that might thereof insue: for it was reported and confirmed by verie credible persons, that when the like happened by chance in another Port, the fish never came to the place

[70] about it, for the space of 7. whole yeere after, by reason of the waters made bytter by the turpentyne, and rosen of the trees, which ranne into the ryvers upon the firing of them. The weather is so hot this time of the yeere, that except the very fish, which is layd out to be dryed by the sunne, be every day turned, it cannot possibly be preserved from burning: but how cold it is in
[75] the winter, the great heapes, and mountaines of yce, in the middest of the Sea have taught us: some of our company report, that in May, they were sometimes kept in, with such huge yce, for 16. whole dayes together, as that the Islands thereof were threescore fathomes thicke, the sides whereof which were towarde the Sunne, when they were melted, the whole masse or heape
[80] was so inverted and turned in manner of balancing, that that part which was before downeward rose uppwarde, to the great perill of those that are neere them, as by reason we may gather. The ayre upon land is indifferent cleare, but at Sea towardes the East there is nothing els but perpetual mistes and in the Sea it selfe, about the Banke (for so they call the place where they find
[85] ground at fourty leagues distant from the shoare, and where they began to fishe) there is no day without rayne, when we have served, and supplyed our necessitie in this place, we purpose by the helpe of God to passe towards the south, with so much the more hope every day, by how much greater the thinges are, that are reported of those Countries, which we go to discover.
[90] Thus much touching our estate.

Now I desire to know somewhat concerning you, but I feare in vaine, but specially I desire out of measure to know how my Patrone Master Henry Umpton doth take my absence: my obedience, and dutie shall alwaies be readie towardes him as long as I live: but indeede I hope, that this journey
[95] of ours shalbe profitable to his intentions. It remayneth that you thinke me to be still yours, and so yours as no mans more. The sonne of God blesse all our labors, so farre, as that you your selfe may be partaker of our blessing. Adewe, my most friendly, most sweete, most vertuous Hakluyt: In Newfound lande, at Saint Johns Port, the sixt of August, 1583.

[100]   Steven Parmenius of Buda,
                                  yours.

COMMENTARY

Richard Hakluyt, *Principall navigations* (1589), pp. 697–99; *Principal navigations*, III (1600), 161–63. The opportunity has been taken here both to annotate the text of Parmenius' valuable eye-witness account of Newfoundland and to draw attention to the qualities of Richard Hakluyt as a translator, a side of his work much neglected. It is possible that he had been able to compare this letter with the almost identical one to Laurence Humfrey (see p. 168, ll. 2–3). If so the discrepancies between Parmenius' Latin and Hakluyt's English which we remark may arise from his trying to elucidate what he knew, from the other source, Parmenius wanted to convey.

1, 1 [1]: *Salve.* Hakluyt, and perhaps Parmenius too, shortened this to "*S.*"
1, 1 [1]: *statueram.* We take this to be an "epistolatory" pluperfect, reflecting an im-
    perfect at the time of writing. P. abandons the convention almost at once, but
    reverts to it at the start of l. 31, where *sunt* has become *erant*; see note. Hakluyt
    does not construe the usage in this way (although he must have been familiar with
    the device from the letters of Cicero), but translates *statueram* as a literal pluperfect.
2, 3 [2]: *superiore ... Iunio.* If Hakluyt had originally intended to occupy, on the
    Gilbert voyage, the role which Parmenius now had, he had been diverted first to
    the Bristol venture, where he had gone to assist Carleill (see above, pp.
    44–5), and then to a diplomatic appointment. For, by the time this letter was
    written, he was probably already preparing for his journey to France as chaplain
    and secretary to the English ambassador, Sir Edward Stafford.
3, 4 [4]: *Humfredo.* Parmenius' letter to Laurence Humfrey has not been found (nor
    indeed has any collection of Humfrey's correspondence).
4, 6 [6]: συνονυμίζειν. Parmenius shows off his Greek again, as in the title to *DNC*
    and the address to the dedicatee of the *Paean* (see pp. 25, 33). This is a made-up
    word which is presumably intended to mean "to write in synonyms" but we
    should expect the fourth letter to be *omega*, as it may indeed have been in P.'s
    original. The point is that, since there will be novelty neither in what he can
    think of to say (*nova meditari*) nor in the way he says it, this letter will come out
    almost word-for-word the same as the one to Laurence Humfrey.
7, 9 [9]: *frater Admiralii.* Hakluyt adds the sidenote *Dominus Ralegh* (Ralegh was not
    knighted until 1585). See above, pp. 45–6. Hakluyt's text omits the "d" from the
    second word.
8, 9 [10]: *subduxit.* See above, pp. 48–9; Edward Hayes in Hakluyt, *Principall navigations*
    (1589), p. 685; Quinn, *Gilbert*, II, 391, 396.

177

9, 11 [11]: *navigavimus*. See above, pp. 49–51. P.'s account of the progress of the *Swallow* can be compared with Hayes on that of the *Golden Hind* (Hakluyt, *Principall navigations* (1589), pp. 685–6; Quinn, *Gilbert*, II, 397–8).

11, 14 [15]: *paucis ante diebus*. Parmenius is quite explicit about the "few days", but Hakluyt ignores this qualifying phrase and translates only the adverb.

11, 14 [15]: *descendissemus*. When vessels sailing to Newfoundland could not count on easterly winds, they had to sail southwestwards towards the Azores, picking up the easterlies there and, farther west, the southerlies associated with the same pressure system. To sail down to 43°N. at least, then run along the latitude until within range of America and finally turn northwards, was quite usual; but it added to the length of the voyage, especially when it was necessary to go as far south as 41°. Edward Hayes (*Principall navigations* (1589), p. 685) confirms P.'s account: "We had winde alwayes so scant from West northwest, and from West southwest againe, that our traverse was great, running South unto 41 degrees almost, and afterward North into 51 degrees."

12, 16 [16]: *suo tempore*. The point is that the winds did not blow even at "their" (*suo*) usual time, which the expedition was trying to anticipate. As Edward Hayes says (*ibid.*): "About this time of the yere the windes are commonly West towards the Newfound land, keeping ordinarily within two points of West to the South or North, whereby the course thither falleth out to be long and tedious after June, which in March, Apriell and May, hath bene performed out of England in 22 dayes and lesse."

Hakluyt's "at any fitte time" seems to miss the force of P.'s phrase.

12, 16 [17]: *Insula*. Sidenote *Insula Penguin* (III (1600), 161, only). Funk Island, lat. 49° 45′ N., long. 53° 10 W.; the birds being Great Auk, *Alca impennis* Linn. (*Pinguinis impennis* (Linn.)), the original Penguin. The best summary account is in H.S. Peters and T.D. Burleigh, *The birds of Newfoundland* (St John's 1951), pp. 246–49; the classical one is S. Grieve, *The great auk or garefowl* (London 1885), and there is a detailed local study by Frederick A. Lucas, "The expedition to the Funk Island, with observations upon the history and anatomy of the Great Auk," U.S. National Museum, *Report for 1887–8* (Washington, D.C., 1890).

14, 18 [19]: *ventis alio vocantibus*. Hakluyt manages to extract from this, or read into it, "the windes serving for our course directed to another place". What it says is "the winds calling elsewhere".

17, 22 [24]: *divum Ioannem*. The large, enclosed, and sheltered harbour of St John's (lat. 47° 33 N., long. 52° 43 W.) had been since the early years of the sixteenth century the clearing house for much of the Newfoundland fishery, and, especially, the centre of the English industry. The following sources show better than modern surveys what the harbour was like before substantial occupation had taken place: Map of St John's Harbour and plan of Fort William, 1698 (B.M., Royal MSS, maps CXIX, 103) and Map of St John's Harbour and fortifications, eighteenth century (B.M., Additional MS 33231.II.14). See also pp. 51–62 above.

18, 23 [26]: *paulo afflictiorem*. Hakluyt takes it that Parmenius is using the comparative form to mean "rather" or "quite" rather than "more". But the qualifying *paulo* (which would otherwise be redundant) suggests that he means a literal comparative. Hakluyt may conceivably have known, from conversation with his friend, that he favoured this idiom of double-qualifications; but it seems more likely that P. is anticipating a comparison of Gilbert's crew with Maurice Browne's, which he goes onto in the next sentence, and perhaps (implicitly) with the rest of the fleet. See n. to l. 21 below for Hakluyt's treatment of another comparative.

19, 25, [27]: amisit. P. alone preserves these details of the Delight's voyage. The sick men were sent home in the Swallow.

20, 26 [28]: Mauricio Browno. On Browne see pp. 38–41 above.

21, 27 [29]: casu quodam. The accident (or perhaps better "incident") took place when some of the Swallow's men were engaged in robbery at sea (see p. 50 above). P.'s indefiniteness may be a deliberate attempt to draw a veil over a discreditable episode, about which he knew more than he cares to say. Certainly it conflicted with the idealistic picture of the expedition which DNC is concerned to create, and ill befitted the magnanimi iuvenes of whom he speaks there (line 237).

21, 28 [29]: longe firmiores. Hakluyt ignores both the comparative form and its qualifying adverb, translating the phrase simply "strong" (cp. note to l. 18 above). P. may mean that they are, paradoxically, "all the fitter for the voyage", or just that they are in better shape than the Admiral's crew. But the nunquam in the next sentence suggests that the comparison here is not directly with the state of Gilbert's men, but with their own state at a previous time.

24, 29 [31]: vendicavit. Details of the ceremony are given by Gilbert (S. Purchas, Pilgrimes, III (1625), 808; Quinn, Gilbert, II, 383); by Hayes and Peckham (Principall navigations (1589), pp. 687, 702; Quinn, Gilbert, II, 402–3, 444–5); and by Whitborne, A discourse (1620), pref., sig. C5 (Quinn, II, 427). For similar ceremonies see Quinn, Roanoke voyages, I, 94–95.

24, 31 [32]: latis ... legibus. Hakluyt expands again, "having made and published". Gilbert had power under his patent of 11 June 1578 (Principall navigations (1589), p. 678; Quinn, Gilbert, I, 191–92) to make regulations for territories occupied so that they "maye be as neare as conveniently maye, agreeable to the forme of the lawes, & pollicie of England".

25, 33 [34]: hilarius et lautius. In his account (Principall navigations (1589), 687), Hayes elaborates this point, and even provides the following "menu": "... we were presented (above our allowance) with wines, marmalads, most fine ruske or bisket, sweet oyles and sundry delicacies. Also we wanted not of fresh salmons, troutes, lobsters and other fresh fish brought daily unto us."

26, 34 [36]: qualibus ... simus. P. uses the perfect tense (in the subjunctive mood because of the indirect question), but his point is presumably that past experience (what they "have" used) will have taught them (docuerit) what the winds "are" like, and can be expected to be like; but see note to l. 27 below for a different interpretation. Hakluyt unnecessarily specifies "contrary" winds, where P. leaves the question open, and omits the note of futurity from docuerit.

26, 35 [36]: potuerimus. Hakluyt's translation, with its introduction of "hereafter", appears to mistake this perfect subjunctive (which directly parallels usi simus, l. 26) for the future perfect (which takes the same form) or even for the future simple poterimus. The point may be that, from their becoming firmiores and sanior on the voyage (l. 21 above), one of the things he has learned is the physical resilience of the human body. We must not suppose, just because he knew Latin and Greek, that P. had never taken any exercise in his life, but he is agreeably surprised to find that men can get quite so exhausted and still recuperate.

27, 33 [35]: *ratio*. Hakluyt takes this to mean the "experience" of the voyage. But the word has strong connotations of "calculation", or "explanation", and it is surely analytical reflection on what happened (their experiences, observations, recordings etc.) which will yield the information P. mentions – partly about the world and partly about themselves. In either sense, however, the clause *certe ... docuerit* does not quite fit in with the rest of the paragraph about how well they are now pro-visioned etc. But if we lay more stress on the tense of *docuerit* and supply *te* (instead of *nos*), the point then becomes: (you can appreciate how much we are enjoying this) because (*enim*) you will have gathered, from considering how long we took to get here (*tam ... ratio*), what poor winds (*qualibus ventis*) we had and how tired and bored with ship's food (*fessi*) we have been able to get (*esse potuerimus*). The translation follows this line. They had taken, of course, some 50 days over a voyage that was often done, as Hayes says (see note to l. 12), in less than half that time. Hayes also elaborates the point that their temporarily sumptuous fare is all the more enjoyable for being unexpected.

27, 36 [37]: *proinde ... deerit*: Hakluyt's expansion of this phrase ("and therefore ... nothing"), and especially the introduction of "therefore" which is not in the Latin, suggests that the taxing of the Spanish and other vessels was a deliberate provision against the rigours and deprivations of future voyages. All that P. says is that their temporary improvement in standard of living (*hilarius ... lautius*) is connected with the intimidated solicitude of the Spaniards and others; see p. 52 above.

28, 37 [38]: *Lusitanicas*. Before 1580 the Portuguese had worked closely with the English in southeast Newfoundland (for example, in supplying them with salt). But, since the Spanish conquest of that year, their position had become dubious as English hostility to Spain grew: see pp. 208–9 below for Spanish reactions to Gilbert's issue of a passport to one of the Portuguese vessels. The Spaniards were mainly Basques who, with their fellow Basques of the French southwest, had their main fishing bases on the south and west shores. Breton and Norman ships fished on the Grand Banks and on the east coast to the north of St John's. No passports issued to French or Spanish vessels have so far been found. On the significance (or lack of it) for the French of Gilbert's visit, see C. de la Morandière, *Histoire de la pêche française de la morue*, 1 (Paris 1962), 267–68.

29, 38 [39]: *Angli*. The English fishermen, who obeyed Gilbert's orders while he was present, had no desire to be tied by his laws or leases: but his authority was, in their eyes, legitimate. They had regarded Richard Clarke as a pirate when he had entered Renews harbour with the *Susan Fortune* in 1582 and seized Portuguese ships there, and had sent testimonials to assist the deprived Portuguese fishermen in their case in the High Court of Admiralty. See *DCB*, 1, 228; p. 51 above.

31, 41 [44]: *erant*. Another epistolary past tense (see note to l. 1), which Hakluyt renders as if P. had written *manent*: "... remayne now to be spoken of." P.'s use of the gerundive (*narrandi*), with its connotation of "ought", reflects his awareness that there were conventions about the order in which the Elizabethan traveller was expected to report on various topics.

32, 42 [46]: *solitudinem*. It is important to compare Parmenius with Hayes. The latter is all enthusiasm (*Principall navigations* (1589), pp. 688–90; Quinn, *Gilbert*, II, 404–408) and the former mainly pessimistic scepticism. It was clearly not wholly "desolate" from the point of view of vegetation, but the absence of inhabitants and organized cultivation makes it seem empty enough. The Golden Age tranquillity for which P. looked (see *DNC* 134–56) was that of amicable human activity, not that of emptiness. He would have appreciated the point of Tacitus' bitter epigram on the so-called *pax Romana*: "where they make a desert they call it peace" (*Ubi solitudinem faciunt pacem appellant*).

32, 43 [46]: *copia*. The contrast of abundant fish and unpromising land helps to explain why fishermen came to St John's each summer but did not settle there, for the bare headlands which enclose the harbour mouth overshadow the vegetation on its western side. At the same time, to Europeans familiar with the shores of northern Europe, including the northern shores of the British Isles, Newfoundland in summer would look both familiar and attractive.

33, 44 [47]: *fundum attigit*. P. specifically mentions the hook touching the bottom, but Hakluyt alters this to "is thrown out" in his translation. Perhaps Hakluyt knew that cod-fishing is done with the hook about a fathom above the sea-bed, and wished to forestall a charge of ignorance against his friend; see H.A. Innis, *The cod fisheries* (New Haven 1940), p. 48. In fact, however, the hook is often (if not usually) allowed to touch the bottom and then withdrawn the appropriate distance. P.'s point is thus that the fish bite even before the hook is at its optimum level.

34, 45 [48]: *Terra universa*. Sidenote "In the south side of Newefound land, there is store of plaine and champion Countrey, as Richard Clark found." This refers to Clarke's description of the southwest coast, which he reached after escaping from the wreck of the *Delight* (*Principall navigations* (1589), p. 701; Quinn, *Gilbert*, II, 425–26). The name is written "Clarke" in III (1600), 161; this spelling has been adopted in *DCB*, I.

36, 49 [52]: *liceat*. The picture of an ageing natural forest is a good one, and again emphasizes the quality of P.'s observation. On the mainland, frequent burning of undergrowth by the Indians to facilitate hunting kept many of the forests open.

36, 49 [52]: *Herbae*. Canada, Department of Northern Affairs and National Resources, *Native trees of Canada* (5th ed.; Ottawa 1958), provides a popular introduction to the tree cover. There is no handy general introduction to the flora of Newfoundland. M.L. Fernald, "The contrast in the flora of eastern and western Newfoundland," *American Journal of Botany*, V (1918), 237–47, is illuminating; the distribution maps of a number of plant species which he prepared for the Labrador Boundary Commission are in the Newfoundland Provincial Archives; his edition of *Gray's manual of botany* (8th ed.; New York 1950) is authoritative for Newfoundland. There are many Newfoundland locations in Henry A. Gleason, *The new Britton and Brown illustrated flora of the northeastern United States and adjacent Canada*, 3 vols. (New York 1958).

38, 51 [55]: *secales*. The recognition may not be specific. Rye-like grasses which he could well have seen are American Beach-grass, *Ammophilia brevilulata*, Fern., and Lyme-grass or Strand-wheat, *Elymus arenarius villosus*, both common on beaches and sand in this area (Fernald, *Gray's manual of botany*, pp. 139, 159).

39, 52 [56]: *assuefieri*. H.1600 reads *assuescere* (as against the 1589 text), but the passive form is more appropriate because the point is that, with suitable treatment, the grass may *be made* to accept cultivation.

Hakluyt is again over-specific in translating *cultura* as "manuring".

39, 53 [57]: *fraga*. What are now the three separate genera *Ribes* (currants and goose-berries), *Rubus* (blackberries, raspberries), and *Fragaria* (strawberries) were not clearly distinguished in the sixteenth century. Thus William Bullein, *Bulleins bulwarke of defence* (London 1562), f. 24v., says: "There be twoo kindes of Strau-berries the greater and the lesser. Also *Rubus idaeus*, a lowe Bramble, called *Ribes*, or *Raspes*, a berie like to the Strauberie." Hakluyt is thus being legitimately cautious in translating "bush-berry". P. may in fact be describing blackberries, which, when red, can be mistaken for raspberries: *rubus* (l. 39) is at any rate classical Latin for the blackberry. However, J.B. Jukes reported that, on the shores of Con-ception Bay, "after a fire in the woods, the first thing that covers the ground is a luxuriant growth of raspberry-bushes" (*Excursions in and about Newfoundland*, I, London 1842, 44–45). The common raspberry in Newfoundland is now Red Raspberry, *Rubus strigosus* Michx.: see Gleason, *New Britton and Brown*, II (1958), 316; Fernald, *Gray's manual of botany* (1950), p. 821. The collective species of the blackberry is *Rubus canadensis* Linn. (Gleason, II, 314). On the varieties of (and the confusion that could arise about) Newfoundland berries even in the eight-eenth century, see Aaron Thomas, *The Newfoundland journal, 1794*, edited by J.M. Murray (1968), p. 146.

40, 54 [57]: *Ursi*. Here, most probably, Polar Bear (*Ursus maritimus* Linn.), rather than Common Bear (*U. americanus* Linn.).

40, 54 [58]: *tuguria*. Spelled *tiguria* in 1584 text (see Plate 11 above). Hakluyt is doubt-ful about the existence of huts on shore so he takes it to refer to the fishermen's "stages". P.'s word (deriving from a verb meaning "to cover") is used by Varro, Cicero, and Virgil for huts or cottages: if P. had wanted to refer to the "flakes" and (or) "stages" (whose purpose was to support rather than to cover), he could have used a word for, e.g., "platform". His evidence is both direct and plausible. Storage huts for barrels and gear, cookhouses, light shelters for men tending the drying fish, conceivably shelters for boats left on land over the winter are all likely structures, though only stages and drying-flakes are clearly indicated elsewhere for the sixteenth century. The picture in 1663 includes huts as essential items in the summer fishery's equipment: "As soon as we resolve to fish there," says James Yonge, "the ship is all unrigged, and in the snow and cold all the men go into the woods to cut timber, fir, spruce, and birch being here plentiful. With this they build stages, flakes [described elsewhere as "boughs thinly laid upon a frame, like that of a table, and here the fish dries"], cookroom, and houses. The houses are made of a frythe of boughs, sealed inside with rinds [bark], which look like planed deal, and covered with the same, and turfs of earth upon, to keep the sun from raning [ruining?] them. The stages are begun on the edge of the shore, and built out into the sea, a floor of round timber, supported with posts, and shores of great timber. The boats lie at the head of them, as at a key. ..." (James Yonge, *Journal*, ed. F.N.L. Poynter (1963), pp. 56–8).

The Latin version of Jacques Le Moyne's account of Laudonnière's expedition to Florida in 1564 uses this word *tiguria* for the very substantial timber cabins which the Frenchmen built, with the aid of the Indians, in their base camp. See Theodor de Bry, *America*, part ii (Frankfurt 1591), 8, and plates 9–10.

41, 56 [60]: *Populus . . . sit.* Parmenius had expressed considerable interest in the American Indian (*DNC*, 52–63): he is now clearly disappointed to find no trace of the Beothuks. His negative evidence is borne out by Hayes (*Principall navigations* (1589), p. 689; Quinn, *Gilbert*, II, 406), who says: "In the South parts we found no inhabitants, which by all likelyhoode have abandoned those coastes, the same being so much frequented by Christians: But in the North are savages altogether harmlesse." Sylvester Wyet, however, in 1594, had his mooring ropes cut by them no further away than Placentia Bay (*Principal navigations*, III (1600), 195; VIII (1904), 165). Most of the information on the Beothuks is collected in J.P. Howley, *The Beothuk Indians of Newfoundland* (1915).

The brackets are lacking from the rhetorical question in *H.1600*, p. 161.

44, 60 [64]: *aspectus.* Where Parmenius says simply "the appearance", Hakluyt expands to "the very colour and hue". Since so much of the view towards the interior was obstructed by trees, Parmenius' *aspectus* must be from the appearance of distant unwooded summits or from the look of nearby shore rocks, islets, and cliffs.

44, 60 [64]: *mineras.* Hakluyt translates "mynes", rather than "minerals". However, in contemporary usage, "mines" often referred to places where minerals might be, rather than actually were, worked. The survey made in the days following by Gilbert's mineral expert, Daniel, provided some evidence of a more concrete character on the mineral resources of the island (cp. Hakluyt, *Principall navigations* (1589), pp. 689–90, 692, 694; Quinn, *Gilbert*, II, 408, 414, 417–18). Gilbert obtained sufficient evidence to convince him that minerals, including silver, were present in quantity; but all his specimens went down with Daniel himself in the *Delight*. The earliest full account of what minerals were readily available is, apparently, Joseph B. Jukes, *Excursions in and about Newfoundland*, 2 vols. (London 1842). He found superficial traces of minerals in various regions: near Port de Grave a bed of "concretionary bog-iron ore"; at Signal Hill, Shoal Bay, south of Petty Harbour (a spot conceivably accessible to Gilbert's metallurgist), "a small vein of sulphuret [apparently galena crystals, natural lead ore] and green carbonate of copper"; Catalina, "abundance of iron pyrites . . . often . . . mistaken for copper or gold"; and in igneous rocks generally, "metallic ores . . . as bunches, nests or strings disseminated through the rocks" (*op. cit.*, I, 44–5; II, 347–8, 237, 203–4).

45, 61 [65]: *authores.* In autographing the copy of *DNC* which he presented to Brumen, Parmenius used the spelling "*autor*" (see Fig. 6, and cp. Fig. 7). This may suggest that what we have here represents Hakluyt's or his compositor's preference, although spelling was sufficiently flexible in the sixteenth century for us not to be able to assume that Parmenius would have been consistent. Both forms are regarded by Lewis and Short (*A Latin dictionary*) as less correct variants of the classical *auctor*. The distinctly informal construction of accusative and infinitive with this word has a precedent in the correspondence of Cicero and Atticus (ix, 10, 5).

48, 65 [70]: *septennium.* It is possible for the destruction of forests along a river to have an adverse effect on fishing off the estuary, but it is not likely to be as a result of resin-pollution. The "floor" of a pine forest tends to act like a sponge, temporarily retaining moisture from rainfall and letting it seep gradually into the stream. If the trees are destroyed, this property of the river basin is lost, so that in some rainfall conditions drainage becomes irregular and the watercourse varies between extremes of flooding and drought. This is in turn disrupts the supply of micro-organisms and other nutrient substances from inland to fish out at sea. It is generally recognized that something like this has happened off the north coast of Africa, but it may be argued that climatic conditions are and were relevantly different in Newfoundland. (We are indebted to Mr T.H. Owen of University College, Bangor, University of Wales, for this explanation.)

50, 68 [72]: *Coelum*. Sidenote: "The great heate of the sunne in summer". Beginning only in the later nineteenth century, modern systematic weather records may not give a wholly accurate picture of the climate of southeast Newfoundland as it was in the sixteenth century. The mean average temperature at St John's for August is 59.8°F., which is moderately high for England if not Hungary. The maximum recorded temperature for the island is 97°; see U.S. Hydrographic Department, *Newfoundland sailing directions* (8th ed.; Washington, D.C., 1958).

50, 69 [73]: *arefiunt*. For the techniques of dry-salting cod, see C. de la Morandière, *Histoire de la pêche française de la morue*, I (1962), 161–84; *The journal of James Yonge*, ed. F.N.L. Poynter (1963), pp. 55–56; E.R. Seary *et al.*, *The Avalon peninsula of Newfoundland* (1968); G.T. Cell, *English enterprise* (1970), p. 4.

52, 72 [75]: *glaciei*. Ice blocked the harbours from January to early May, and sometimes, with on-shore winds, well into June. After a hard winter, icebergs could be seen floating freely (though melting fast) throughout June and into July and even, very occasionally, into August (cp. R.G. Lounsbury, *The British fishery at Newfoundland 1634–1763* (New Haven 1934), pp. 7–10, and the literature cited in Canada, Department of Mines and Technical Surveys, Geographical Branch, *Selected bibliography on sea ice distribution in the coastal waters of Canada* (Bibliography Series, no. 18; Ottawa 1957).

53, 73 [78]: *orgyas*. The word P. uses here for a "fathom" is a transliteration from Greek and occurs only in Late Latin (A. Souter, *A glossary of later Latin to 600 A.D.*, 1949). Sixty fathoms (360 feet) is not an unusual depth for an iceberg. This description of them is graphic, even though at second hand, and indicates that P. was good at collecting materials from others as well as recording what he saw.

57, 77 [84]: *Bancum*. For sketch-maps of the Banks see Innis, *Cod fisheries* and Louns-bury, *The British fishery*. Canadian Hydrographic Service, Chart 4490, shows the greater part of the Banks.

58, 79 [86]: *ferme*. Hakluyt ignores P.'s qualifying "almost".

59, 80 [86]: *pluvia*. P. is correct. Both sea-fog (*nebulae*, l. 57), from the mixing of cold and warm currents and the melting of ice, and rain frequently envelop the Grand Banks and the Newfoundland coasts: Lounsbury, *The British fishery*, pp. 17–18; Robert Perret, *La géographie de Terre-Neuve* (Paris 1913), pp. 116–27.

59, 82 [87]: *progrediemur*. Parmenius is anxious to leave what is, for him, an inhospit-able shore; his interests are already focused on the lands to the southward. For the course of their short and ill-fated voyage *in Austrum*, see pp. 58–9 above.

63, 87 [92]: *Untonus*. Hakluyt uses "Umpton" (as did John Dowland later in *La-chrimae* (John Windet, 1604): "Sir Henry Umptons Funerall"). The family more often used "Unton" (cp. Nichols, *The Unton inventories, passim*); but Henry was not consistent, sometimes signing himself (as in Lambeth MS 654, f. 136, January 1596) "Henry Vmpton."

64, 88 [94]: *quamdiu*. *Principal navigations*, III (1600), 161, reads *quandiu*, a spelling which is classically less frequent but not less "correct".

65, 89 [95]: *instituto*. The meaning of *institutum* is invariably abstract in classical usage (as it is in the Preface to *DNC*, line 26), and would thus refer here to Unton's "purpose" or "intention" in fostering exploration, the arts and learning. But by the sixteenth century the word may have acquired a transferred, concrete sense much nearer that of its English derivative. In which case it would mean his circle of associates and protégés, no less than fifty-seven of whom (including Laurence Humfrey) contributed literary memorials to *Funebria . . . D. Henrici Untoni* (Oxoniae, excudebat Iosephus Barnesius, 1596). See also above, pp. 10–11.

66, 91 [97]: *eatenus*. The 1600 reprint reads *hactenus*, which suggests (inappropriately) that the point referred to has already been reached.

67, 91 [97]: *participare*. Hakluyt's expansion "be partaker of our blessing" is curious. It is natural to supply a pronoun-object referring back to *labores*, in which case P.'s prayer seems clearly to be that God may bless their activities even to the extent of enabling Hakluyt to come and join in "them". Cp. line 2, *putabas te . . . nos subsecuturum*.

67, 92 [98]: *et nos ama*. Hakluyt's translation ignores P.'s valedictory request.

68, 95 [99]: *Sancti Iohannis*. Though literally "St John", we may follow Hakluyt's "Saint Johns" as already the accepted English form of the name for the famous harbour.

68, 95 [99]: *6 Augusti*. If one of the English fishing vessels on which Gilbert felt he could rely was returning home at once, it is likely that P.'s letters to Humfrey and Hakluyt, together with Gilbert's of 8 August to Sir George Peckham (Purchas, *Pilgrimes*, III (1625), 808; Quinn, *Gilbert*, II, 383), and, no doubt, something from Maurice Browne, went together to England. Or it may be that they, and others like them, had to wait for the *Swallow* and so were appreciably delayed. The "sable alive" which Sir Humphrey sent to his brother Sir John (Quinn, *Gilbert*, II, 407) was apparently never delivered. Hakluyt may not have received his letter before he left England, and it may have had to follow him to Paris. He first cited it in "A particuler discourse," completed in the early autumn of 1584 (see p. 67 above, and Fig. 1).

APPENDIXES

1 The Longleat Letters of Maurice Browne

The letters of Maurice Browne, preserved at Longleat, Wiltshire, record one half of a very interesting and lively correspondence, the other half of which, that by John Thynne, the younger, to Browne, has wholly disappeared. In this selection only those parts directly relevant to the plans of Sir Humphrey Gilbert for an American colonizing expedition, on which they form a commentary, are extracted. Browne was a rapid writer who rarely re-read what he had written and he will be found to have made a number of mistakes. A minimum of re-punctuation, and a small amount of consequent re-capitalization, have been found necessary.

1: 6 July 1582   MAURICE BROWNE TO JOHN THYNNE[1]

Good Master Thynne my meaninge was that yow should have receyved awnswere from me of your letters, had George Walker called for my letter as I thought he would have donne. Sence the writinge thereof I have had conference with one of excellent knowlegd and expeairence in navigatione and in Cosmographye[2] about the goodnes and exactnes of the sea carde yow sent me.[3] It is very exacte for all the hethermost partes of Europe Asia and Affrica which are usually Navigable, but for America it is though[t] very exact from the Strayght of Magellan all alongest the cost of America till yow come to [blank] degres a[t] this side the lynne to the north warde but further to the northward there is noe certeynety in it, which at this day is

1 Longleat, Thynne Papers, v, ff 204ʳ–205ᵛ. From "Tower Streate." Extract.
2 This might very well have been Dr John Dee who was at this time actively concerned with American cartography.
3 The chart had apparently belonged to John Thynne the elder, d. 1580, and had been lent to Browne by his son. An old Portuguese world chart, it might seem from the description to have belonged to the period c. 1550–70. Dr R.A. Skelton did not think the particulars precise enough for identification. It was possibly a map of the type of the Lopo Homem map of 1554 (see L. Bagrow and R.A. Skelton, *History of cartography*, 1964, Plate M, which omits the southern part of South America and gives no help with the supposed Northwest Passage).

189

most desired to be knowen and discovered. Further for all the cost within the
strayte of Magellan of Peru and Mexico, it is altogether uncertaine. The cause of
theise uncerteyne[4] is, for that, at such tyme as this Carde was made (which is longe
sence) it was not lawfull for the Portingall (where this carde was made) nor for any
spaniard by A lawe made by theise kinges that none of there subjectes should
discover any further of any part of America then so many degres northward as
afore sayed.[5] And for all the costes within the strate of Magellan in Mare del Sur
theise have bin of purpose made uncerteyne because the spaniard nowe and Portingall in tymes past wold not have any to discover those partes for that they dowbted
that the traficke they had in the former places discovered wold be quiet over growne.
And ther did never stand in so greate feare thereof as now the kinge of spayne doth,
who wold be lord of the hole world, but I trust se the day when he shall have litill
to doe in those partes. He was never so well shott at by England as now he is. For
by the meannes of Sir Frauncis Drake who hath discovered all that part of America
within [the] straite of Magellan in Mare del Sur as also by meannes of such
excellent Navigators as are at this tyme on the seaes (god send them good successe)
as likwise such as intent to interprise the lyke with as much speed as conveniently
as they can, noe dowbt by godes good successe but all that North and North West
part of America with the portes and passages thereof into Mare del Sur wilbe
discovered, accordinge at the Opynione of the best learned in Cosmography and
Navigatione doth judge and write. But for this carde (which I thancke yow) I have
I am gyven to understand is as necessarye A carde as one can have, for to confer
with other newer cardes, and for Navigation very good, but very uncerteyne
whether the north west part of America with the portes and Ilandes lyinge alongst
that cost be placed true; and howe they lye in latitude is most uncerteyne. I am
promysed with as much speid as it can be procured to have one of the newest
cardes[6] and at such convenient tyme as I can have, I will apply my tyme in the

4 "uncertainties."
5 In 1573 Philip II's ordinances had codified earlier provisions on discovery, conquest,
and settlement (*Colección de documentos inéditos para la historia de España*, ed. Fernández de
Navarrete *et al.*, 112 vols., Madrid, 1842–95, XVI, 142–8). They provided that for
new discoveries a licence must be obtained from the Crown. Cp. C.H. Haring, *The
Spanish empire in America* (1947), pp. 11–12; H.R. Wagner, *Spanish voyages to the
Northwest coast of America in the sixteenth century* (1929), p. 168: Thus Richard Hakluyt:
"I have hearde my selfe of Merchants of credite that have lived long in Spaine, that King
Phillip hath made a lawe of late that none of his subjectes shall discover to the North-
wardes of five and fortie degrees of America." (*Divers voyages*, ed. D.B. Quinn, 1967,
Sig. *2ᵛ.) Browne probably got his information from Hakluyt's book which had come
out in May and which may have been, in part at least, the cause of his interest in
America.
6 The only map of North America which was new at the time of writing and available

studdy of Cosmography, and the art of Navigatione. And if oure Voyage do not procede as it is dowbted[7] when you come to London at [f.204^v] Mychelmas next (by the grace of god) we will device to have somme convenient tyme notwith-standing all your great affayres and cawses, to have an excellent fellowe who dwelleth here at London to read Cosmography and to instruct us and to make us learned in the art of Navigation,[8] that with the more easines we may come to the full knowlege thereof by experience. And it will be A very good exersice to spend the werisome winter withall, and much for oure profittes, and estimatione.

As concerninge your man Lowe your Trumpitter let hym not lose any good voyage that may be for his profitt,[9] but only this I will desire you, that at what tyme it shalbe my good hap to take any such voyage in hand, I may (If he be in England in good health) make account to have hym with me and he shall be in account with me for your sake. in the meanne tyme I will pleasure yow with A younge youthe which was with me the last sommer at the Ilandes of Tersera. And soundes upon the dromme all the poyntes of warre every[10] well not the like in England of his yeeres beinge but xij yeeres of age. I had hym here at London with me ever sence before Ester and have kept hym all this while at stable[11] with the excellentest fellowe in all London accounted to make hym perfectt one the dromme, and he makes me beleve the boye will prove excellent in his profession. Besides the mony I have bestowe[d] one his master for his teachinge he hath bin very profittable to his maister for that he hath gayned hym money at playes and dyvers other showes. Truly the boy hath a very good witt and A good conditioned boye. My cosen Thomas Baker, and lykewyse Sir Thomas Perrott have bin very earnest with me to have hym, but I have reserved him him for yow to be your page if so yow please, trustinge that at such tyme as I shall proceide one my voyage I shall request hym of yow for that tyme. And if I may here from yow I will send hym to yow.

in London, so far as can be ascertained, was Michael Lok's which was prepared, with Robert Thorne's, for *Divers voyages* and had appeared in May. It is by no means certain that all copies were supplied with both maps (the Longleat copy, see p. 195 below, lacks both maps) so that Browne may have seen one not containing Lok's map and have been promised one separately. Of course an older map (e.g. one by Ortelius or Mercator) may have come on to the English market at about this time.

7 Browne had been in the Azores and may have been involved in a plan for a further voyage to assist Dom Antonio, perhaps that of William Hawkins the elder, who had links with the Portuguese claimant. Hawkins' American expedition did not leave until November by which time Browne was committed elsewhere (J.A. Williamson, *Hawkins of Plymouth*, 1949, pp. 217–20).

8 Either Thomas Harriot or Thomas Hood is suggested above (p. 39) as his possible instructor.

9 See below, pp. 199–200.

10 "very."   11 "table."

2: 20 August 1582 MAURICE BROWNE TO JOHN THYNNE[1]

Good master Thynne:

I receyved your frindly letter sent by your boye also my geldinge and old broke your nagge for that I am uncerteyne of my cominge doune to yow which wilbe I trust now within this fower dayes. I have bin stayed here sence sir Rowlandes[2] departure from london, by A matter that happyned within three dayes after which I thought of as much as of the Pope of Rome, as the proverbe. I had thought veryly the next day after Sir Rowlandes departure from London to have Ryden into Essex and within two dayes after to have begonne my jorny towardes yow. But what man determyneth god disposeth at his goodwill and pleasure and I trust all for the beast. But godes will be donne. Master Smith[3] and I beinge together it was told us that Sir humfry Gylbert was at his house in London, who I assure yow I had thought had bin at sea towardes his voyage of A newe discovery a moneth before as it was certeynly told me his was. And I thought veryly he was not in London, bu[t] beinge certyfed of the certeyntie thereof by one who desco[vered?] Master Smythes and my good worde unto Sir Humfry in his behalf, where upon Master Smithe and I went to Sir H. Gylbertes howse where we found hym. And after we had disspached with him for that we came. We fell to discoursinge with Sir H. of his voyage. and in that discourse kept o[n] so longe, that he wolde neades have us staye to supper, a[t] which tyme we were with hym we had noe other talke, but of the frutfullnes and great riches that was in that country where he intendeth by godes assistance to goe unto. We both lykede so well of his discourses, and of the large Awthoritie that the Queene hath graunted hym for the furtheraunce of his voyage that our awnswere was we were sory that we had not knowlege of those matters in tyme for if we had we wold have made provysion to have accompanyed hym, and so we departed from hym, not thinckinge to have senne hym any more before his departure. The next morninge Sir Humfry sent his man very early unto our lodginge, very earnestly desiring us to suppe with hym that nyght. Within A whyle after our cominge to hym we fell into oure former discour[s]es, where upon he shewed us his graunt from her majestie under the great seale of England, further

---

1 Longleat, Thynne Papers, v, ff. 212ʳ–213ᵛ. Postscripts omitted.
2 Sir Rowland Heyward, John Thynne's father-in-law, one of the most prominent City merchants.
3 This may have been Customer Thomas Smythe but it is more likely to have been his son, then about twenty-four years of age and so a contemporary of Maurice Browne. He was to be the Sir Thomas Smythe who was so prominent in the East India and Virginia companies. He was probably also "my cosen Smith" whom Browne was trying in July 1582 to persuade to come to Longleat with him (f. 203)

he shewed us the card of the whole cuntry[4] where he ment to settill hym self, which country was the last yeere with great commodities there in discovered by A cunning Navigator which Sir Humfry sent thether, which man goeth as chefe pylat for his voyage,[5] and offereth to bringe Sir Humfry and his company (by godes good assistaunce) into that parte of the country, (which lyeth in the North west of America) which is the most richest place for gold, silver, and pearle, as also for all frutfulnes of the soyle, and a boundannce of all kind of wylde cattell and beastes necessary for meannes vse for victuall as also for great profitt and in lyke sort for other frutes trees, and woodes, in which countrye are aboundannce of goodly freshe ryvers replenyshed aboundantly with all kinde of freshe fyshe. But which is the greatest he is veryly of opynion, that there is A passage that way by the west in to the sowth sea, which will prove the greatest matter of importaunce for the wealth of the state of England that can be in the world. For the wealth, and fructfulnes of the country aforesayd he offereth to aprove true upon the losse of his lyfe, and for the passage there is as great lyklyhode as can be. All which is confirmed by one Davy Ingram,[6] who was left seven yere sence, by master Hawkinges with aboue three score more in the gowlfe of Mexico & there set a land in the sowth part of America. This Davy Ingram with two more in his company only determyned to travell towardes the North of America, hopinge that way to have come to newe found land, where in the tyme of the yere he hopped to have found englyshe shipes there, and so to have come into England, they traveled throwght all the West of America, and travellynge toward the north, he had passage over A great ryver above twentie leages over, in A kind of bote of that country called a *Canoas*. It is thought this is the Ryver of May[7] one the North side whereof he travelled in that country above Three monethes, in which country he found most Aboundannce of all the wealth frutes beastes and commodities aforesayed, in more aboundannce then in all the travell he passed throught the country which laye one the west side of that Ryver of May, where he travelled eyght monethes. In the hole his travell one foote was eleven monethes. This man hath lykwyse confessed as aforesayed first to Sir Humfry and next unto my Master who hath his confessione in writing, And

4 Sir Humphrey Gilbert's chart is reproduced in Quinn, *Gilbert*, II, 374.
5 Simão Fernandes in 1580 took the *Squirrel* to New England and back, but he was not to accompany Gilbert in 1582 having sailed with Fenton in April.
Nothing is known of a successful voyage in 1581 nor of a master pilot who was to take Gilbert back across the Atlantic in 1582. It seems not unlikely that Browne has got confused about names and dates, but it is not impossible that Gilbert was deliberately misleading him about Fernandes. (See Taylor, *Fenton*, p. 157.)
6 David Ingram's tale is mentioned above, p. 40, and some account of it is to be found in *DCB*, I, 380–1.
7 St. John's River, Florida.

offereth, with godes assistaunce sending hym lyfve to bringe Sir Humfry to these places of wealth and all other commodities upon ye losse of his lyfve, if they prove not true when [he] comes to lande.[8]

The particularyes of all theise matters I am throwghly instructed. Sir Humfry performes this voyage at his owen charge saving three or fower of his frindes which in all, beinge but certeyne comodities of smale price, in all their venture is not A Hundreth pound. Sir Humfry hath two shippes & three pynesses; he caryeth About A eleven score men with him, and meaneth to plant hym self there, and to contynewe there this yeere. But After he hath bin there a whyle and had under-standinge of the wealth and state thereof: He intendeth to send backe one pynyse (by godes grace) into England frayt with the comodities of the country, as also one to declare the state of the country unto the Qweenes Maiestie, and her Pryvy counsell. My Master is the only counsellour in England that Sir humfery hath made acquanted with his voyage,[9] and he is the only man Sir Humfry doth relye hym self one. The Qweene hath promysed Sir Humfry At what tyme he doth retourne newes of his landinge and of the commoditie of the country her Maiestie will send hym as much shippinge and men, and other necessary thinges for his strenngh and furtheraunce of his intentes as he will write vnto her Maiestie for to send hym.[10] My Master hath protested by his honor to further the same and to se it performed. Here upon Sir Humfry told my master that he wanted, A sufficient man to be the messenger (as he trusted in god) of the good newes that should send to her Majestie, and his honour. And desired my master to healp hym with A man for that purpose. In this meanne tyme not knowinge of this matte[r] Sir Humfry very earnestly moti[o]ned me of this voyage and to undertake this matter. I lyked very well of the voyage, as also of his most frindly offer, only relyuing[11] my self upon the good liking and perswatione of my Master thereunto. Where upon Sir Humfry presently wrote unto my master requestinge my masters lawfull favore if he thought me sufficien[t] to discharge such A matter to goe with hym to be the man to retorne (as he trusted in god) with happye newes. My master presently talked with me and showed me of his lykinge of this voyage and of his likinge for me to goe this voyage and of the profitte in divers respectes that might there[by] redound unto me. I told my master that I holy relyed my self upon the lyki[ng] of his honor, and

8 Ingram accompanied Gilbert in 1583 and survived the voyage (Quinn, *Gilbert*, II, 452).
9 Sir Francis Walsingham, Secretary of State, and Gilbert's principal supporter at Court.
10 This perhaps is the source of Gilbert's optimism on his return voyage (Quinn, *Gilbert*, II, 418) which it has hitherto been possible to dismiss as wishful thinking.
11 "relying"?

that I was very glad to undertake the voyage in r[es]pect his honor did favore the same. Here upon my master used me with very honorable wordes and countinaunce and presently my master wrote A letter to Sir Humfry in my behalf. I wold I were such A one as he commended me vnto Sir Humfry for and howe well he liked of and therewithall desired hym to have an especiall care of me – so yow se how I am disposed of. We are ready and shall take shippinge at Sowthamton or else I thincke rather at Plymoughe in Devonshire. So that within this fower dayes (god will[inge]) I will beginnge my jorny towardes Longleat to se yow before my departure. And if [you wi]ll be A venturer,[12] ether in mony or corne, as wheat especially or whyt pease, I will be your factor for them to your commoditie I trust in god. I pray yow let me request of yow A crasbowe and arrowes. Thus Have I declared unto yow how unlooked for, god I trust to somme good ende hath stayed me from yow all that while. Wherein the old proverbe is verified that many thinges chaunce betwene the cuppe and the lyppe, but godes will be donne, and I trust in god that he hath appointed this for the best, A meanne for me After ward to lyve with yow quietly, to enjoye your frindship and company which I protest before god I wyshe only.

And so comending my self holy to yow to my good gouernes A[nd] litill Tom. Tell my governes she is the only cause [of my] travilinge for that she will not provyde me A clogge and shackell to make me kepe home lyke A stayed man. The only fault is hers. I was longe Agoe redy to have bin bestowed, if it had pleased her upon A wyfe And A very excellent good one. My suertie will not fayle to stand bound for me, that I wylbe awnswerable *Ad omnia quare.*

And so hartely I committ yow to god. Tower streat this xxth of August 1582

Your faithfull lovinge frinde

M Browne

12 The Longleat copy of Hakluyt's *Divers voyages* was quite possibly sent down by Maurice Browne to John Thynne in the first flight of his enthusiasm for Gilbert's venture, though it contains no inscription. It lacks the maps, which may not have been present in all copies. Further, the Zeno narrative (a fabrication) has been torn out, the first page, which backs up the last page of Verrazzano's letter, being heavily scored through in ink, and "Finis" inserted in the same ink at the end of Verrazzano. The hand is very like that of John Thynne as seen in marginal notes to letters (in Thynne Papers, v) which he received, though a single word is too little for certainty to be possible. Beside the list of things which the elder Hakluyt recommended Pet and Jackman to take by way of the Northeast Passage to Cathay are pencilled crosses, "Taffeta hats", "the large mappe of London" and "A painted Bellowes" being singled out (Sig. I2^v, I3^r, I4^v). It is conceivable, if quite unprovable, that these were made when Browne (during his visit to Longleat) and Thynne were considering what trade goods they should adventure in the Gilbert voyage.

3: 21 [September] 1582   MAURICE BROWNE TO JOHN THYNNE[1]

Good master Thynne:

I am Apon further occation offered me to use your friendship and credit, at this present, which at my last departure from yow vpon your most frindly offere, I told yow that if occation where that myght be for my profitt I wold carve[2] your frindship, of which I never dowbted. So it is y^t for my better adventure and credit, I wold request your letter of credit vnto William Staveley[3] to whom I did your commenda⸗ tions, And told him yow thought your self much beholdinge vnto hym for the wynne he sent yow of credit, and that A bout Mychelmas yow wold se hym satisfied. The man is an Alderman of Sowthampton of great wealth And A very honest man And the best howse keeper in the citie of A comminer. He told me he always was much beholdinge to Sir John Thynne, And did always serve hym of wynne. He told me that my Lady Thynne and master Rawley[4] deales hardly hym about wynne they had longe sence. Thus having speach with hym I told hym I was to use your frindship and credit, About Sowthampton to the Valewe of twentye poundes, for provysion of corne about Sowthamton for this my Voyage. And I told hym he myght shewe me great pleasure if he wold shewe me so much favore as to take your bill for twentie poundes for half A yeere, to the which he awnswered me very frindly that he wold accept of your bill or letter for as much as he was worth very honestly. Wherefore in respect aforesayde I desire your bill or letter creditt for twentie poundes, for half a yere or till oure lady day. And god willinge accordingly I will take order for the savinge of yow harmeles. And as yow shall here by greatly benefitte me so will I if, god make me able, as I trust in god he will requit it assuredly, in the meanne tyme contynewe as thanckfull and lovinge A mynde towardes yow as yow can wyshe A frind to bearere [sic] yow. And Thus desiring god to prosper your procedinges and myne to his honor, with my hartye commenda⸗ tions to my good Governes litill Tom & lastly your self I committ yow all to god. This xxj^{th} day At nyght 1582

Your faythfull lovinge frind ever

M Browne

---

1 Longleat, Thynne Papers, v, ff. 238^r/-9^v. Extract. The failure to complete the date is typical of Browne's haste in writing. If Sir Humphrey Gilbert's ship, mentioned here as delayed, reached Southampton about October 16 or 17 (see p. 199 below), then the month is apparently September.   2 "crave."

3 William Stavely was an alderman and one of the mayor's assistants in Southampton, 1575–80 and at the time of his death, having been mayor 1580–1; *The third book of remembrance of Southampton*, ed. A.L. Merson, III (Southampton 1965), 63–5.

4 Carew Ralegh, Walter Ralegh's brother and Gilbert's half-brother, had married Lady Thynne, John's father's widow.

POSTSCRIPT

The shipp which Sir humfry Gylbert loked for to come from the Dounes hath bin by most contrary wyndes kept backe, but At this present the wynd serves very well beinge all this day easterly but nowe flatt east so that if god contynewe this wynd but two dayes the ship will Aryve in Hampton roode, by the grace of god.

After my departure from yow that nyght I lay at Rumsey six myles from Hampton, where I fell into reckning with my pursse, And I found contrary to my expectatione, that sence my first departure from yow to hampton, of the mony receyved of yow that thereof I have spent xl*s*, And I thincke I shall About thend of this next weake ryde unto Devonshire, six score myles from Hampton,[5] to increase my charge and expense, wherefore if yow have any spare mony to sende me it will stand me steade and be very welcome.

We have very certeyne newes from Lyme by A ship that Aryved there from the Iland of Tersera, that the Kinge of Portingall hath had most wounderfull good successe a gaynst the Kinge of Spayne[6] ...

4: [September] 1582   MAURICE BROWNE TO JOHN THYNNE[1]

I doe not here but that master Norrice most wonderfully scaped withowt any great hurt his soldyers had A very great spoyle of the eneymy, And Master Norrice so gallan[t]ly did gather his men together and did behave hymself in so good order, that after the conflict and all ended, Monshire and the Prince of Orrannge and the chefe of the citie did receyue hym with all the honor that might be,[2] Monshire gave hym for rewarde A Thowsand poundes, which presently Master Norrice gave his gentilmen a soldyers. All theise ill successes that happens towardes the Kinge of Spayne, makes the most for oure voyage & for oure quietnes that may be which make Sir H. Gylbert glad and all his company, godes will be donne.

The plage increseth in London there died the last weake 160 of the plage god of

5 The object was to join the expedition when it left Dartmouth, which had been appointed for a rendezvous after leaving Southampton.
6 Browne's optimism was unfounded. His report on Terceira has been omitted, as has his account of Norris's behaviour at Ghent (see next letter).

---

1 Longleat, Thynne Papers, v, f. 236ʳ–237ᵛ. As the Norris episode is mentioned in a postscript to the previous letter, we may date this late in September.
2 John Norris's gallantry at Ghent on 29 August is well documented (*Calendar of state papers, foreign, 1582*, pp. 295–6, 400, 420). The letter is valuable as showing Browne's strong anti-Spanish leanings and his attempt to link up Gilbert's voyage with the events in the Netherlands as equally directed against Spain. "Monsieur" is the Duc d'Alençon.

his mercye seace it, The terme is adjorned.[3] I have letters from London since my cominge from yow that the plage is very hott in fraunce, and that they make tentes in the feyldes for the sicke. god be mercifull unto us & them to. Thus have yow all the newes I here And my self yow shall have ever your fayfull and lovinge freind

M Browne

I send my man to Bristowe to cause all my thinges I have there[4] to be brought to Sowthamton.

[Addressed]

   To the worshipfull assured good freind
   Master Iohn Thynnes Esquier

[Endorsed]

   M. Browne to M^r. 1582.

5: 1 November 1582 MAURICE BROWNE TO JOHN THYNNE[1]

Good Master Thynne, I had thought longe sence to have written unto yow could I had A messenger to my mynde, to have signified vnto yow of the recept of your letter to Master Staveley in my behalf. The same nyght I receyved your letter Master Staveley fell sicke sodenly being by the water side of A deade palsey, and within fower dayes after died, so that I never delyvered your letter and I made fension of my desire.[2] Yow have lost the best frind of A townnesman in Southampton, where he lyved with the love and likinge of all that knewe hym and his death greatly lamented. Sence the death of this man I haue dealt with one master Richard Godarde one of the substantialest marchauntes in Southamton,[3] who maryed one master Heyers dawghter of Wilshire. And she doth knowe yow. Master Godard is

---

3 The progress of the plague in and around London in September and October (*Calendar of state papers, domestic, 1581–90*, pp. 70, 73, 75–6), may have been one of a number of factors which held Gilbert back from sailing in the autumn of 1582.

4 We do not know why Browne's baggage should have been at Bristol. Perhaps he had expected to begin an earlier voyage (see p. 191 above) from there.

---

1 Longleat, Thynne Papers, v, ff. 233^r–234^v. Extracts.

2 This does not make sense: he probably intended to write "I never made mension of my desire".

3 Richard Goddard's career as a local official can be followed in *The third book of remembrance of Southampton*, ed. A.L. Merson (Southampton 1952–65), 3 vols. He had been steward in 1575–6, water-bailiff in 1576–7, and was to have been mayor for 1583–4 (*ibid.*, III, 62–3). As Browne wrote "Thomas" and crossed it out before writing "Richard" he may not have known Goddard well.

willinge to pleasure me in supplyinge my wannt if yow will write your letter of credit unto hym wherfore I pray yow in such sort as yow wrote your letter unto master Staveley (which by this bearer I send yow). Write the like to master Godard in my behalf addinge not only corne but also any other necessarye thinge which I shall wannt to that somme which yow please to set doune for the which god willinge I will take order yow shall be noe loser if yow can increase the somme to twentie poundes. Sence the cominge of Sir Humfry Gylbertes ship to Sowth-ampton, which was fortnyght sence there hath bin such foule weather till this fyve dayes past that men could not worke on her nether could she take any of her ladinge. The maior of Sowthampton and the Burgesses doe venture with Sir Humfry about 300^{ll} such good likinge have they of his proceidinges And he doth incorporate the company of adventurers with hym the staple for ever to be kept at Sowthampton.[4] I trust in god we shalbe redye to depart within this 8. or 9. dayes. I wold have bin with yow or this but oure departure hath bin so often tymes deferred and all for the betteringe of oure voyage. And I trust in god yeat will have good successe to the benifitt of all Englande.

Yow shall understand of oure procedinge as often as I can fynd A messenger to send to yow. After our departure from Sowthampton we shall touche at Dartmouth and I thincke we shall stay senyght there so that I judge it will be 3 weakes before we shall depart from England. We are almost pursse penilesse, but I dowte not the lowe ebbe will have as hye a flowde, which god graunt if it be his will. I pray yow let me intreat yow to perswade your name[5] Lowe[6] to goe with me in the company of Sir Humfry, And shall retornne with me, I dowt not by godes grace, to his very great profit and he shall after be more able to lyve in your service with conntynaunce. Yf yow speake but A worde to hym I knowe he will goe, and for such matters as he hath in lawe or in controversy by your good meannes there may be good order taken notwithstandinge Lowes absence, and also his wyfe may be by your frindship provyded for in his absence. In sendinge hym with me I veryly thincke that yow cannot doe A thinge more for his benifit, and here after more inablyed every way to do you service. If he come to Dartmouth to Sir John Gylbertes[7] in Devonshire, he shall there have Sir Humfry Gylbert, which is the best place for hym to come to, and whether he shalbe very welcome. I have written to Lowe to perswade hym

4 The agreements between Gilbert and the town of Southampton were sealed on 2 November, when £500 was recorded as having been adventured by Southampton men, Richard Goddard being down for £40 (Quinn, *Gilbert*, II, 313–35).
5 "man."
6 See p. 191.
7 Sir John Gilbert's house, Greenway, was near Dartmouth. Sir Humphrey Gilbert intended his fleet to call at Dartmouth.

(with your good likinge) to goe this voyage. If he be here within this 7 or 8 dayes he shall have Sir H. here at Sowthampton. If you can healp Sir H. with A good fremason he will gyve hym interteynment to his contentment.[8]

I resieved A letter from Capten Ricardes from the iland of Tersera he hath hym hartily commended to yow and to his cosen your wyfe. He writes me nothing at large of the proceadinges of the Kinge of Portingal, but only that the Frenche men were overthrowne by the K. of Spaynes flete.[9] ... Here is noe other newes.

Thus desiringe yow ever to account me most myndfull of all your frindship with my most harty commendations to your self and good mistris Thynne my only good Gouernes and litell Tom. I comite yow to god. Sowthampton this first of November 1582

Your assured faithfull frind

M. Browne

[Addressed]

To the worshipfull his very good frind Master Iohn
Thynne esquier at Longleat in Wilshire
dd/this

[Endorsed]

Mr. Brownes lettre 1° Novembris 1582

6: 17 December 1582 MAURICE BROWNE TO JOHN THYNNE[1]

Good Master Thynne I receyved your most freindly letter wherby I vnderstand how greatly yow have bin mysinformed of the proceydinges intent & dealinges of Sir Humfrey Gylbert & his company. The Lyngeringe here yow write of, god hath bin the only cause of, as All those which hath had occasion to marke the wyndes can to their great charge to[2] well testify the same, the lyke tempestious and stormy weather contynewinge this fower monethes Sowthwest hath not by the most

---

8 The bringing of a mason with the expedition might suggest Gilbert proposed to build a post and leave men behind at this destination.
9 The Spanish admiral Santa Cruz had defeated the French under Strozzi in the decisive battle of the Azores on July 25–6, new style. A further passage on the Azores is omitted. For Richards see pp. 38–9 above.

---

1 Longleat, Thynne Papers, v, ff. 231ʳ–232ᵛ. Sir Humphrey Gilbert's letter, which follows, is written on the second page of Browne's, before the address leaf.
2 "so" is most probably meant.

Auntiauntes men of this Towne heretofore bin seen. But at this present Sir H. is ready to set sayle, & I trust god hathe cleared the heavens of All stormes and now will send us large wyndes in the North, & east to bringe us to the place we desire to Aryve at wherein godes will be donne to his honour & glory. There was never greater expectations and good hope conceyved of this voyage by her Majestie and those of her counsell which deale therein then At this present. There is great preparation of A present supply to be sent After Sir H. by certen consortes gentilmen of great account. Of all matters here, And of all the proceydinges of this voyage, this gentilman Master Stowghton[3] A master of Art and A very learned preacher who doth gooe with Sir H. can at a large asserteyne yow. he is my very frend of whose company I take great comfort. I pray yow let hym be very welcome to yow. Thus beinge redy to goe A ship borde, and to hawsth sayle towardes Dartmought. I ever pray to god for your prosperous eastate. I wold longe sence have certyfyed yow how master Richard Godard hath accepted of your letter very freindly and I have as it doth apeare, under my hand tha[t] I have receyved Tenne poundes in lynine cloth of his credit. If yow have occation to deale with any marchaunt of Sowthampto[n] yow cannot deale with a more honester & A substantiall marchaunt. Thus commendinge my self holye to your frendship and to my good governes, And Tom. I committ yow to god, desiringe all to to [sic] pray to god to blesse us And send us mery meetinge. Sowtha[m]ton this 17th of December. 1582.

Your assured faythfull freind, noe man more

M Browne

I pray yow send Lowe your Trumpyter to Sir John Gylberte by Dartmought.

[Addressed]

To the worshipfull my estemed good freind
Master John Thynne esquier at Longleat, Wilshire.

[Endorsed]

Mr Browne. 17° Dec' *1582*

3 The Reverend Mr Stoughton was apparently John Stoughton. John Stoughton, M.A., appears in the Buttery Books of Christ Church (information from Dr J.F.A. Mason) on 25 December 1579, in a list which includes Hakluyt. He is also most probably the man celebrated in William Gager's catalogue of the masters and students (i.e. fellows) of Christ Church, 29 September 1583, in which Richard Hakluyt appears (B.M. Additional MS 22583, f. 63v). He would therefore have come under Hakluyt's influence and could well have been inspired by him to join Gilbert's company though he evidently became discouraged and did not sail with him at the end. Another man of the same name had entered Christ Church in 1551, graduated B.A. in 1553, and was vicar of Godalming, Surrey, 1553, and Felpham, Sussex, 1559, dying in 1598, so that there is a slight possibility of a confusion between the two men. (Cp. the entries in Joseph Foster, *Alumni Oxonienses*, IV, 1892, 1432.)

7: 17 December 1582   SIR HUMPHREY GILBERT TO JOHN THYNNE[1]

good master thyn I commend me moste hartely vnto yow and to your wyeffe as to the daster of a deyd mother that I louyed and honerid mytche,[2] for your soundery commendations I dow moste hartely thancke yow. for soundery mens folishe opineons either of my Jorne, or of my longe abode in Hampton, or of my geuynge over of the Jorne, or of any dyshonest course that I shoulde mean to rune. I answer yow as my freynde, to tell them from me, that I nether caer for ther lykynges nor myslykynge but if any of them shall daer to Injure me at my retorne, I will answer them or sonner if that they will saye it to my faese whom am boeth as honest and as worshipfull as the beste in this land of my callynge and lesse I esteym not of my selffe.[3]
and so faer yow well as my good Frend. Hampton the 17 of desember 1582.
                    Yours hoelly
                    H Gylberte

8: 19 December 1582   MAURICE BROWNE TO JOHN THYNNE[1]

Good Master Thynne I pray yow pardon me for the stay of your boy Edward, for this two dayes hath him so extreme fowle weather, as Sir Humfrey Gylbert hath not bin able to goe aborde his ship till this day, and of purposse I stayed hym to bringe the certeynty, of Sir H. intent to depart from hence (god willinge) with the wynd to carry his shipes to Dartmought. Untill which tyme Sir H. is determyned not to come, or at the lest lye owt of his ship a shore, so that we only depart when it shall please god with a good wynd to carry us from hence. This last nyght Sir H had a messenger from Sir George Peckham and others of his good freindes that there is dyvers good shipes preparinge to follow Sir H, As A newe supply to assist hym in this Action. My master with all the meannes possible doth advaunce the same, Sir H. will not stay for any, but I doubt not but within one moneth after our arryvall on that cost where we (god willinge) determyne to land to have A eyght or nyne sayle of very good ship[s] well appoynted for defence. In the meanne tyme we will commit oure selves to god, and ever after ...[2]

1 Longleat, Thynne Papers, v, f. 231ᵛ. On the verso of the first leaf of the preceding letter. Gilbert's spelling and his hasty writing are characteristic of him.
2 Nothing is known of Gilbert's relationship to Sir Rowland Heyward's late wife.
3 The letter, not hitherto noticed, gives a typical example of Gilbert's impetuous and violent reaction to criticism.

1 Longleat, Thynne Papers, v, ff. 233ʳ–3ᵛ. Extracts.
2 The determination of Gilbert on a winter sailing if possible shows he was now willing

Further the cause of stay of your footeman was to conduct master Stowghton to your howse, who told me at his departure he wold ryde to or three myles owt of the way From this town is³ cominge to your howse. The boy was here on sonnday at dynner. Thus desiringe yow contynually and in lyke manner my good Governes to pray for my good successe as for hym who doth wyshe yow both all happynes & felycitie. And so I commend my self howly to yow both and us all to god. desiringe hym to send us a joyfull meetinge to our comfortes, makinge me able (if it be his will) accordinge to my mynd to requite all frendshipes receyved of yow in the meane tyme except as thanckful A mynd as may be. From Sowthampton this 19ᵗʰ of December 1582.

Your Assured faithfull freind

M Browne

[Addressed]

> To the worshipfull my very good freind master
> John Thynne esquier

[Endorsed]

> Mʳ Browne. 19⁰ Decembris 1582.

9: [Between 25 April and 3 May 1583] MAURICE BROWNE
TO JOHN THYNNE¹

Good Master Thynne one day this weake I ryde to Sowth[amp]ton where Sir Humfry Gylbert is redy with all his shipes very excellently appointed to depart on his voyage. I trust god hath appointed this his stay for Sir Humfreys most good, for he was never half so well appointed for excellent shipes of streanthe & conntinaunce as nowe he is. Sir Humfreys brother Water Rawley (who at this present hath her

---

to make the long voyage round by the Caribbean so as to be at the site of his proposed colony on Narragansett Bay in the early summer of 1583. The readiness of Peckham to assist him and Walsingham's continued support must have given him some encouragement. Nevertheless it cannot have been much later before the expedition was abandoned and Gilbert returned to London. He was at his house in Red Cross Street on 7 February 1583 when he began to renew pressure for another attempt (Quinn, *Gilbert*, II, 339–40). A passage of personal news and a similar postscript have been omitted.

3 "in" apparently intended.

1 Longleat, Thynne Papers, v, ff. 252ʳ–253ᵛ. Extracts.

majestes favore above all men in the court) hath at his owne cost and charges bought a newe ship of Master Owttred at Hampton: she is of bourden twelfe score tonnes, redy furnyshed of all thinges belonginge to her & victuled for .60. men. The setting owt of this ship will cost Master Rawley two thowsande marckes.[2] Sir Humfrey doth goe in her and is the Admyrall. Also Sir Humfrey hath another ship of seven score tonnes as good A ship as any is in England of that bourden which Master William Wintter goeth in for that he is at half the charge[3] in setting owt that ship.[4] [crossed out: Further my Lord Vycount Byndon doth send A ship with Sir Humfry of six score tonnes. A very excellent ship as any is of that bourden and A newe ship, throughly appoynted, wherein my selfe doth goe and have charge of her. I wo[ld not] wyshe I assure yow to goe in a better ship.[5]] Sence the writing of this letter I have receyved intelligence that my Lord Vicount accordinge to his old humor of fantasticalines hath disappointed Sir Humfrey and my self of his ship. But I hope to be shipped to my contentment.[6]

Besides theise [Sir] Humfrey hath three pynasses, of good bourden, In A present supply divers of the cheife marchauntes of London, and the marchauntes of Bristowe dooe joyne in consort, and doth send fyve sayle more of good shipes with provision and men to Sir Humfrey my Master,[7] and Master Rawley doth joyne together to further this Actione by all the meannes they can, so that Sir Humfrey havinge two good supporters (at this time provided of god) I hope it will have great good successe. The Qweenes majestie hath used Sir Humfrey with very great favore, with promyse unto hym that upon awnswere from hym, he shall not want any thinge that may be for his assistaunce in this action, After Sir Humfrey had

2 For Henry Oughtred see Letters of the fifteenth and sixteenth centuries, ed. R.C. Anderson (Southampton 1921), and The troublesome voyage of Captain Edward Fenton, ed. E.G.R. Taylor (Cambridge, Eng., 1959). The information that the Bark Raleigh had been his ship is new. Richard Clarke, who was to be master of the Delight in the 1583 voyage, had been in command of Oughtred's ship, the Susan Fortune, in a Newfoundland voyage in 1582 (DCB, I, 228–9). The rumour was that Raleigh spent £2000 (not £1330. 6s. 8d.) on his ship, the Bark Raleigh, and her lading, Browne giving her tonnage as 240, Hayes as 200 (Quinn, Gilbert, II, 365, 396).
3 The Delight was rated at 120 tons by Edward Hayes, who said Winter was part-owner and Captain (Quinn, Gilbert, II, 396); Browne is a little more specific.
4 The sentence following, in square brackets, is crossed out and the next sentence interlineated.
5 Henry Howard, Viscount Bindon, not otherwise known to have been associated with Gilbert. His withdrawal was an addition to many other misfortunes.
6 Browne was to be offered and to accept command of the Swallow.
7 The reference is to the supporting squadron being organized under Walsingham's auspices by Christopher Carleill and Richard Hakluyt. Thus Browne makes it clear that it was not in any sense a rival venture. This modifies the views expressed in Quinn, Gilbert, I, 76–81, 94–5.

taken his leave of her majestie and gon doune to Hampton, the Qweene sent Sir Humfrey as A token of her especiall good favore A very excellent Jewell.[8] The device was An Anckor of gold set with .29. diamondes with the Portracture of A Qweene holdinge the ringe of the Ancor in one hand the flux of the Ancor in The other hand. In the breast of which picture there is set A very greate poynted Diamonde, and in the Crowne that standes on the head is set A very greate ruby and at eache end of the ankor A great peare. On the back side of the ankor is written as followeth, *Tuemur sub sacra ancora*. Which Jewell doth hange at two smale cheynes devised with roses set with rubyes and diamondes which was tyed with two pointes of heare couler tagged with gold and inamile and A scarffe of white silke Ciperous[9] egged with A fayer lace of Gold and silver. And here with receyved A letter of very great favore, so that I Assure yow I hope god hath sent all theise former delayes as a meannes for the better performaunce of this Actione for Sir Humfrey never had her majesties favore more hyghly nor ever had so great meannes to contynewe the same, for the bringinge of his Actione to good effect, which god graunt if it be his will.

Master Water Rawley is in very hyght favore with the Qweenes majestie, nether my Lord of Lecester nor Master Vicchamberlayne, in so [sho]rt tyme ever was in the like, which especiall favore hath bin but this half yeere. But the greatest of all hath bin within this two monethes. I have harde it credibly reported that Master Rawley hath spent within this half yeere above 3000[11]. He is very soumptous in his Aparell, and as I take it he hath his diet owt of the pryvy chychen,[10] but all the vessell with which he is served his at his stable[11] is silver with his owne armes on the same. He hath attendinge on hym at lest .30. men who[se] lyveryes are chargable, of which number half be gentillmen, very brave fellowes, divers havinge cheynes of gold. The hole court doth followe hym. By means of Sir Humfrey Gilbert and for that I followe hym in this Actione Master Rawley doth love me very well, I did one nyght suppe with hym and did lye with Sir Humfrey Gylbert in Master Rawleys loginge. His lodginge is very bravely furnyshed with Arrace; the chamber where in hym self doth lye hath A feild bedde all covered with greine velvett layed with broade silver lace and upon every corner and one the toppe set with plumes of whit feathers with spangles. He hath all other delyghtes and pleasure aboundantly and above all he behaveth hym selfe to the good likinge of every man. I have had

---

8 Cp. Raleigh's description on 16 March 1583 (Quinn, *Gilbert*, II, 348). Browne gives much more detail on the jewel, which was probably lost at sea with Gilbert himself.

9 Cypres or cypress, a light, transparent material, resembling cobweb lawn or crape, used for scarves or women's hoods.

10 "privy kitchen."

11 "table."

occatione divers and sundry tymes to come to master Rawley and he doth use me
with all the kindnes that may be. But especially because Sir Humfrey doth use me
aswell as my self can desire, and doth put me in truste to followe all his causes here
at the court as also to receyve such mony as he hath here and to buy dyvers provisions for hym, and to send them to Hampton. Sir Humfrey did let his brother
understand that I was there kinsman, my mother and Sir Humfreys mother where
sisters chyldren.[12] Truely master Rawley doth shewe hymself A very honest and A
kind brother to Sir Humfrey and myndfull of the freindship which Sir Humfrey
heretofore hath showed hym, for Sir Humfrey may have any thinge at his handes
that he will require. And Sir Humfrey regardes as litell on the other side his
brother Carew Rawley. All this tyme of Sir Humfreys beinge at London I never
hard Sir Humfrey once aske for hym or speak of hym, and they never spoke one to
the other at there beinge here last in London. There was never any lykinge between
Sir Humfrey and Carewe Rawley.[13]

I was one day At dinner at my cosen Bakers where master Thomas Gorge at that
tyme dined, And by chaunce talkinge of yow master Gorge inquired how yow and
Carewe Rawley agreed. I annswered that I hard yow say that all differences betwene
yow and hym wold be ended by master Attorny Generall and by master solicitor,
where upon master Gorge told me openly that the Qweene sent hym t[he] last
terme to my Lord Chaunceller with A message that my L[ord Chaun]celler
should doe master Carewe Rawley justice in the c[ause] dependinge betwene yow
and hym, But withall master Gorge sayed that her majestie did require that justice
should be donne with equitie to yow bothe. Whereby it did appeare althoughe her
majestie was informed against yow yeat her majestie did not gyve credit that yow
did hym upon[14] wronge but did require my Lord Chauncellor to doe equitie to
both partyes. I wold yow could ryde your handes of hym, and pursue hym owt of
Corsley althought yow gave hym must[15] as it were worth and withall purchace

12 The precise relationship of Maurice Browne to Walter Raleigh has not been determined. The mother of both Gilbert and Raleigh was born Katherine Champernown,
   daughter of Sir Philip Champernown of Modbury, whose wife, Katherine Carew, is
   not known to have had a sister. Maurice Browne's mother is given in the *Visitation of
   London, 1568* (Harleian Society, CIX–CX, 1957–8, p. 49) as Christian, daughter of
   William Carkett of London. Carkett may be a corruption of Carew and the connection a more distant one.
13 John Thynne was on bad terms and in legal controversy with Carew Raleigh, who
   had married his father's widow (cp. p. 196 above). The long passage cited is not
   directly relevant to the voyage but is given to illustrate the network of personal and
   political influence in which the participants and investors in the voyage were involved,
   and how significant such matters appeared to Browne at a time when his interests
   might well have been confined more strictly to the voyage to which he was committed.
14 "open."   15 "much."

your ease. For I dowbt yow shall never have hym so freindly as yow wold wyshe hym, especially as longe as my Lady lyveth. Wherefore considering the great and especiall favore that Water Rawley is in with her majestie, whereby yow shall be sure that duringe the controversies betwene yow, and his brother, yow shall Water but your heavy freinde wherein he may displeasure yow, and not wanntt the other alwayes to put hym in mynde who will with the advise of his lady ever be prac- tisinge agaynst yow, and by all the meannes they can to the vttermost countinaunce [of] your adversaryes which are in that shire or country agaynst yow in all causes. Wherefore I wold wyshe yow to streayne your self hereafter for your owne ease and if yow can by any meannes purchace Corsley into your owne Possession withall ye landes that my lady hath there. And withall I wold not wyshe yow to over buy any of those landes or any thinge else of them, but to the uttermost what they are worthe gyve, not buyinge gold, nor your pleasure and ease to deare or payinge for there freindship more then it is worth.

Yow have of longe tyme neclected your honorable freindes in not goinge to them at your cominge to london, especially my Lorde of Leycester whome yow have vowed to followe and have required his countinaunce and freindship in all your just causes. You shall have adversaryes plenty to diswade hym and others agaynst you, and your owne longe absence will be somme meannes to farther the same. My lord of Lecester is the only man that can command or perswade with master Water Rawley who are supporters the one to the other. Wherefore comminge to my Lorde often and usinge his countinaunce with famylyarytie will greatly stay master Rawley from doinge you that hurt which otherwise havinge occatione he wold. And agayne I wold wyshe yow if yow see that master Rawley dothe seke to informe her majestie agaynst yow, I wold let my Lord of Lecester understand thereof, desiringe his lordship (for that yow relyed your self on hym) to perswade master Rawley to desist from the same. And by lettinge my lorde of Lecester understand of the matter wherein Carewe Rawley doth you wronge in mysinforminge them In all your just causes I wold let my Lord understand that you looked for his favore and countynaunce. And the meannes to contynewe the same is to follow your old freinde Sir John Hubandes if he be here, if not speake your selfe for by usinge my lorde yow shall contynewe my Lordes freindship.[16] And it is more wysdomme to

<hr/>

16 Browne's cousin Baker (see above, p. 191) has not been identified. The persons referred to below are Thomas Gorges, a groom of the privy chamber; Sir John Popham, later prominently associated with the Virginia Company, Attorney General; Thomas Egerton, later Lord Chancellor Ellesmere, Solicitor General; Sir Thomas Bromley, Lord Chancellor, and a subscriber to the Gilbert expedition as was the Earl of Leicester (Quinn, *Gilbert*, II, 329); Carew Raleigh had commanded a ship in Gilbert's 1578 voyage and was still reckoned a contributor to Sir Humphrey's enterprise (*idem*,

kepe A freinde then to gett A freinde[17] . . .

Sir as I was writinge hereof I receyved A letter from yow which yow sent to Hampton dated the xiij[th] of Aprill, and receyved it the 25[th] of the same, wherefore I though[t]e good to deferre the sendinge of this letter unto you [un]till my cominge to Sowthampton which was one Maye Day last I underst[and] by Sir Hymfrey Gylbert that yow are well contented [that] your man Syssell should goe one this voyage with hym. I wold your busines wold by any meannes suffer yow to come to Sowthampton[18] . . .

I pray do my most harty commendations to my good Governes with thanckes A Thowsande fold for my butter and cheeses and marmylade and to my litell [master] great suertye, wishinge to you all three as to my owne soule. With my commendations I committ yow to God who send us all good successe and joyful meeting. this [   ] of [19] May 1583 your assured fayfull friend

M Browne

---

p. 332); "my Lady" is his wife, the former Lady Thynne – they lived at Corsley, not far from Longleat; Sir John Huband of Warwickshire was knighted in 1574 (W. A. Shaw, *The Knights of England*, II, 1906, 76), but little seems to be known of him; John Thynne's man Syssell (Cecil) has not been identified and it is not known whether or not he went with Gilbert.

17 A passage relating to Thynne's private business has been omitted.
18 Ditto.
19 The date must have been shortly after 1 May. The blank is in the original.

2 Sir Humphrey Gilbert in Newfoundland

1: 27 October 1583   GONZALO ESTEVEZ TO PHILIP II[1]

SIRE

From persons who have come this year from the Newfoundland [*Terra Nova*]
fisheries it has been learnt that there went to that coast certain English ships which
had for commander one Huiz,[2] a great lord of England, who took possession of
certain ports, saying that they were to be settled, and that those who went to fish in
those parts were to pay him duty. And it is also said that they were going to winter
at Cape Breton [*cabo de bertão*] and from thence go to Florida.[3] It seemed necessary
to give an account of this to your highness as these lands are held to be of your
conquest. And for greater certainty I acquired a public instrument which I am
sending with this, together with a passport in English which they were giving to
each ship. Our Lord preserve the Catholic and royal person of your majesty and
enlarge his realms and states. From Aveiro, 27 October 1583.

Gonçallo Estevez

Addressed: To our lord the king. From the municipal judge of the town of Aveiro.

1 Archivo de Indias, Seville, A.G.I. Patronato 2–5–1/20, no. 40, Portuguese and
  Spanish texts. I am indebted to Dr Alastair McFadyen for help with the translation.
2 The Spanish has "Luiz". "Huiz" is either what a fisherman made of "Humphrey
  Gilbert", or indicates that he had encountered Edward Hayes as Gilbert's officer and
  mistook his name for that of the leader of the expedition.
3 Maurice Browne had learnt in 1582 of Gilbert's intention to follow a reconnaissance
  by a winter settlement (pp. 193-4 above), so it is likely he intended to pursue a similar
  course in 1583. There is no need to take Cape Breton literally as its intended site,
  though whether Gilbert used the word Florida for his ultimate objective is doubtful.
  Iberian usage of "Florida" to cover eastern North America up to at least 40° N. lat.
  could equate Florida with Gilbert's Norumbega, though by 1574 Juan López de
  Velasco (*Geografía y descripción universal de las Indias*, Madrid, 1894, p. 171) had begun
  to differentiate the *Costa de la Florida* from the *Costa de Bacallaos*, or Norumbega, making
  the dividing line 41° or 42° N. lat.

Note added that the letter has been translated into Spanish (from Portuguese) by Tomas Gracián Dantisca, notary public and servant to the king.
Covering paper to say that these papers were in Portuguese and have been trans-lated into Castilian. To this is added an endorsement in a contemporary or nearly contemporary hand: "1583. Advices how the English have discovered a strait in Newfoundland at the cod [*Bacallaos*] fishery, from whence they pass into the South Sea and take possession of those ports."

2 : 7 August 1583   PASSPORT ISSUED BY SIR HUMPHREY GILBERT TO TOMAS ANDRE[1]

To whomsoever it may concern, know that I, Humfrey Gilbert, knight [*Humberto Guilberto cauallero de armas*], in the name and under the authority of her majesty, the queen of England, give and concede to Tomas Andre of Avero in the kingdom of Portugal that he may have free access to and liberty in the fishing and trade of the Newfoundland. Requiring all those who may be associated with me in any way that they should not harm or annoy him, but rather that they should help and protect him and his ships and goods as much as they are able. Given in St John's [*Sot Rones*][2] after my taking possession of Newfoundland, 7 August 1583.
H. Guilberto[3]

1 Enclosed in no. 1. The original English version has gone and the Spanish version alone is left. It is impossible to restore its wording precisely as no original has survived.
2 The Spanish is possibly a misreading for "St Ihones".
3 Gilbert would have signed "H. Gylberte" (cp. p. 202 above).

3 Camden "accepts" Parmenius

Letter-draft by William Camden to an unknown correspondent (? Richard Hakluyt at Oxford), mentioning Parmenius: see pp. 12–13 above, and Fig. 8. Transcribed from Brit. Mus., Additional MS 36294, f. 2 r. & v. The MS is rubbed and has a number of marginal lacunae. In the text, we have used roman characters to indicate doubtful readings and square brackets to show conjectures. Since what Camden writes is not fully articulated in its syntax and is only informally punctuated, any coherent translation must be something of a reconstruction and paraphrase – quite apart from textual lacunae. Where our translation is more than usually speculative we have used italics. The notes immediately follow the text and translation.

Litterae tuae suavissimae xi Martii datae, una cum Savili quaestione, me ...
[*c*]*redentem duodecimo post die* excep*erunt, gratissimae illae quidem, mihi* m[*ultisque*]
[*h*]*ominibus, sed mitte quaestionis illa prolegomena, (et) securus de amicitia nostra,*
Responsum itaque non aliud addam, quam quod hic omnibus in ore de
5 *Principe Auriaco, Habe* tu *paucis, ut ab optimo, et mihi amicissimo Antwerpiae*
laesae, *Mercatore accepi, Die dominico superiori xviii Martii*
adulescentulus Hispanus, a tabulis accept*is et* expens*is*
Gaspari Castane*to Mercatori Hispano, qui paucis ante dies Antwerpiae foro cessit spe*
xxv millia scutatorum aur[*eorum*]*, quae Rex Catholicus illa constituerat nuper cum*
in subl[*ime*]
10 *Auraici caput pretio addiceret, in Auriaci aedes irrepsit cui statim a*
prandio in cubiculum secedenti, una manu libello supplicem exhibet altera scl[*opetum*]
in eius faciem exoneravit, cuius globulus (venenatus ut nonnulli male metuunt) su[*per*]
maxillam dextram penetrans, ad maxillam *sinistram, exitum soli patefecit*
(Princeps) paxque abfuit, quin princeps defluctu in arteriam asperam sanguine
15 *suffocaretur, Percussor, cum educto gladio se defenderet, e vestigio* transverbera[*tus*]
aiunt, frustatim concisus est, licet signaculis, crucibus, et amuletis munitissimus erat,
ubi primum hoc in vulgus emanivit, quod iam Alenconio infensiss*imum erat, ob*
[*comm*]*issationem* sacrific*ius* seductus *(Michaelis in monasterium Pontificique*
concessit) statim intonu*erunt*
in Gallos exclamationes, imprecationes, passimque iact*abatur (tumultuat) iam Gallus*
Parisiensem
20 *lanienam, ut Bartholomei festum redintegratum sed sub noctem re comperta*
siluer*unt turbae, et resedit tumultus, contristavit hic eventus in aula nostra plurimos,*
Alenconium vero acerbissime afflixit, et etiam ut ferunt lachrimas
excussit; qui iam magna pompa Gaudendum *cogitavit, ubi in eius honore signati*

Your charming letter of 11 March, along with Savile's question, reached me *believing* [? *the worst*] twelve days later. They were indeed most welcome, to me and many folk; but *let him* send me the background to the question – "in the security of our friendship". So I will add no other answer than that
5 all the talk here is about the Prince of Orange: here it is briefly, as I had it from my great friend the good Mercator in troubled Antwerp.

Last Sunday, 18 March, a young Spanish lad (*according to documents that had been acquired and paid for on behalf of one* Gaspar Castanetus, a Spanish merchant, who went out of town from Antwerp a few days earlier, hoping
10 for the 25,000 gold écus which the catholic King had put up for him recently, since he was setting that price on Orange's noble head) – this youth crept into Orange's palace, and, when the Prince was retiring to his bedroom straight after dinner, presented himself, small book in one hand, as a suppliant, but with the other discharged a pistol in his face. The bullet
15 from it (poisoned, as some pessimistically fear) went in above the right jaw-bone towards the left one and made a gaping hole on its way out. [The Prince] and peace were gone – except that the Prince was [still] being suffocated by blood flowing down into the throat. Although the assailant defended himself with drawn sword, he was immediately set upon, they say,
20 and hacked in pieces – even though he had been well equipped with crossings, crucifixes and charms.

When this first leaked out in public, since it was now very dangerous for Anjou, he was taken away *as a scapegoat for what had been done* (he retreated to St. Michael's monastery *and to the Pope*); shouts and curses immediately
25 thundered against the French, and there was turmoil on all sides [...]. Now a Frenchman *has made, they said,* a Parisian slaughter like a repetition of the feast of St. Bartholomew, but with the affair discovered before night was out; the mobs became quiet and the tumult subsided. This turn of events grieved many people in our Hall; indeed it affected Anjou most sharply, even to the
30 extent, they say, of drawing tears. He had been looking forward, at the time,

[eran]t nummi, in quorsum reversa haec legalis inscriptio ...

25 *[...] parte.*

Hodie abducuntur (in Essexiam ad iudicium) e Turri Londiniensi Payne
sacrificulus, et Ludlo *famulus*

Comitissae Pembrochiae Senioris quos Eliot laesae maiestatis accusavit, Dominum
Parmenium Budensem, quod mihi commendasti beneficiam, Savilo a me plurimas
salutes, cui haec catholicati poetae carmina, – (e) fossila Campiani, cum haec

30 *communicaveris tradita, e Martyrio Campiani hic nuper impresso, describenda (mihi)*
curavi.

De quaestione tua acumine plena et vere Saviliana gratias meo Savi[lo]
postac agam, nunc valere iubeo. In adornanda profectione
componendis sarcinis totus sum, iam talaria indiu et bonis arcibus Eboracum a [...]
et inde natale solum Savili mei aulam Bradleianam cogito hoc [...]

35 *datis [litteris] iussit optimus senex D. Garth cui aliquid denegare im[par].*
Vale 5 Aprilis Londinii. D. Hottomano meo nom[ine]
salutes plurimae,

to a very lavish Festival at which coins were *to be* struck in his honour – *for which purpose* this official [legal] inscription has been turned round. ...

Today Payne is being taken (to Essex for trial) from the Tower of London as a sacrificial victim, and also one of the *Ludlow* household of the elder
35 Countess of Pembroke, whom Eliot has accused of treason. I will look after Master Parmenius of Buda since you have commended him to me. Many good wishes from me to Savile, whom I have also encouraged to transcribe (for me) these verses by a catholic poet – the 'remains' of Campion, out of the Martyrdom of Campion recently printed here – when you have handed it
40 [? them] over and let him in on it [? them].

I will thank friend Savile later for the question you sent, which is very shrewd and in the true Savile tradition; for the present I bid you farewell. I am completely taken up with packing bags in preparation for my journey. For some time now I have had a mind for travel – for York*shire with its fine*
45 *cities* [...] and then for my friend Savile's native heath, the house at Bradley. That grand old man Master Garth has issued orders to this effect [? in a recent letter], and it would be unfair to deny him anything. Goodbye; 5 April, London. Many good wishes in my name to Master Hotman.

COMMENTARY

1, 1: *Savili quaestione.* We can identify Thomas Savile's question as that contained in his short letter to Camden, dated 11 March, which Smith prints as his no. xi (see p. 13 above, and note to l. 3 on *securus*, below). He has been studying the first book of *De bello Gallico* and is puzzled by why the route-blocks should have been set up at a certain stage of the campaign in the way Caesar describes. He gives detailed reasons for thinking that they were not wisely deployed and would not have been effective. A good deal of the surviving correspondence between Savile and Camden is concerned with such scholarly points that they have come across in their reading.

3, 3: *illa.* Although the reading looks like *ille* at first sight, referring to Savile, sense would then require *mittat* instead of *mitte*, "let him send (me) …". And some of Camden's final *as* elsewhere are scarcely distinguishable from his *es*.

3, 4: *securus … nostra.* This phrase clinches the identification made in the first note, because it is a repetition of words that Savile had used, at the very beginning of his note, to excuse the fact that he had not replied for a long time to a "most handsomely penned" letter from Camden. *"Securus de amicitia nostra"*, he says, *"suavissime et optime Camdene, literis iamdudum elegantissime a te scriptis, nihil respondi"*; and then a little later, *"Accipe quaestionem"* – "Here's the query".

5, 5: *tu.* Perhaps read *ita*, anticipating the *ut*.

6, 6: *laesae.* Somewhat speculative reading: but cp. how closely the form resembles that of this word in the phrase *laesae maiestatis* (line 27 below).

7, 7: *adulescentulus.* The youth's name was Juan Jauréguy, and he was employed as clerk by the merchant mentioned below. An accessible account of the circumstances of the attempted assassination and its immediate consequences is in C.V. Wedgwood, *William the Silent* (London 1944), pp. 213–35.

7, 8: *acceptis … expensis.* The final *ss* are speculative, but reading the case-endings as genitive is problematical, something having to be "supplied".

8, 8: *Gaspari Castaneto.* Reading doubtful. The merchant's name was in fact Gaspar Añastro, and he was Portuguese rather than Spanish; his trade was in furs. A few days before the attack, he had acquired a permit to go out of Antwerp (*Antwerpiae foro*, below) and into the Walloon provinces on business. He went, in the event, to the Duke of Parma at Tournai and boasted to him that he had set up an assassin.

8, 9: *paucis.* If this reading is right, Camden seems to be wavering between *paucos ante dies* and *paucis ante diebus*, the latter of which is more common.

9, 10: *xxv millia ... constituerat.* Philip II of Spain had proclaimed Orange an outlaw
and settled this blood-money on his head in June 1580.

10, 11: *Auraici.* Obviously Camden meant to write *Auriaci*, but the metathesis in the
second syllable is quite clear in the MS.

11, 13: *libello.* Wedgwood (p. 230) does not mention the "little book" – if indeed that
reading is right.

13, 16: *exitum ... patefecit.* "By an extraordinary chance", says Wedgwood (p. 232),
"the bullet which had passed from right to left at an upward angle through the
cheeks and palate had struck no vital organ and broken no bone ... But ...
there was more than a chance that the maxillary artery had been grazed." Camden's phrase perhaps means literally "laid open a (its) way out to the daylight",
though the dative of motion would be unusual.

16, 21: *licet signaculis ...* Cp. Wedgwood, p. 231: "Jauréguy's pockets contained some
cheap metal crosses, such as the poor devout buy at places of pilgrimage, a prayer
written on a torn shred of paper, two little pieces of beaver skin ... and a green
wax candle-end." He had also taken the precaution of saying his confession early
in the morning and receiving the last sacrament.

17, 23: *Alenconio.* Queen Elizabeth's "little Frog", the Duc d'Alençon or Duke of
Anjou, had been installed at Antwerp only weeks earlier as Protector of the
Netherlands against Spain. Neither he nor his *entourage* was popular, and the
people were quick to see in the assassination attempt a French plot (*intonuerunt in
Gallos ...*) and to turn against him. For this reason he was advised to stay in-
doors after the attack; but the retreat to a monastery, if that is what Camden
means, is not mentioned in Wedgwood.

23, 30: *lachrimas excussit.* Anjou's detractors have questioned the cause of the tears. The
attack took place on his birthday, to mark which Orange had arranged lavish
festivities (*magna pompa ...*); so Wedgwood comments (p. 231), "Anjou may
have been genuinely upset, for William's death at this moment would be fatal to
his hopes [of usurping control of the country]; he beat his head three times against
the wall and broke into loud tears. Or was it merely annoyance at the loss of his
birthday party?" Perhaps the *inscriptio* mentioned in line 24 is the legend that was
to be on the commemorative coins.

26, 33: *in Essexiam.* Payne was taken to Chelmsford in the county of Essex for trial
and execution. According to R. Challoner, *Memoirs of missionary priests* (London,
1924), pp. 39–44, the contemporary account by Cardinal William Allen entitled
A briefe historie of the glorious martyrdom of xii reverend priests ... (Rheims 1582)
gives 20 March for Payne's removal from the Tower and agrees with Stow's date
of 2 April for his death. The date which Camden puts at the end of his draft
may indicate only when it was finished: but this part can hardly have been written
on 20 March, because he has had time to hear from Mercator about the events of
the eighteenth in Antwerp. Stow, however, gives the wrong date (1 September
instead of 1 December) for Campion's execution: see his *Annales ...* (1615),
p. 695.

Camden's reference to the Pembroke family remains obscure, since the household
which Eliot had accused, along with Payne, was that of Lady Petre in Essex,
who had once employed them both.

27, 35: Eliot. George Eliot seems to have been a particularly unsavoury priest-hunter. He had turned to this trade in order to secure his release from prison to which he had been sent for rape and homicide. From his cell he had written to Leicester informing against various people, and especially accusing Payne of plotting a "horrible treason" which included unspeakable actions against the Queen's person and the attempt to put Mary in her place. It was also he who had run down Campion in July 1581 at Lyford Grange in Berkshire – a house which stands no more than six miles eastwards of Wadley where P. stayed with the Untons: see E. Waugh, *Edmund Campion* (second ed. 1947 and 1953), pp. 121–29. Thus the first of the poems about Campion's martyrdom, which Camden is passing on indirectly to Savile (see line 29 below), contains the line "Repent thee, Eliot, of thy Judas kisse."

29, 38: carmina. The syntax of what Camden says about these poems and the tract on Campion's martyrdom is particularly sketchy, so the translation is doubtful. Although we can be almost certain that the tract referred to is the anonymous S.T.C. 4537 (see p. 13 above), it is not clear whether the poems are the ones "annexid" thereto or a separate set.

The combined volume, which gives no author nor place of publication, is often catalogued as printed at Douay (S.T.C., Brit. Mus., Bodleian), but A.C. South- ern's detailed study, in his *Elizabethan recusant prose* (London 1950), pp. 279–83 and 376–9, argues that Thomas Alfield wrote its prose account of Campion's trial and death, that three other hands composed the verses "by sundrie persons" and that the printing was done at Richard Verstegan's secret press in London, with Stephen Vallenger's assistance, in February 1582 (cp. *hic nuper . . .*). The printer's note at the very end asking the reader to "beare with the workmanship of a strainger" does not, therefore, reflect overseas production, but only a non-English printer. Southern quotes a contemporary account of the consequent government discovery and destruction of the guilty press. The principal author, Alfield, him- self a priest, was eventually executed in 1585 for disseminating seditious literature.

The phrase *e Martyrio* ... (l. 30) suggests that the poems are to be transcribed "out of" the work on the martyrdom. If we read *tradito*, it looks as though the whole volume is to be (or has been) "handed over" – and the poems do not seem to have been published separately. Perhaps we should read *tradita*, referring to the poems, and suppose that the final *-o* is a slip anticipating the ablatives of the next phrase.

To confuse matters, there was a separate set of verses about Campion's life, in Latin this time, added to Alfield's *True reporte* ... when Allen reprinted it as part of his *Briefe historie* ... (see note to l. 26 above) which appeared in the late summer of 1582: see Southern, pp. 383–5. This poem may perhaps already have been circulating separately in England, and Camden is more likely to want Savile to make a copy of Latin verses than of English. He would hardly say, however, that these additional verses were *e Martyrio* ..., unless perhaps in the loose sense of "arising from", "consequent upon".

29, 38: (e). We suppose that Camden intended to strike out this word, along with the capital N following, when he decided to delay the phrase which now starts *e Martyrio* ... in the next line.

34, 45: *Bradleianam.* Bradley is a small village in Yorkshire, some 40 miles northwest of York.

35, 46: *D. Garth.* In the preface to the first edition of *Principall navigations*, Hakluyt describes his friend Richard Garth as "one of the Clearkes of the pettie Bags". Garth collected botanical specimens brought back from the western voyages, and himself cultivated rare plants.

36, 48: *D. Hottomano.* See p. 12 above.

BIBLIOGRAPHY

1 MANUSCRIPT SOURCES
2 THE WORKS OF STEPHEN PARMENIUS
3 HUNGARIAN PUBLICATIONS ON
STEPHEN PARMENIUS, 1889–1968 (IN CHRONOLOGICAL ORDER)
4 WORKS CITED IN THE COMMENTARIES

I

1 Manuscript Sources

BUDAPEST: National Széchenyi Library
"A dunamelléki egyházkerület terul etén született azon egyének névsora, kik a külföldi egyetemekre látogatták 1522–1600-ig." MS Fol. HUNG. 1734.

LONDON: Public Record Office
Licences to go abroad. State Papers, Domestic, Elizabeth, S.P. 12/154, 5.

Letters from Simão de Verro, October–December 1581. State Papers, Foreign, Portugal, S.P. 89/1, 199, 201, 205.

Cases relating to Edward Hayes. High Court of Admiralty, Book of Acts, H.C.A. 3/18, 24 June 1580; Libels. H.C.A. 24/52, 145.

Maps of St. John's Harbour, Newfoundland, 1750. Maps, MPHH 274.

LONDON: British Museum
Letter from E. Pryn to the Earl of Leicester, 16 November 1581. Cotton MS, Vespasian C. VII, f. 386.

Letter (draft) from William Camden to [Richard Hakluyt?], 5 April, [1582].
Additional MS 36294, f. 2.

Letter (draft) from William Camden to Thomas Savile, n.d. *Ibid.*, f. 6ᵛ.

Letters (15) from Thomas Savile to William Camden, various dates. Cotton MS, Julius C. V., passim.

William Gager's complimentary verses to members of Christ Church, Oxford, 1583, Additional MS 22583, f. 63ᵛ.

Map of St. John's Harbour and Plan of Fort William, Newfoundland, 1698. Royal MSS, maps CXIX, 103.

Map of St. John's Harbour and its fortifications (eighteenth century). Additional MS 33231. II. 14.

LONDON: Somerset House

Will of John Browne. Prerogative Court of Canterbury. P.C., 30 Lyon.

LONGLEAT, WILTSHIRE: Manuscripts of the Marquess of Bath

Letters of Maurice Browne, 1582–83. Thynne Papers, V.

Personal accounts of John Thynne the younger, 1583. Thynne Papers, LV.

OXFORD: Christ Church

Buttery Books, 1579–80.

T. V. Beyne, MS lists of Senior Members.

OXFORD: Merton College

Merton College Register.

NEW YORK: New York Public Library

Richard Hakluyt, "A particuler discourse" (1584) (known as "Discourse of Western Planting"). Division of Manuscripts.

SEVILLE: Archivo General de Indias

Letter (with enclosures relating to Sir Humphrey Gilbert) from Gonzalo Estevez to Philip II, 27 October 1582. Patronato 2–5–1/20, no. 40.

WASHINGTON, D.C.: Library of Congress

John Mackeclean, Map of St. John's Harbour, Newfoundland (eighteenth century). Photostat in Map Division, 13. 15. F. 67.

2 The Works of Stephen Parmenius

PAEAN

PAEAN STEPHA⁄|NI PARMENII BVDEJI| Ad psalmum Dauidis CIV. conformatus, & gra⁄|tiarum loco, post prosperam ex suis Panno⁄|niis in Angliam peregrina⁄tionem, | Deo optimo & termaximo | seruatori consecratus. | [Ornament.] | LONDINI, | Excudebat Thomas Vautroulerius Typographus. | 1582.

COPIES

1 British Museum. 11630. ff. 2 (bound as part of a collection of tracts). 24.1 cm. by 17.1 cm.
2 Eton College Library, Fa. 4.9. With inscription by the author to Thomas Savile | on the title⁄page. 25.2 cm. by 18 cm.
Collation: A⁴.

BIBLIOGRAPHY

DE NAVIGATIONE

DE NAVIGATIONE / ILLUSTRIS ET MAGNANIMI / Equitis Aurati
Humfredi Gilberto, ad deducen⁄dam in novum orbem coloniam / susceptâ,
carmen / ἐπιβατικὸν / STEPHANI PARME⁄ / NII BVDEII. / LONDINI, /
Apud Thomam Purfutium. / An. 1582.

COPIES

1 British Museum. 1070.m.31.3. (bound as part of a collection of tracts: epistle
misplaced at end). 18.25 cm. by 12 cm., trimmed, affecting text of A2ʳ.
2 Henry E. Huntington Library. 17387 (modern binding, E.D. Church bookplate).
20.05 cm. by 14.5 cm. With inscription by the author to Geoffroy le Brumem on the
title⁄page.
Collation: A–B⁴, C².

LATER PRINTINGS

De navigatione Humfredi Gilberti ... carmen. Massachusetts Historical Society, *Ameri⁄cana* series (photostats), no. 78 (British Museum copy); no. 78a (Huntington Library
copy). Boston, 1922.
De Navigatione ... 1583. In Richard Hakluyt, *Principal navigations,* vol. III (1600), pp.
137–43.
De Navigatione ... 1583. Reprinted in *Hakluyt's Collection of early voyages, travels, and
discoveries of the English nation.* 4 vols. London, 1809–12. Vol. III, pp. 173⁄83.
De Navigatione ... 1583. Reprinted in Richard Hakluyt, *Principal navigations,* edited
by Edmund Goldsmid. 16 vols. Edinburgh 1884–90. Vol. XII, pp. 311–20.
De Navigatione ... 1583. Reprinted in Richard Hakluyt, *The principal navigations.*
12 vols. Glasgow 1903–5. Vol. VIII, pp. 23–33.

TRANSLATIONS

"A poem of Stephen Parmenius of Buda, in celebration of the Voyage of the illus⁄trious and valiant knight, Sir Humphrey Gilbert, undertaken for the purpose of con⁄ducting a colony to the new world."
[Translated and edited by Abiel Holmes.] Massachusetts Historical Society, *Collec⁄tions,* 1st series, IX (Boston 1804), 53–75.
"A Marine Poem of the Expedition Undertaken by the Glorious and Valiant Golden
Knight Sir Humphrey Gilbert for colonizing the New World."
Henry E. Huntington Library. Typescript, bound, with bookplate of E.D. Church.
Shelved with *De navigatione* (1582) (shelf number 17836). Anonymous translation,
prior to 1907.
" 'Embarkation Ode' ... a somewhat free translation ... omitting some of the less
pertinent parts." In W.G. Gosling, *Sir Humphrey Gilbert* (1911), pp. 216–21.

NEWFOUNDLAND LETTER

"A letter of the learned Hungarian Stephanus Parmenius Budeius to master Richard
Hakluyt." [From Newfoundland, 6 August 1583. Latin and English.] In Richard

225

Hakluyt, *Principall navigations* (1589), pp. 697–99.

"A letter …" In Richard Hakluyt, *Principall navigations* (1589), a facsimile, edited by D.B. Quinn and R.A. Skelton. 2 vols. Cambridge, England, 1965. Vol. II, pp. 697–99.

"A letter …" In Richard Hakluyt, *Principal navigations*, vol. III (1600), pp. 161–3.

"A letter …" In *Hakluyt's Collection of early voyages, travels, and discoveries of the English nation.* 4 vols. London 1809–12. Vol. III, pp. 205⁄6.

"A letter …" In Richard Hakluyt, *Principal navigations*, edited by Edmund Gold⁄smid. 16 vols. Edinburgh 1884–90. Vol. XII, pp. 358–63.

"A letter …" In Richard Hakluyt, *Principal navigations.* 12 vols. Glasgow 1903–5. Vol. VIII, pp. 78–84.

"A letter …" In *Hakluyt's voyages*, edited by John Masefield. 10 vols. London 1927–1928 (English only.). Vol. VIII, pp. 363–6.

"A letter …" In E.G.R. Taylor, *The original writings and correspondence of the two Richard Hakluyts.* 2 vols. London 1935. Vol. I, pp. 199–202. (English only. From *Principall navigations* (1589).)

"A letter …" In D.B. Quinn, *The voyages and colonising enterprises of Sir Humphrey Gilbert.* 2 vols., 1940. Vol. II, pp. 379–83. (English only. From *Principal navigations*, III (1600).)

3   Hungarian Publications on Stephen Parmenius, 1889–1968 (in chronological order)

[Professor Harrison Thomson, Mr Philip Barbour and Dr György Pajkossy guided the editors' early steps in this unknown field. Dr István Gál and Mr Tivadar Ács have most generously made it possible for us to record the results of their own bibliographical researches.]

KROPF, LAJOS. "Budai Parmenius István", *Egyetérés* Budapest 4 January 1889
    "Budai Parmenius István", *Századok*, XXIII Budapest 1889, 150–4
HAVASS, DEZSŐ, ed. "Magyar Földrajzi Könyvtár", *Bibliotheca Geographica Hungarica* Budapest 1893, pp. 357–59
MÁRKI, SANDOR. "Amerika und Hungarn", *Ungarische Geographische Gesellschaft* Budapest 1893
— *Amerika und Hungarn.* Budapest 1893
— *Földrajzi Köslemények*, II Budapest 1893, 60
SZINNYEI, JÓZSEF, ed. *Magyar irók*, X Budapest 1905, cols. 409–10
PIVÁNY, JENŐ. "Magyarok Amerikaban 1000–1800", *Amerikai Magyar Népszava* New York, May 1912
— *Magyar⁄Amerikai történelmi kapcsolatok.* Budapest 1926
— *Hungarian⁄American historical communications from pre⁄Columbian times.* Budapest 1927

KENDE, GÉZA. "Ki volt az elsö magyar ember Amerikában?" *Magyarok Amerikában* Cleveland, Ohio, 1927

HORVATH, KARÓLY. "Angol-Magyar kapcsolatok. Budai Parmenius István", *Historia* Budapest 1928, pp. 13–14

—" Historical links between England and Hungary. István Parmenius of Buda", *Hungary, a quarterly review* Budapest 1930, pp. 1–20

HALÁSZ, GYULA. *Öt Világrész Magyar Vándorai.* Budapest 1936

PIVÁNY, JENŐ. "Hungarians of the 16th and 17th centuries in English literature", *Angol Filölogiai Tanulmányok,* 11 Budapest 1937

— *Hungarians of the 16th and 17th centuries in English literature.* Budapest 1937

KEZ, ANDOR. "Parmenius István", in *Felfedezők Lexikona,* pp. 104–5. Budapest n.d.

CLAUSER, MIHÁLY. "Budai Parmenius István", *Debreceni Szemle,* April 1940

ÁCS, TIVADAR. *Akik elvándoroltak.* Budapest 1942

HALÁSZ, GYULA. *Magyar Világjárók. Az Ezeréves Magyarorsszág.* Second edition, Budapest 1940

SZENTKIRÁLYI, JÓZSEF. "Magyar-amerikai történelmi kapcsolatok", *Magyar Tájékoztató Zsebkönyv,* ed. Elemér Radisics, pp. 979–80. Second edition, Budapest 1943

HALÁSZ, GYULA. *Ungarische Entdecker,* p. 5. Hamburg and Budapest 1944

— *Magyarok Északamerikában,* pp. 4–5. Budapest 1944

PIVÁNY, JENŐ. *Hungary and the Americas.* Budapest 1944

GÁL, ISTVÁN. *Magyarország, Anglia és Amerika.* Budapest 1945

ÁCS, TIVADAR. "Egy tengerbe veszett magyar humanista költo a XVI. században", *Filölogiai Közlöny* Budapest 1962, pp. 115–22

RÁZSÓ, GYULA. *Felfedezők, kalózok, gyaramatositók. Angol utazók a XV.-XVIII. században.* Budapest 1936

LÁNG, DEZSŐ. "Budai Parmenius István", *Magyar Hirek* Budapest, 23 November 1967, p. 9

ÁCS, TIVADAR. "Ki volt Budai Parmenius István", *Magyar Nemzet* Budapest, 24 January 1968, p. 3

4 Works Cited in Introduction and Commentaries

ALCHINDUS, JACOBUS. *De imbribus, sive de mutationibus temporis.* Venice, P. Liechtenstein, 1507

ALFIELD, THOMAS [attrib.]. *A true reporte of the death and martyrdome of M. Campion Jesuite and prieste, ... wheruuto is annexid certayne verses made by sundrie persons.* London, R. Verstegan, 1582.

ANDERSON, R.C. ed. *Letters of the fifteenth and sixteenth centuries.* Southampton 1921

ADAMS, CLEMENT. *Nova Anglorum ad Moscovitas navigatio.* London 1554; reprinted in C. Marnius and J. Aubrius, *Rerum Moscoviticarum auctores varii* (Frankfurt 1600)

ALLEN, WILLIAM. *A briefe historie of the glorious martyrdom of xii reverend priests ...* Rheims, J. Fogny, 1582

ARBER, EDWARD, ed. *A transcript of the registers of the Company of Stationers of London, 1544–1640.* 5 vols. London and Birmingham 1875–94

ARMSTRONG, A.H. *The intelligible universe in Plotinus.* Cambridge, Eng., 1940

BEA, AUGUSTIN. *Le nouveau psautier latin.* Paris 1947

BEST, GEORGE. *A true discourse of the late voyages of discoverie.* London, H. Bynneman, 1578

BINDOFF, S.T. *Tudor England.* Harmondsworth, Middlesex, 1950

Biographia Britannica. 7 vols. London 1747–66

BIZARRI, PIETRO. *Pannonicum bellum, ...* Basle, S. Henricpetrus, 1573

BOURNE, WILLIAM. *A booke called The treasure for travelers.* London, for T. Woodcocke, 1578

BRADNER, LEICESTER. *Musae Anglicanae: A history of Anglo-Latin poetry.* New York 1940

BROWNE, R.A. *British Latin selections, A.D. 500–1400.* Oxford 1954

BRUNO, GIORDANO. *La cena de le ceneri.* London, J. Charlewood, 1584

BRY, THEODOR DE. *America.* Part II. Frankfurt 1591

BUCHANAN, GEORGE. *Opera omnia.* Ed. T. Ruddiman. 2 vols. Edinburgh 1725

— *Paraphrasis psalmorum Davidis poetica.* London, T. Vautrollier, 1580

— *Rerum Scoticarum historia.* Edinburgh, A. Arbuthnet, 1582

BULLEIN, WILLIAM. *Bulleins bulwarke of defence.* London, J. Kyngston, 1562

BUXTON, JOHN. *Sir Philip Sidney and the English renaissance.* London, 2nd edition, 1964

Calendar of patent rolls, 1558–9. London 1939

Calendar of state papers, colonial, East Indies, China, and Japan, 1513–1616. London 1862

Calendar of state papers, domestic, 1581–90. London 1865

Calendar of state papers, foreign, 1581–2 (London 1907), *1582* (1909); *1583 with addenda* (1913); *1583–4* (1914)

Cambridge Modern history. 13 vols. Cambridge, Eng., 1902–26

CAMDEN, WILLIAM. *V. cl. Gulielmi Camdeni et illustrium virorum ad G. Camdenum epistolae.* Ed. Thomas Smith. London 1691

— *Remaines concerning Britaine.* London, G. Eld for S. Waterson, 1605

CAMOENS, LUIS DE. *The Lusiads.* Translated by W.C. Atkinson. Harmondsworth, Middlesex, 1952

CAMPION, EDMUND. *Rationes decem, quibus fretus certamen adversariis obtulit in causa fidei.* Antwerp, A. Radaeus, 1582

Canada, Department of Mines and Technical Surveys, Geographical Branch. *Selected bibliography on sea ice distribution in the coastal waters of Canada.* Ottawa 1957

Canada, Department of Northern Affairs and National Resources. *Native trees of Canada.* 5th edition. Ottawa 1958

CAREW, RICHARD. "The excellency of the English tongue"; in William Camden, *Remaynes concerning Britaine.* London, J. Legett for S. Waterson, 1614

CARTIER, JACQUES. *A shorte and briefe relation of the two navigations and discoveries to the northwest partes called New France.* Translated by John Florio. London, H. Bynneman, 1580

— *See also* D.B. Quinn, *Richard Hakluyt, editor*

CASAS, BARTOLOMÉ DE LAS. *Brevíssima relación de la destrucción de las Indias.* Seville, 1552

— *Seer cort verhael destructie van d'Indien.* [Brussels or Antwerp], 1578
— *Tyrannies et cruatez des Espagnols.* Antwerp, 1579 (reprinted Rouen 1580; Paris 1582)
— *The Spanish colonie.* Translated by M.S. London, T. Dawson for W. Broome, 1583
CASSIRER, E., KRISTELLER, P.O., RANDALL, J.H., JUNIOR, edd. *The renaissance philosophy of man.* Chicago, 1948
CELL, GILLIAN T. *English enterprise in Newfoundland, 1577-1660.* Toronto 1970
CHALLONER, RICHARD. *Memoirs of missionary priests.* London 1924
CHAPMAN, GEORGE. *The works of George Chapman.* Edd. R.H. Shepherd and A.C. Swinburne. 3 vols. London 1874-75
CHEW, SAMUEL C. *The crescent and the rose.* New York 1937
CHURCHYARD, THOMAS. *A discourse of the Queenes Majesties entertainement ... whereunto is adjoyned a commendation of Sir H. Gilberts ventrous journey.* London, H. Bynneman, 1578
— *A generall rehearsall of warres.* London, E. White, 1579
— *A prayse, and reporte of Maister Martyne Forboishers voyage to Meta Incognita.* London, for A. Maunsell, 1578
COLE, W.A., ed. *A catalogue of books relating to the discovery and early history of ... America forming a part of the library of E.D. Church.* 5 vols. New York 1907
—"Elizabethan Americana", in *Bibliographical essays: a tribute to Wilberforce Eames.* Cambridge, Mass., 1924
COLLINS, ARTHUR, ed. *Letters and memorials of state.* 2 vols. London 1747
COPERNICUS, NICHOLAS. *De revolutionibus orbium celestium.* Nuremberg 1543
DEANE, CHARLES. *Documentary history of Maine.* 1st series, vol. II. Boston 1877
Dictionary of Canadian biography. Vol. I. Toronto 1965
Dictionary of national biography. 65 vols. London 1885–1900
DORMER, E.W, "Two historic portraits at Burlington House", *Berkshire Archaeological Journal,* XXXVIII (1934), 33–36
DORSTEN, J.A. VAN. *Poets, patrons and professors: Sir Philip Sidney, Daniel Rogers, and the Leiden humanists.* Leiden 1962
DOWLAND, JOHN. *Lachrimae.* London, J. Windet, 1604
ELLIS, THOMAS. *A true report of the third and last voyage into Meta Incognita.* London, T. Dawson, 1578
EPSTEIN, MAX. *The early history of the Levant Company.* London 1908
FERNALD, M.L. "The contrast in the flora of eastern and western Newfoundland", *American Journal of Botany,* V (1118) 237–47
— *Gray's Manual of botany.* 8th edition. New York 1950
FICINO, MARSILIO. *Opera Omnia.* 2 vols. Basel 1561
FIRMINUS. *Repertorium de mutatione aeris.* Paris, J. Kerver, 1539
FERNÁNDEZ DE NAVARRETE, et al., edd. *Colección de documentos inéditos para la historia de España.* 112 vols. Madrid 1842–95
FORSTER, L. *Janus Gruter's English years.* Leiden and London 1967
FOSTER, JOSEPH. *Alumni Oxonienses.* 4 vols. Oxford 1891–2
GÁL, ISTVÁN. "Sir Philip Sidney's guidebook to Hungary", *Hungarian studies in English,* IV. Debrecen 1969.

GENTILI, SCIPIO. *Paraphrasis aliquot psalmorum Davidi.* London, T. Vautrollier, 1581
— *In xxv. Davidis psalmos epicae paraphrases.* London, J. Wolfe, 1584
— *T. Tassi Solymeidos liber primus latinis numeris expressus a S.G.* London, J. Wolfe, 1584
GILBERT, SIR HUMPHREY. *A discourse of a discoverie for a new passage to Cataia.* London, H. Middleton for R. Johnes, 1576
GLEASON, HENRY A. *The new Britton and Brown illustrated flora of the northeastern United States and adjacent Canada.* 3 vols. New York 1958
GOSLING, W.G. *The life of Sir Humphrey Gilbert.* London 1911
GRAFTON, RICHARD. *A chronicle.* London, H. Denham for R. Tottle and H. Toye, 1569
GRAVES, ROBERT. *The Greek Myths.* Revised edition. 2 vols. Harmondsworth, Middlesex, 1960
GRIEVE, S. *The great auk or garefowl.* London 1885
HAKLUYT, RICHARD. *Divers voyages touching the discoverie of America.* London, T. Woodcocke, 1582
— *See* D.B. QUINN, *Richard Hakluyt, editor*
— *Divers voyages.* Edited by John Winter Jones. (Hakluyt Society, 1st series, 7.) London 1950
— *Discourse on western planting.* Edited by Charles Deane. Boston 1877
—"Discourse of western planting", in E.G.R. Taylor, *The original writings and correspondence of the two Richard Hakluyts.* Vol. II, 211–326. (Hakluyt Society, 2nd series, 77.) London 1935
— *The principall navigations, voiages and discoveries of the English nation.* London, Deputies to Christopher Barker, 1589
— *The principall navigations, 1589.* Edited, in facsimile, by D.B. Quinn and R.A. Skelton. 2 vols. Cambridge, Eng., 1965
— *The principal navigations voyages traffiques and discoveries of the English nation.* 3 vols. London, G. Bishop, R. Newberie and C. Barker, 1598–1600
— *The principal navigations.* 12 vols. Glasgow 1903–5
HARING, CLARENCE H. *The Spanish empire in America.* New York 1947
HARVEY, SIR PAUL, ed. *Oxford companion to classical literature.* Oxford 1937
HASTED, EDWARD. *A history of Kent.* 2nd edition. 12 vols. Canterbury 1797–1801
HÄUSER, HELMUT. "Zu Verfasserfrage des Faustbuchs von 1587: Stephanus Parmenius", *Philobiblon*, XV (Hamburg, 1971), 105–17.
HESSELS, J.H., ed. *Abrahami Ortelii et virorum eruditorum ad eundem et ad Jacobum Colium Ortelianum epistulae.* (Ecclesiae Londino-Bataviae Archivium, I.) Cambridge, Eng., 1887
HESSUS, HEOBANUS. *Psalterium Davidis carmine redditum per H.H.* London, T. Vautrollier, 1581
HIGHFIELD, J.R.L. "An autograph manuscript ... of Sir Henry Savile", *Bodleian Library Record*, VII (1963), 73–83
HOLINSHED, RAPHAEL, et al. *The chronicles of England, Scotland and Ireland.* 2nd edition. 3 vols. London, for J. Harrison [etc.], 1587
HOLLAND, HENRY. *Herωologia Anglicana.* Arnhem 1620
HOLMES, ABIEL. "Memoir of Stephen Parmenius", in Massachusetts Historical Society, *Collections*, 1st series. Vol. IX, pp. 49–52. Boston 1804

HOTMAN, JEAN and FRANÇOIS. *Epistolae.* Amsterdam 1700

HOWARD, J.J. and ARMYTAGE, G.J., edd. *Visitation of London 1568.* London 1869; new edition 1958

HOWLEY, J.P. *The Boethuk Indians of Newfoundland.* Cambridge, Eng., 1915

HUMFREY, LAURENCE. *Oratio ad serenissimam Angliae reginam Elizabetham in aula Woodstochiensi habita, anno 1575, Septembri 11.* London, H. Binneman for G. Bishop, 1575

HURSTFIELD, JOEL. *The Elizabethan nation.* London 1964

— *Elizabeth I and the unity of England.* London 1960

INNIS, HAROLD A. *The cod fisheries.* New Haven 1940

JACOB, ERNEST F., ed. *Italian renaissance studies.* London 1960

JUKES, J.B. *Excursions in and about Newfoundland.* 2 vols. London 1842

KER, N.R. "Oxford college libraries in the sixteenth century", *Bodleian Library Record,* VI (1959), 459–515

KEYMIS, LAWRENCE. *A relation of the second voyage to Guiana.* London, T. Dawson, 1596

KIRK, R.E.G., and KIRK, E.F., edd. *Returns of aliens, London, 1571–97.* (Huguenot Society of London, 10, part II)

KRAUS, HANS P. *Sir Francis Drake.* Amsterdam 1970

KRISTELLER, P.O. *The philosophy of Marsilio Ficino.* New York 1943

LE FANU, W.R. "Thomas Vautrollier, printer and bookseller", Huguenot Society of London, *Proceedings,* LX (1906), 12–25

LEWIS, C.S. *The discarded image.* Cambridge, Eng., 1964

LLWYD, HUMPHREY. *Commentarioli descriptionis Britanniae fragmentum.* Ed. Abraham Ortelius. Cologne 1572

— *Angliae regni florentissimi nova descriptio.* London, R. Johnes, 1573

LÓPEZ DE VELASCO, JUAN. *Geografía y descripción universal de las Indias.* Madrid 1894

LOUNSBURY, RALPH G. *The British fishery at Newfoundland, 1634–1763.* New Haven 1934. Reprinted 1969

LUCAS, FREDERICK A. "The expedition to the Funk Island, with observations upon the history and anatomy of the Great Auk", United States, National Museum, *Report for 1887–8.* Washington, D.C., 1890

MCCANN, FRANKLIN T. *English discovery of America to 1585.* New York 1952

MADGE, S.J., ed. *Abstract of inquisitions post mortem, London, 1561–77.* London 1901

Massachusetts Historical Society. *Proceedings, 1791–1835.* Boston 1879

MATTHEW, SIR TOBIE. *Concio apologetica adversus Campianum.* Oxford, L. Lichfield for E. Forrest, 1615

MERBURY, CHARLES. *A briefe discourse of royall monarchie.* London, T. Vautrollier, 1581

— *Proverbi vulgari.* Ed. Charles Sperone. University of California Publications in Modern Philology, XXVIII, Berkeley 1964

MERCATOR, GERARDUS. *Atlas.* Duisburg 1595

MERSON, ALAN L., ed. *The third book of remembrance of Southampton.* 3 vols. Southampton 1962–65

MORANDIÉRE, CHARLES DE LA. *Histoire de la pêche française de la morue dans l'Amérique septentrionale.* 3 vols. Paris 1962–6

MULCASTER, RICHARD. *The first part of the elementarie.* London, T. Vautrollier, 1582
MUNBY, A.N.L. *Phillipps studies.* 5 vols. Cambridge, Eng., 1951–60
NEILSON, G., ed. *George Buchanan: Glasgow quatercentenary studies, 1906.* Glasgow 1907
The New Cambridge Modern History. (14 vols.) Cambridge, Eng., 1957–70
NICHOLS, JOHN. *Queen Elizabeth's progresses.* 3 vols. London 1788–95
NICHOLS, JOHN GOUGH. *The Unton inventories . . . with a memoir of the family of Unton.* London 1841
ORTELIUS, ABRAHAM. *Theatrum orbis terrarum.* Antwerp 1570
PARADIN, GUILLAUME. *De motibus Galliae et expugnato receptoque Itio Caletorum anno MDLVIII.* Lyons 1558
PARKS, GEORGE BRUNER. *Richard Hakluyt and the English voyages.* New York 1928. Reissued with additional bibliography 1961
PATTERSON, GEORGE. "The termination of Sir Humphrey Gilbert's expedition", Royal Society of Canada, *Proceedings and transactions*, 2nd series, III (1897), section II, pp. 113–27
PERRET, ROBERT. *La géographie de Terre-Neuve.* Paris 1913
PETERS, H.S., and BURLEIGH, T.D. *The birds of Newfoundland.* St John's 1951
PICO DELLA MIRANDOLA, G. *De hominis dignitate.* Basel 1572
POLLARD, ALFRED FREDERICK. *Tudor tracts, 1532–88.* London 1903
POLLARD, A.W., and REDGRAVE, G.R. *A short-title catalogue of books printed in England, Scotland and Ireland, 1475–1640.* London 1926
PURCHAS, SAMUEL. *Hakluytus posthumus, or Purchas his pilgrimes.* 4 vols. W. Stansby for H. Fetherston, 1625
— *Hakluytus posthumus, or Purchas his pilgrimes.* 20 vols. Glasgow 1905–7
PUTTENHAM, GEORGE. *The arte of English poesie.* London, R. Field, 1589
QUINN, DAVID BEERS. "The argument for the English discovery of America between 1480 and 1494." *Geographical Journal*, CXXVII (1961), 279–85
—"Edward Hayes, Liverpool colonial pioneer." Historic Society of Lancashire and Cheshire, *Transactions*, CXI (1959), 25–45
— *The voyages and colonising enterprises of Sir Humphrey Gilbert.* 2 vols. (Hakluyt Society, 2nd series, 83–84.) London 1940. Reissued, 1 vol. Liechtenstein 1967
— *The Roanoke voyages, 1584–90.* 2 vols. (Hakluyt Society, 2nd series, 104–5.) Cambridge, Eng., 1955. Reissued, 1 vol. Liechtenstein 1967
— *Richard Hakluyt, editor.* (A study introductory to the facsimile edition of Richard Hakluyt's *Divers voyages* (1582) and *A shorte and briefe narration of the two navigations to Newe Fraunce* (1580).) 2 vols. Amsterdam 1967
RALEGH, SIR WALTER. *The discoverie of the large and bewtiful empyre of Guiana.* Ed. V.T. Harlow. London 1928
RAMUSIO, GIOVANNI BATTISTA. *Navigationi et viaggi.* 3 vols. Venice 1550–9
REEDS, L.G. *Land-use survey: Avalon Peninsula.* Ottawa 1953
REESE, GERVASE. *Music in the Renaissance.* Revised edition. New York 1959
ROBINSON, HASTINGS, ed. *Zurich letters.* Second series. Cambridge, Eng., 1845
ROSENBERG, ELEANOR. *Leicester, patron of letters.* New York 1955
ROWSE, A.L. *Ralegh and the Throckmortons.* London 1962
RUDDIMAN, THOMAS. *A vindication of Mr George Buchanan's paraphrase of the book of Psalms.* Edinburgh 1745

RYAN, W.P. *Map of St John's.* St John's 1932

SABIN, JOSEPH, et al. *A dictionary of books relating to America.* 29 vols. New York 1868–1936

SALUSTE DU BARTAS, GUILLAUME DE. *L'Uranie.* Translated by Thomas Ashley. London, J. Wolfe, 1589

SAVILE, SIR HENRY. *H. Savilis commentarius de militia Romana ex Anglico Latinus factus.* Heidelberg 1601

SEARY, E.R., et al. *The Avalon peninsula of Newfoundland.* National Museum of Canada, Bulletin 219. Ottawa 1968

SETTLE, DIONYSE. *A true reporte of the laste voyage by Capteine Frobisher.* London, H. Middleton, 1577

SHAW, W.A. *The knights of England.* 2 vols. London 1906

SIDNEY, SIR PHILIP. *Apology for poetry.* Ed. G. Shepherd. London 1965

SOUTHERN, A.C. *Elizabethan recusant prose.* London and Glasgow 1950

SPARROW, JOHN. "Latin verse of the high renaissance", in E.F. Jacob, ed., *Italian renaissance studies.* London 1960

STONE, LAURENCE. *The crisis of the aristocracy, 1558–1641.* Oxford 1965

STOW, JOHN. *Annales, or A generall chronicle of England ... continued by Edmond Howes.* London 1631 (–2)

STRECKER, K. *Introduction to mediaeval Latin*, translated and revised by R.B. Palmer. Berlin 1957

STRONG, ROY. "Sir Henry Unton and his portrait", *Archaeologica* XCIX (London 1965), 53–76

TASSO, TORQUATO. [See *s.v.* GENTILI, S.]

TAYLOR, EVA G.R. "Instructions to a colonial surveyor in 1582", in *The mariner's mirror,* XXXVII (1951), 48–62

— *The original writings and correspondence of the two Richard Hakluyts.* 2 vols. (Hakluyt Society, 2nd series, 76–7.) London 1935

— *The troublesome voyage of Captain Edward Fenton.* (Hakluyt Society, 2nd series, 113.) Cambridge, Eng., 1959

THAYER, HENRY O. "A pioneer voyager of the sixteenth century: Sir Humphrey Gilbert", Maine Historical Society, *Collections,* 3rd series, II (1906), 51–73

THOMAS, AARON. *The Newfoundland journal ... 1794.* Edited by Jean M. Murray. London 1968

THOMPSON, H.L. *Christ Church.* London 1900

TILLYARD, E.M.W. *The Elizabethan world picture.* London 1943

TREMELLIUS, J., and JUNIUS, F., translators. *Testamenti veteris biblia sacra, quibus etiam adiunximus novi testamenti libros.* London, H. Middleton for C. B[arker], 1580

TREVOR-ROPER, HUGH. "George Buchanan and the ancient Scottish constitution", *English historical review,* Supplement III (1966)

TURNER, WILLIAM. *Avium praecipuarum.* Cologne 1544

— *Turner on birds.* Translated by A.H. Evans. Cambridge, Eng., 1903

UNCIUS, LEONHARDUS. *Poematum libri septem de rebus Ungaricis.* Cracow 1579

United Kingdom, Hydrographic Office. *Chart of St John's Harbour, 1816.* (Copies in P.R.O., C.O. 700/Newfoundland; W.O. 78/307)

UNTON, SIR HENRY. *Funebria nobilissimi ac praestantissimi equitis D. Henrici Unton a musis Oxoniensibus apparata.* Oxford, J. Barnes, 1596

VAN TIEGHEM, P. *La littérature latine de la Renaissance.* Paris 1944

VENN, J., and J.A. *Alumni Cantabrigienses.* 4 vols. Cambridge, Eng., 1922–7

VERESS, ENDRÉ, ed. *Matricula et acta Hungarorum in universitate Patavina studentium, 1264–1864.* Budapest 1915

— *Fontes rerum Hungaricarum*, vol. I. Budapest 1915

Victoria county history of Berkshire. vol. IV. London 1924

WAGNER, HENRY R. *Spanish voyages to the northwest coast of America in the sixteenth century.* San Francisco 1929. Resisued, Amsterdam 1966

WATERS, DAVID W. *The art of navigation in England in Elizabethan and early Stuart times.* London 1958

WATSON, THOMAS. *Amintae gaudia.* London, W. Ponsonby, 1592

— *The Hecatompathia; or The passionate centurie of love.* London, J. Wolfe for G. Gawood, [1582]

WAUGH, EVELYN. *Edmund Campion.* London 1947. 2nd edition 1953

WEDGWOOD, C.V. *William the Silent.* London 1944

WEISS, ROBERTO. *The spread of Italian humanism.* London 1964

WHITBOURNE, RICHARD. *A discourse and discovery of New-found-land.* London, F. Kyngston for W. Barret, 1620

WILLIAMSON, JAMES ALEXANDER. *Hawkins of Plymouth.* London 1949

— *The Cabot voyages and Bristol discovery under Henry VII.* (Hakluyt Society, 2nd series, 120.) Cambridge, Eng., 1962

WILLES, RICHARD. *The history of travayle in the East and West Indies.* London, R. Jugge, 1577

WILSON, ELKIN CALHOUN. *England's Eliza.* Cambridge, Mass., 1939

WIND, EDGAR. *Pagan mysteries in the renaissance.* 2nd edition. Harmondsworth, Middlesex, 1967

WINSOR, JUSTIN. *Narrative and critical history of America.* 8 vols. Boston and New York 1889

YATES, FRANCES A. "Giordano Bruno's conflict with Oxford", Warburg Institute, *Journal*, II (1939), 227–42

—"Queen Elizabeth as Astraea", in Warburg and Courtauld Institutes, *Journal*, X (1947), 27–82

— *The art of memory.* London 1966, and Harmondsworth, Middlesex 1969

YEAMES, A.H.S. "The grand tour of an Elizabethan", in British School at Rome, *Papers*, VII (1914), 92–113.

YONGE, JAMES. *The journal.* Ed. F.N.L. Poynter. London 1963

Index

Celtae 90 *see* France

centaurs 126

Ceres 148

Chaledonidum 84, 112 *see* Scotland

Champernown, Katherine 206n

Champernown, Sir Philip 206n

Chancellor, Richard (*d* 1556) 23, 69, 134, 135

Chapman, George (*d* 1634): *De Guiana carmen* 69–70, 132

Charities (Three Graces) 94, 95, 127

Chelmsford, Essex 217

Christ Church, Oxford 8, 11, 14, 19, 35, 36, 130, 168, 169, 201n; prayerbook 33, n

Church, E.D., book collector 29; catalogue *see* Cole, G.W.

Churchyard, Thomas (*d* 1604) 122, 136

Cicero (*d* 43 BC) 24n, 26n, 107, 109, 157, 177, 182, 183

Cimmerii 102, 135 *see* Russia

Clarke, Richard (*fl* 1596) master *Delight* 48, 51, 52, 59, 61, 180, 181, 204n

cod *see* St John's

Colchis 110, 126

Cole, George Watson: ed. Church catalogue 72n; translation *D.N.C.* 106, 107, 109, 116, 119, 120, 127

Columbus, Christopher (*d* 1506) 84, 85, 102, 103, 137

Conception Bay, Newfoundland 51, 182

Copernicus, Nicholas (*d* 1543), *De revolutionibus* 36n

Corsley, Wilts 206, 207, 208n

Corte Real, Gaspar (*d* 1501) 54

Cossa, Francesco del (*d* 1477), painter 128

Coverdale, Miles (*d* 1568) 31n

Cox, William, master *Golden Hind* 59, 62

Cracow, Poland 125

Croatia 86, 118, 119

Croesus 137

Cronus 118

Cyrus the Great (*fl* 558–528 BC) 104, 105, 137

Dacia 86, 118 *see* Rumania, Transylvania

Dalmatia 118

Daniel, mineral expert 55, 56, 57, 183; death 59

Dantisca, Tomas Gracián, notary public 210

Danube, River 47, 93, 125

Dartmouth, Devon 41, 47, 197n, 199, n, 201, 202

Deane, Henry: *Discourse on western planting* 72

Dee, John (*d* 1608) 19–20, 189; map 20

Delia 94, 127 *see also* Diana

Delight see ships

Delos, Island of 127

Demeter 136

Deptford, England 110, 126

Devonshire 195, 197, 199

Diana 68, 95, 127, 128, 130, 150

Dionysius the Areopagite (*fl* AD 492): *De Ecclesiastica hierarchia;* pseudo-Dionysius 116, 121

Dionysus, god 136–7

Dodona, grove 126

Dominicans 5n

Dominus Parmenius Budensis 4, 13, 214 *see* Parmenius

Dorsten, Jan A. van 7n

Douai or Douay, France 218

Dowland, John (*d* 1626?): *Lachrimae* 185

Downs, Kent 40–1, 197

Drake, Sir Francis (*d* 1596) 20, 23, 39, n, 68, 110; circumnavigation 10, 38, 102, 103, 132, 134, 136, 190

Dudley, Robert, earl of Leicester (*d* 1588) 30, 39n, 130, 205, 207, n, 218

Dutch church, London 11

East India Company 192n

Eboracum 214 *see* York

Edinburgh, Scotland 19n, 112

Edward VI, king of England 33

Edward, footman 202

Egerton, Thomas (*d* 1617), solicitor general 206, 207n

INDEX

Hall, Christopher: journal (1576)   126
Hampton *see* Southampton
Hannibal   118
Harborne, William (*d* 1617), ambassador
   130
Harriot, Thomas (*d* 1621)   39n, 191n
Hawkins, (Sir) John (*d* 1595)   27, 40,
   122, 134, 193
Hawkins, William (*d* 1554?)   39, 191n
Hayes, Edward, captain *Golden Hind*   5n,
   26n, 204n, 209n; career   22
– voyage (1583)   46, 48, 49–50, 51; in
   Newfoundland   52, 56, 57, 180, 183;
   off Sable Island   59–60, 62; return to
   England   62, 66
– account of voyage   49–50, 115, 133,
   178, 179, 183; comment on Browne
   47; on Parmenius   21, 22, 67
Hebrus, river   86, 87, 118
Hector   94, 95, 113
Heidelberg University   6, 7, 16, 107, 125
Helicon, mountain, Greece   125, 129
Henricum Untonum   24n *see* Unton,
   Henry
Henry VIII, king of England   33n, 127
Hera   126
Herbert, Anne, countess of Pembroke
   (*d* 1588)   214, 215, 217
Hercules   85, 102, 103, 113, 115, 134, 136
Hermes   156
Hermeticism   35, 156
Heroic Age   118, 121
Hesiod: *Works*   118, 162
Hessus, Heobanus: *Psalterium* (1581)   31
Heyer, of Wiltshire   198
Heyward, Sir Rowland (*d* 1593)   40,
   192, n, 202
Hibernia   90, 122 *see* Ireland
Hippocrene, sacred spring   125, 129
Hispania   84 *see* Spain
Hoby family   22
Holland, Henry (*d* 1650?); *Herωlogia*   121
Holmes, Abiel, clergyman: trs. *D.N.C.*
   71, 106, 108, 126–7
Homem, Lopo: map   189n
Homer: *Iliad*   68n, 114; *Odyssey*   111, 126

Hood, Thomas (*d* 1598)   39n, 191n
Hooker, *alias* Vowell, John (*d* 1601), cited
   109, 126
Hooper, John (*d* 1555)   120
Horace   25: *Odes*   25, 122, 124, 128,
   129, 137
Hotman, Jean, Sieur de Villiers St Paul
   12, 13, 14, 214, 215, 219
Hotman, François (*d* 1590)   12n, 13
Howard, Henry, Viscount Bindon
   204, n
Huband, Sir John   207, 208n
Hudson, R.   64
Huguenots   12, 19
Huiz, 209, n *see* Gilbert, Sir H.
Humanism   3, 6, 7, 24n, 31, 34, 131, 160;
   humanists   13–14, 109 *see also* Ficino,
   Pico, Pomponazzi
Humfrey, duke of Gloucester (*d* 1447)
   24
Humfrey, Laurence (*d* 1596)   30, 185;
   Oratio   10, 133; verses on Unton's
   death   10–11, n
   associated with Parmenius   9, 11–13,
   18; letter from Newfoundland   12, 55,
   64, 168, 169, 174, 177
Hungary   16, 22, 36, 62, 110, 143, 157,
   184; history   87, 99, 118–19, 125, 131;
   scholars   3, 6, 77, 134 *see also* Parmenius
Huntington Library, California   27, 29,
   72
Hurstfield, Joel; cited   114, 129
Hydra   136
Hyperion   110

Iacchus   112, 136
Iberi (Spaniards)   98
Iberia   3, 131 *see* Portugal, Spain
Iberus   90, 131 *see* Spain
ice *see* Newfoundland
Illyricum   118
India   10, 102, 103, 136, 138
Indians, American   123, 133, 181, 183;
   origins of   117 *see also* Beothuk
Ingolstadt, Germany   16

241

– *Delight*, William Winter captain, Richard Clarke master, with Gilbert (1583) 46, 204, n; becomes flagship 47; voyage to Newfoundland 47–9, 51; at St John's 52–3; Parmenius transfers to 55, 57, 58; Maurice Browne captain 58; wrecked off Sable Island 3, 59, 61, n, 62, 64, 66, 183; ship's company 53, 56, 59, 64, 169, 174, 179

– *Golden Hind*, Francis Drake captain 110

– *Golden Hind*, Edward Hayes captain, William Cox master, with Gilbert (1583) 22, 46; voyage to Newfoundland 49–51, 178; leaves St John's, 58; off Sable Island 59; return to England 62, 64, 66

– *Squirrel*, Simão Fernandes master, voyage to New England (1580) 19, 30, 40, 193n; [William Andrews captain] with Gilbert (1583) 46; voyage to Newfoundland 49, 51; Gilbert transfers to 58; off Sable Island 59; return to England, lost at sea 62, 64, 66

– *Susan Fortune*, Richard Clarke captain: voyage to Newfoundland (1582) 48, 180, 240n

– *Swallow*, Maurice Browne captain, with Gilbert (1583) 46; Parmenius on board 47; voyage to Newfoundland 48–51; William Winter captain, return to England 55, 58; ship's company 48–50, 58, 169, 174, 179

– *Swallow*, John Fisher owner 22

ships' company 56–7, 194 *see also Delight, Swallow*

ships' provisions 46, 51, 52, 57, 58, 62, 179, 204, 206

Shrewsbury, Lord *see* Talbot, George

Sidney, Sir Henry (*d* 1586) 19, 122

Sidney, Sir Philip (*d* 1586) 16, 34n, 111, 125–6, 130; dedication *Divers voyages* 20n, 21, 30, 31n; investor in Gilbert's voyage 39

Sidney, Robert (*d* 1626) 16

Signal Hill, Newfoundland 183

Silver Age 118

Sixtus v, pope (1585–90) 31n

Smalcald, Diet of (1578) 11

Smith, Thomas: *V. cl. Gulielmi Camdini* (1691) 12n, 13n, 113, 216

Smythe or Smith, Thomas (*d* 1591), customer of London 39, n, 192, n

Smythe or Smith, Sir Thomas (*d* 1625) 39, n, 192, n

South America 189n

South Sea 193 *see* Pacific

Southampton: merchants 40, 41, 46, 196, 198, 199, n, 201 *see also* Goddard, Oughtred, Stavely

– base for Gilbert's fleet 47, 109, 110, 195, 196n, 197, 199, 201, 203, 204, 206 *see also* Browne, M.

Southern, A.C.: *Elizabethan recusant prose* 218

Spain 3, 62, 68, 699

– In America 54, 85, 115, 132, 133, 190; in Azores 38, 200, n; in Netherlands 91, 119, 122, 131, 197, n, 217

– shipping at St John's 52, 170, 171, 175, 180

Sparta 156

Spenser, Edmund (*d* 1599): *Faerie Queene* 124; *Prothalamium* 110

Squirrel see ships

Stafford, Sir Edward (*d* 1605), ambassador 66, 177

stages *see* St John's

Statius 24, 25, 26; *Silvae* 106, 126, 132; *Thebaid* 124, 127, 157

Staveley, William (*d* 1582), alderman 40–1, 196, n, 198–9

Stephanus Budaeus 5, 6; S.P. Budeis 4; S.P. of Buda 9 *see* Parmenius, Stephen

Stephen, Robert, printer 123

Stertson, Drite (*fl* 1582) 13n

Stoics 162

Stoughton, John, BA (*d* 1598), clergyman 201n

This book
was designed by
WILLIAM RUETER
under the direction of
ALLAN FLEMING
and was printed by
R&R Clark, Ltd, Edinburgh
for
University of
Toronto
Press